OUR LIVING TRADITIONS

OUR LIVING TRADITIONS

An Introduction to American Folklore

Edited by *TRISTRAM POTTER COFFIN*

BASIC BOOKS, Inc., Publishers
New York   *London*

This book is dedicated to the memory of
WILLIS L. JAMES
who was to have been a contributor
and to the memory of
MACEDWARD LEACH
who was

Preface

In my wittier moments, I like to describe folklore as a bastard field that anthropology begot upon English. And the Victorian vignette of the *nouveau riche* father who has deserted his child and the aristocratic mother who fosters an offspring she never really wanted is not an inaccurate one. It summarizes the history of folk studies in American universities quite succinctly. It is particularly appropriate to the University of Pennsylvania.

Folk studies at the University of Pennsylvania began over twenty years ago, when the late MacEdward Leach, influenced by his training as a medievalist and his friendship with anthropologist Frank Speck, began converting already established English courses into studies of the ballad and of the use of folklore by British, American, and Celtic authors. By 1962 Leach's enthusiasm, sound scholarship, and Celtic charm had created such an ardent clique within the Department of English that something had to be done to answer its particular needs. Thus, the Graduate Group in Folklore and Folklife was born. It is that Group, along with the Voice of America, which sponsored the Forum out of which this book has grown. Seven of the contributors, in addition to the editor, are part of what is sometimes referred to as "Mac's Pennsy Gang."

What has happened at Pennsylvania has also happened at other places, sometimes with equal success, more often to die a-borning. Folklore at Indiana University, once the only American institution to offer a full program in the field, has flourished under the leadership of first Stith Thompson and now Richard M. Dorson. The Interdepartmental arrangement at U.C.L.A., the brain child of Professor of German Wayland D. Hand, is "fat and healthy," as is the Cooperstown Graduate Program of the New York State University College at Oneonta, run by Louis C. Jones and Bruce Buckley. Soon Mody Boatright, Américo Paredes, and Roger Abrahams will have an independent program at Texas, while William Bascom and Alan Dundes have made strides in the same direction at Berkeley, as have Thelma James and Ellen Stekert at Wayne. But generally there is one enthusiast, like Francis Lee Utley at Ohio State or Archie Green at Illinois, a worker in the dawn, whose program blossoms under his energy, only to wither when he retires or moves on. Harold Thompson and his work at Cornell offer a classic case in point. Such persons, usually working with administrators who haven't the foggiest idea what the scientific study of folklore embraces, have been unable to do what Leach, Stith Thompson, and Hand have done.

Folklore has seldom been accepted rapidly in a university that reveres the Teutonic, nineteenth-century-oriented humanities program. Most persons trained in these schools never studied folklore and they aren't inclined to feel it necessary for others to study it. Even at Pennsylvania, where folklore has been taught since World War II, my colleagues in other programs still think I concern myself with some sort of "antik bric-a-brac." Folklore has always gained most rapid acceptance where the administrator can tie it to local pride, regional history, or politics. Harvard, Yale, Princeton, Columbia, Brown, Cornell, N.Y.U., Wisconsin, Michigan, Northwestern, and Chicago make an impressive list of graduate schools in America. Not one of them has an established folklore program or any intention of having one. This is of course incredible, especially when one realizes that folk literature is the only literature that a vast percentage of the world has ever known, when one realizes that it is the base from which all other literatures have grown. Besides needing it to know thoroughly history, language, literature, anthropology, psychology, sociology, and all studies those disciplines suggest, one needs it for no other reason than to understand his or another's culture. A man trained in folklore draws immediate and accurate parallels between the stubborn belief in water-witching and the current flying-saucer scare; he understands the reaction to an

execution such as that of Carryl Chessman in 1961 in terms of
Western outlaw tradition; he sees the relationships between a
society governed by the proverb and our legal system; he knows
why the American Negro is embarrassed by a man like Sonny
Liston, even though Liston's public image is that of most Negro
folk heroes. And persons trained in folklore seldom make "ugly
Americans."

Thus, when the United States Information Agency, through
Theodore Wertime, Director of the Voice of America Forum
Lectures, asked me to coordinate a series on American folklore,
I was delighted. I saw a golden opportunity to get the leading
folklorists in America to write readable, but accurate, essays on
various aspects of this often misunderstood field, and I knew
those essays would get the widest sort of distribution. Big hopes
for this book have resulted. I want it to do its part in educating
more and more people to what the scholarly pursuit of folklore
means, so that the intelligent among us will be able to distinguish
between the moral, maudlin nonsense that is hawked in bright
packages to the commercial market and the genuine oral traditions through which ethnic, occupational, and regional groups
maintain their individual cultures. I want the book to reach the
hands of the troubled members of our national legislature, who
in Report 652 of the 87th Congress, First Session, listed folklore
as unrelated to the purposes of the National Defense Education
Act, which supports sister fields such as anthropology, linguistics,
written literatures, and history. I want it to reach the hand of
the prominent Harvard professor of American civilization (no
less) who in reviewing Dick Dorson's *American Folklore* called
the field "the most sentimental, and the most anti-intellectual
scholarly discipline in America today." I want it to reach these
persons, and the others like them, because they need help. I
want intelligent people to know that the mass markets are
glutted with fake, ersatz products designed to look like folklore,
as these markets are glutted with poor novels, phony medical
studies, and sloppy legal advice. But I want intelligent people
to know also that there is a scientific way of studying folklore,
just as they know there is a scientific way of studying Fielding
and Faulkner; scrofula and dandruff; wills and torts.

The essays that follow have been divided into three groups.
Part I is a general introduction to the history and techniques of

folk studies, including descriptions of folklore in this country, as well as remarks on how it may be collected and later studied. Part II covers the main genres that flourish in America. Obviously some things had to be left out of the fourteen essays that comprise this section. It would have been useful, for example, to include a lecture on folk drama. However, Southwestern drama, the *Coloquios, Los Pastores,* is Mexican, or Mexican-American at best, and derive directly from medieval Spanish literature; British drama, the St. George's and Robin Hood plays, is for all practical purposes no longer found in America, in spite of the one or two remarkable discoveries of Marie Campbell in Kentucky; and drama that has developed from and developed into song, game, and festival is easily taken care of in essays on these subjects. Perhaps it was also unfair to ask Edson Richmond to cover all American lyric song (the work songs, the love lyrics, the game and dance songs) in one brief essay. But these are the usual problems of space. After finishing Part II, the reader will have a pretty good grasp of the genres folklorists find and study in America. Part III acknowledges the role folklore plays in shaping and augmenting highly literate, urban life. As the levels of education have reached deeper and deeper into American society, the markets for folklore, pseudo-folklore, and the products derived from folklore have increased. Writers, labor organizers, singers, churchgoers have capitalized on the varied folk heritage of this country, stressing its patriotic appeal to hawk and dove alike; cultivating its rural, old-fashioned atmosphere for nostalgic minds; relying on its time-tested entertainment value. Of course, much of the commercial opportunism described in Part III results in misconceptions about the field and about folklore as a science. It would not hurt if this portion of the book were "conned in great swarths" by administrators and teachers across the land.

But whether it is or not, whether or not the book rises to my hopes, the project has been great fun, and I want to thank Theodore Wertime, the Director of the Voice of America Forum Series, and his assistant Joy MacFadyen, not only for their assistance but also for their boundless energy and cheer. I also want to thank former Dean of the Graduate School of Arts and Sciences at the University of Pennsylvania, Roy F. Nichols, for supporting my idea that the Graduate Group in Folklore at

Pennsylvania co-sponsor the Forum. And I want to tip my hat to Irving Kristol of Basic Books; to Miriam Strawser, my hardworking secretary for the project; and to all the scholars who contributed so willingly and fortunately.

January 1968   TRISTRAM POTTER COFFIN

The Authors

ROGER D. ABRAHAMS is Associate Professor of English and Folklore at the University of Texas and a former fellow of the Guggenheim Foundation. The author of *Deep Down in the Jungle, Negro Narrative Folklore from the Streets of Philadelphia* (1964), and a number of articles in folklore publications, he has recently completed a study of Anglo-American folksong style with George Foss. Abrahams is a talented musician and singer. He has made a number of recordings and appears frequently on television and radio.

HORACE P. BECK, well known both as a deep-sea sailor and folklorist, is Professor of American literature at Middlebury College. Primarily a student of New England folklore, Beck has written *The Folklore of Maine* (1957) and *The American Indian as Sea-Fighter in Colonial Times* (1959), and edited *Folklore in Action* (1962) and *Gluskap the Liar and Other Indian Tales* (1966). He is well known as a lecturer, as a television personality, and as an active member of the American Folklore Society. Currently, he is President of the New England Folklore Society.

RAY B. BROWNE, Associate Professor of English at the Bowling Green Ohio State University, has published some thirty articles on aspects of literature, popular culture and folklore, has prepared a critical study of Herman Melville, and has edited half a dozen books, including the two-volume *Critical Approaches to American Literature* (1965), with Martin Light, and *Popular Beliefs and Practices from Alabama* (1958).

BRUCE R. BUCKLEY is Professor of American Folk Culture in the Cooperstown Graduate Programs of the State University of New York, College at Oneonta. He is a past President of the Hoosier Folklore Society and a current member of the executive board of the New York Folklore Society. A regular contributor to the *New York Folklore Quarterly*, he has had articles published in various state and regional journals of folklore and history. His educational film *Canals: Towpaths West* received a number of awards, including the American Film Festival Blue Ribbon Award and the CINE Golden-Eagle Award. His record album *Ohio Valley Ballads* was released by Folkways Records.

TRISTRAM POTTER COFFIN is Professor of English and Vice-Dean of the Graduate School of Arts and Sciences at the University of Pennsylvania. A former Secretary-Treasurer of the American Folklore Society, he has published many books and articles in the field of the ballad, folklore as literature, and folklore in American culture. He has hosted over one hundred television programs on folklore and Shakespeare, among them the nationally shown "Lyrics and Legends." A Guggenheim fellow, Dr. Coffin is best known for his complete finding index to the *Journal of American Folklore* (1958), his bibliographical study of ballad story variation, *The British Traditional Ballad in North America* (1963), and the widely read anthology *Folklore in America* (1966), edited with Hennig Cohen.

HENNIG COHEN is Professor of English at the University of Pennsylvania and editor of *American Quarterly*. Formerly, he was Secretary of the American Studies Association (1956–1961). Dr. Cohen is the author of the *South Carolina Gazette, 1732–1775* and editor of *The Battle Pieces of Herman Melville* (1962), *Selected Poems of Herman Melville* (1964), and *White-Jacket* by Herman Melville (1967), *Humor of the Old Southwest* (1964) with W. B. Dillingham, and *Folklore in America* (1966) with Tristram Potter Coffin.

RICHARD M. DORSON is Professor of History and Folklore at Indiana University and Director of its Institute of Folklore. His books include *Jonathan Draws the Long Bow* (1946), *America Begins* (1950), *America Rebels* (1953), *Negro Folktales in Michigan* (1956), *Negro Tales from Pine Bluff, Arkansas and Calvin, Michigan* (1958), *American Folklore* (1959), and *Buying the Wind: Regional Folklore in the United States* (1964). He is General Editor of the series *Folktales of the World* and has recently completed *The British Folklorists, A History*. Currently, he is President of the American Folklore Society, Vice-President of the International Society of Ethnology and Folklore, and Chairman of the Executive Board of the Society for Asian Folklore.

ALAN DUNDES, Associate Professor of Anthropology and Folklore at the University of California at Berkeley, has written *The Morphology of North American Indian Folktales* (1964); edited an anthology of essays, *The Study of Folklore* (1965); and contributed to the *Book of Knowledge*, the *Encyclopedia Britannica*, and a large number of folklore and anthropology journals. He is especially interested in folklore theory and method, an area in which he has become an internationally known authority.

KENNETH S. GOLDSTEIN is Associate Professor of Folklore in the Graduate Folklore Program at the University of Pennsylvania. He is the

Secretary-Treasurer of the American Folklore Society, President of the Pennsylvania Folklore Society, and Executive Editor of Folklore Associates, Inc. A Fulbright scholar in Scotland 1959–1960, Dr. Goldstein is the author of *A Guide for Field Workers in Folklore* and co-editor of *Two Penny Ballads and Four Dollar Whiskey: A Pennsylvania Folklore Miscellany*. He has produced, edited, and annotated over 500 long-playing recordings of folk music.

ARCHIE GREEN is Associate Professor of Labor and Industrial Relations at the University of Illinois. For many years he has studied and collected labor lore. Mr. Green is currently a member of the United Brotherhood of Carpenters and Joiners of America and has served as secretary of Shipwrights, Joiners, Boatbuilders Local Union 1149 in his home city of San Francisco. His works have appeared in such periodicals as *American Speech, Ethnomusicology, Industrial Relations, Labor History, Textile Labor*, and the *Journal of American Folklore*.

JOHN GREENWAY is Professor of Anthropology at the University of Colorado. His *American Folksongs of Protest*, published in 1953, was the pioneer work in this area of folk scholarship. Dr. Greenway conducted field research among the Australian aborigines under a grant from the National Institute of Mental Health in 1965–1966. As a lecturer and folksinger he has done considerable radio and television work in the United States and abroad and has made nine phonograph record albums. His most provocative work is his analysis of the American national character, *The Inevitable Americans* (1964).

WAYLAND D. HAND is Professor of German and Folklore at the University of California at Los Angeles. Since 1944 he has been working on a multi-volume *Dictionary of American Popular Beliefs and Superstitions*. He has served as editor of the *Journal of American Folklore*, helped found the California monograph series "Folklore Studies," and has just resigned from twenty-five years of editorial service on *Western Folklore*, the last twelve as editor. Dr. Hand was President of the American Folklore Society from 1957–1958, and in 1964 was elected to a five-year term as Vice-President for North America of the International Society for Folk Narrative Research.

BRUCE JACKSON is on the faculty of the State University of New York at Buffalo. He edited *Folklore and Society* (1966) and *The Negro and His Folklore in Nineteenth Century Periodicals* (1967). His most recent work, *The Criminal Experience*, is a study of how people learn to be criminals. His articles, fiction, poetry, and reviews have appeared in the *Journal of American Folklore, Atlantic Monthly, New York Folklore Quarterly, Western Folklore, Comparative Literature*, and *Minnesota Review*.

WILLIAM HUGH JANSEN is a member of the faculty at the University of Kentucky. Before joining the academic world; he amassed experience as a tour guide, steel worker, editor, and baseball manager.

Dr. Jansen was a Fulbright lecturer at Ankara University in Turkey (1951–1952) and a Ford Faculty Fellow (1955–1956). Widely known in folklore circles for his versatility as a collector, archivist, editor, and analyst, his articles have appeared in folklore journals around the world. He has served as president of three folklore societies, editor of four folklore journals, and is a past Vice-President of the American Folklore Society.

G. MALCOLM LAWS, JR., is Professor of English at the University of Pennsylvania. The American Folklore Society is the publisher of his two definitive books, *Native American Balladry* (1964) and *American Balladry from British Broadsides* (1957). Dr. Laws is also known for his work in Victorian studies, particularly in the literary ballad of the nineteenth century.

MACEDWARD LEACH, who died in the summer of 1967, was one of the world's foremost folklorists. He developed the folklore program at the University of Pennsylvania. From 1941 to 1960 Dr. Leach was Secretary-Treasurer of the American Folklore Society and from 1960 to 1962, its President. He inaugurated the Bibliographical and Special Series published by that group. Always an active collector, Dr. Leach went into the field all over North America and brought together collections from Virginia, Nova Scotia, Newfoundland, and Jamaica. He edited *Amis and Amiloun* (1937); the widely read *The Ballad Book* (1955); *The Critics and the Ballad* (1961) with Tristram Potter Coffin; and *Folk Ballads and Songs of the Lower Labrador Coast* (1965). Just before he died, he completed the revised ballad bibliography for Wells's *Manual*.

RAVEN I. McDAVID, JR. is Professor of English at the University of Chicago. He is the editor of the forthcoming *Linguistic Atlas of the Middle and South Atlantic States* and is Vice-President of the American Dialect Society. The best known of his many scholarly publications is his 777-page abridgment of H. L. Mencken's *The American Language*. In 1965 he was a Senior Fulbright Lecturer at the University of Mainz in West Germany.

BRUNO NETTL, Associate Professor of Music and Acting Chairman of the Division of Musicology at the University of Illinois, specializes in the study of folk and traditional music. Among his publications are *Music in Primitive Culture* (1956), *North American Indian Musical Styles* (1954), *An Introduction to Folk Music in the United States* (1960), *Theory and Method in Ethnomusicology* (1964), and *Folk and Traditional Music of the Western Continents* (1965).

AMÉRICO PAREDES is Professor of English and Anthropology at the University of Texas. He is a Guggenheim fellow in folklore. He has been Visiting Professor of Latin American Culture in the National Defense Education Act program at West Virginia University, folklore bibliographer for the *Southern Folklore Quarterly*, and book review editor for the *Journal of American Folklore*. His fields of specialization are the folklore of Latin America and folklore in crosscultural relationships among ethnic groups in the United States. For a number of years he was director of the University of Texas' Folklore Archives.

W. EDSON RICHMOND is Professor of English and Folklore at Indiana University. He has served as a lecturer in folklore at the Salzburg Seminar in American Studies in Austria, and as a visiting professor at Helsinki University and Abo Akademi in Finland. He also was a Fulbright Research Professor attached to the Norsk Folkeminnesamling in Oslo, Norway, during 1953–1954. He has published widely in the field of ballad studies and in recent years has concentrated his attention on Norwegian ballads and folksongs. Dr. Richmond edited *Midwest Folklore* from 1950 until 1963, was bibliographer for the American Folklore Society from 1952 until 1965, as well as having served as Review Editor and Acting Editor of the *Journal of American Folklore*.

LEONARD W. ROBERTS is Chairman of Languages and Literature at West Virginia Wesleyan College. He taught at Berea Foundation High School, where he began collecting the tales that culminated in *South from Hell-for-Sartin* (1955), *Up Cutshin and Down Greasy* (1959), and a series of booklets. Since his Berea days he has served as head of the English Department at Union College, as Chairman of Languages and Literature at Morehead State College, and at West Virginia Wesleyan in his present post. His most recent works are *In the Pine: Folksongs of Appalachia*, and *Old Greasybeard (Folktales of the Cumberland Gap Area)*.

BRIAN SUTTON-SMITH is Professor of Psychology at the Teachers College of Columbia University. He was born in Wellington, New Zealand, but became an American citizen in 1962. A child psychologist, he has published two children's novels and a book, *The Games of New Zealand Children* (1959), as well as many articles on children's folklore and child psychology.

JOHN F. SZWED is Assistant Professor in the Department of Anthropology at Temple University and was a former jazz musician and film maker. He was a Research Fellow at the Newfoundland Institute of Social and Economic Research from 1962–1964 conducting research in isolated communities. He has also carried out research on Afro-Spanish religious cults and music in Trinidad. Dr. Szwed is author of a monograph, *Private Cultures and Public Imagery: Interpersonal Relations in a Newfoundland Peasant Society*, has published in *Ethnology*, *Phylon*, and *Jazz Review*, and is currently one of the editors of *Jazz* magazine.

FRANCIS LEE UTLEY is a member of Ohio State University's Department of English, and the recipient of three Guggenheim Foundation fellowships. He has published two books and a number of articles in professional journals, including research studies on Thoreau, Chaucer, Biblical literature, political words and phrases, myth and folklore, and structural linguistics and aesthetics. Dr. Utley was president of the American Folklore Society from 1950–1952. In 1950 and 1962, he was president of the Ohio Folklore Society, which he helped found. In 1950 he became a sponsor and charter member of the American Name Society (ANS), which is devoted to the study of personal and place names.

D. K. WILGUS is Professor of English and Anglo-American Folksong at the University of California at Los Angeles. He has written *Anglo-American Folksong Scholarship since 1898* (1959) as well as a host of articles on balladry, spirituals, and general folklore. From 1955–1961, he edited the *Kentucky Folklore Record,* and since 1949 he has been Record Review editor for the *Journal of American Folklore.* Professor Wilgus has held a Guggenheim Fellowship, won the Chicago Folklore Prize, directed the UCLA Folk Festival three times, served as Secretary of the John Edwards Memorial Foundation, and founded the Western Kentucky Folklore Archives.

DON YODER is Chairman of the Graduate Program in Folklore and Folklife at the University of Pennsylvania. He has for most of his academic career been studying American regional folk culture, especially the folk life of the Pennsylvania farmers. He was one of the founders of the Pennsylvania Folklife Society and is now editor of *Pennsylvania Folklife.* A specialist in folk religion, he is author of *Pennsylvania Spirituals* (1961), a study of the religious folksongs of the Pennsylvania Dutch Country.

Contents

I

FOLKLORE
AS A
FIELD
FOR
STUDY

A Definition
of Folklore

FRANCIS LEE UTLEY

Almost everybody who has heard the word "folklore" knows in-
stinctively what it is, just as everybody who has seriously read
"poetry" knows what *it* is. Yet both these words are hard to define
with the clarity, say, that one can achieve for "electron" or
"sodium chloride" or "lion." Once I tried to do so, and came
out with the definition that folklore was "literature orally transmitted." This was what is called an operational definition—that
is, a definition workable for (at least) myself, a student of both
oral and written literatures who comes from the United States
and hence belongs to a special branch of Western civilization.

Apparently the definition has worked for others, even for those
who might want to approach oral literature with different tools
from the ones I know best: literary analysis of form and content
and the study of the folktale from a historical and cultural point
of view. Most of us agree on one thing: that the field of folklore
has to be defined if it is to be the subject of serious study. If it
is merely another form of written literature it should simply be
studied as such, and certainly "Cinderella," in the presence of
Shakespeare's *King Lear*, might get second billing. Yet both
Cordelia and some folktale Cinderellas tell their fathers that their
love is like salt, and the vain and arrogant fathers, who do not
realize the value of that prosaic addition to our daily diet, re-

3

pudiate the daughter whose love is so great that it is honest and needs no flattery. Literary men must not similarly repudiate folklore.

We also have to separate folklore from anthropology. Europeans may not understand this as a special American problem. To a German, for instance, *Volkskunde* is the study of the culture of the Germanic and European *Volk*, with emphasis on the peasants and the plain people. It more or less corresponds to English "folklore." *Völkerkunde*, on the other hand, means what we call "ethnology." It is the study of the cultures of peoples outside Europe, both those of high civilizations (Chinese, Hindu) and those of arrested cultures (Pueblo, Trobriand Islander, African pygmy). In America, it is often said, we have no peasants. Sometimes this is a mere boast of the upward mobility of our farming classes, and of the relatively few pockets where the dominant economic and cultural structure has not penetrated: rural Negroes, Appalachian hill folk, migrant workers. What one can say accurately is that farm traditions in the United States are in no sense so strongly based as they are in Europe. Too much has been lost in the transatlantic voyage. Surely in Europe and in Asia there is also today a tendency for the cities to swallow up the farm folk. Yet Americans believe, when they visit other lands and witness a wealth of local festivals and folksongs, that the city has not devoured so much of the older culture as it seems to have done in America. As for Western civilization, we must remember that it is not everywhere so dominant as it is in Europe and America. They say that when Mahatma Gandhi was asked what he thought of Western civilization, he replied that he thought it might be a good idea.

Despite this quip Americans still believe that they have a civilization against which we can also measure one or many folk cultures, differing in some measure from the dominant culture of modern science and industry. It has, however, been much harder to train a corps of professional folklorists here than in Europe, in which many countries are inspired by simple homogeneous nationalism to establish archives and to record the traditions which are even there fading, or at least evolving as all human institutions do, under the influence of education and social change. Closely related to the folklorist, however, is the anthropologist. In this country, as contrasted to Europe, he has no scanty body of data. There are still a host of thriving American Indian linguistic and cultural families: Eastern Woodland, Iroquois, Plateau, Plains, Californian, to name a few. Whatever the history of the relationship of American whites to Indians, and it has not always been a proud story, the role of the anthropologist with his tolerance of other cultures than his own has been a valuable one. Anthropologists have traditionally been the people in this country who have studied the primitive lore of the Indians with both clarity and affection, and who have therefore championed them against exploitation and indifference.

Seeking for disciplinary models, folklorists in America have often turned toward the American anthropologist as well as toward the European student of folk literature. It is not surprising that they have often accepted the anthropologist's view that folklore is merely "folk literature." To the student of the Indian, who describes a total culture, folklore can be specialized in meaning to "literature." The term "primitive lore" is often applied by folklorists to this total culture, though anthropologists have claimed, rightly, that Pueblo Indians and Bushmen and Andaman Islanders have been evolving as long as we have, and that the term primitive is not an accurate one. Be that as it may, it is likely that the indigenous literature of a non-Western culture plays a somewhat different role in that culture from the oral literature which exists on the outskirts of an industrial culture like our own. If we cannot use the term "primitive lore" to cover the tales which Longfellow levied upon in his "Hiawatha" and to distinguish them from the tales which Richard Chase has collected in Virginia and named for their hero "Jack," we may lose sight of certain basic functional differences.

American folklorists have learned much indeed from the collections and analyses which Franz Boas has provided for North Pacific Indian tribes like the Tshimshians and the Kwakiutls. In recent years American anthropologists themselves have sought for systematic accounts of folklore, and found it in the work of Finnish folklorists like Krohn and Aarne, and in their many disciples, like Reidar Christiansen of Norway and Stith Thompson and Archer Taylor of the United States. There is also in this country an older tradition, which concentrates on the folk ballad rather than the folktale. It too has its European counterparts, most especially in Denmark with Grundtvig, Olrik, and Dal, or in Germany with Erk, Böhme, and John Meier. Until the 1930's it was centered on the work of Francis James Child, a Harvard professor who demonstrated the continuity between British and American tradition. "Child" ballad collections, like those of Phillips Barry, Arthur Kyle Davis, or Helen Flanders, long dominated the scene. Lately, under the influence of John and Alan Lomax and D. K. Wilgus, the focus has shifted to a more clearly American tradition in balladry, including the notable contribution of the American Negro.

Faced with this body of professional work in folk literature, the anthropologist and some of his folkloristic admirers, including the writer, have tended to exclude from folklore anything but "literature orally transmitted." We have been neither unanimous nor consistent. An anthropologist like William Bascom of the University of California once accepted the narrow definition, but later came to believe that "verbal art" was a better phrase than "folklore," since it did not exclude music or proverbs or weather sayings.

These definitions, "operational" and useful for defining a division of labor among specialists, may play havoc with the general field of folklore studies. Should we exclude from folklore or "verbal art" arts such as the dance, crafts such as weaving and the stacking of hay, customs such as Plough Monday processions, or beliefs such as the counsel to plant grain in the light of the full rather than the waning moon? All folklorists have known the value of such expressions of the human spirit, but many of them have been willing to turn them over to the anthropologist for systematic description. But though the anthropologist has been helpful in giving us models for the comprehension of literary texts, like the Freudian and sociological readings of Clackamas texts of Melville Jacobs or the "structural" readings of Alan Dundes, inspired by the Russian Propp and the French Lévi-Strauss, he has not been especially helpful in the study of folk culture as a whole in America. In some measure he has studied the Negro (Melville Herskovits and William Bascom are notable examples), but his work has been mainly with African origins. We owe the Negro a recognition of his past, but in stressing it too heavily we may be making the same mistake as earlier enthusiasts for English and Scottish origins for American balladry—a slavishly genetic rather than a contemporary point of view. And if the anthropologist has ignored the folk literature of the United States, he has similarly ignored the folk life, just as reprehensibly as has the folklorist proper.

The study of "literature orally transmitted," then, is a highly respectable subject, calling upon the talents of men trained both in folklore and in literature. But it is too narrow for the whole field which this book is to explore. Our schools of folklore are beginning to pay more attention, for instance, to the vital aspect of material culture and folklife. Warren Roberts and his study of domestic architecture, Louis Jones and his model village at Cooperstown, Austin Fife's classification of haystack types, and Don Yoder and his work with Pennsylvania German culture—all of these show the enrichment of folklore which can come by adding to the still central and significant area of folk literature the physical conditions which in actuality surround it. Nor must we neglect custom and belief. Many students, critical of badly planned and unauthenticated collections of "superstitions," have been tempted to declare the mass of tiny details without structure and best ignored. But we should have heeded the excellent folklore atlases of Germany and Switzerland, as one of our number, Wayland Hand, did. His two volumes of *Popular Beliefs and Superstitions from North Carolina*, the last of the seven excellently edited volumes of the Frank C. Brown Collection of North Carolina Folklore, show what can be done for the structured arrangement and authentication of 8,500 such beliefs, from "If a rooster crows on the banister it is a sign of death" to "Fish will not bite on a northeast wind."

One man may, therefore, confine his intensive work to the folktale and the ballad, but he cannot without assurance send out his students without teaching them something of the other literary genres, as well as the non-verbal folk arts, and the traditional beliefs, customs, crafts, and the way of life associated with those people and subcultures we call the "folk."

But we still must identify the "folk," and the processes by which they pass on tradition, whether it is the manufacture of a homemade wooden pitchfork, a Mardi Gras celebration, or a folktale like the model for Mark Twain's "The Golden Arm: 'You Got It!'" In some sense we all are the "folk," since none of us is without tradition and oral heritage. But all of us are not creative members of the folk, or re-creators such as are called "active tradition-bearers." Only in sections of the country where books (and perhaps mass media) are of minimal influence, such as isolated hill and mountain communities like the Ozarks and the Kentucky Hills, island communities like the Georgia Sea

Islands or Newfoundland, underprivileged farmers like those in the Black Belt, migrant workers like the fruitpickers of California, the lumberjacks of Maine and the Maritime Provinces, the cattle herders of the West, only here do we find a dependence on oral tradition which creates a true folk culture or, better, subculture. The dominant culture always presses in, but we folklorists have found that some of our earlier fears that these viable cultures would disappear have been unwarranted. They even survive when, with the rush to the cities, their members leave the isolated communities.

Another strong force in American folklore has been the immigrant groups: Greeks, Polish Jews, Scots, Chinese, Japanese, Italians, Irish, and a host of others. In the 1920's their efforts went into the founding of societies for "Americanization." The same societies today are likely to be most preoccupied with returning to an appreciation of the culture of their parents and grandparents. Whether this is properly the task of American folklorists, as Thelma James of Detroit has argued and demonstrated with the work of her students in Polish folksongs and Armenian folktales, or the work of European folklorists who come to the United States for an extension of their work at home, like Linda Degh with Hungarian immigrants or Jonas Balys with Lithuanians, it is one of the more exciting prospects in America.

In defining the folk as a subculture, we must learn not to be snobbish. To speak only of "folk survivals," for instance, is to suggest that the subject is a merely antiquarian one, and that the people of the Ozarks and the Black Belt are woefully out of touch with modern civilization, and always to their disadvantage. Many of their customs and crafts and works of art are functional, in the sense that they play a significant part in the lives of the isolated folk who preserve them. Indeed many a city dweller has grown enthusiastic over a country ham, well smoked and cured with pepper in a way long forgotten by the assembly-line meat packer. The Mardi Gras of New Orleans is not without its commercial aspects, and yet there is something about that particular festival which still wins the heart of those who no longer understand the relation of carnival to Lenten austerity. The popularity of American folksinging, now become a worldwide export and a money-making home product, shows that "Little Mattie Groves" and "Barbara Allen" and "John Henry" and "Birmingham Jail" are as important to city dwellers as they are to the folk who have preserved and re-created them.

From the point of view of scientific description it is just as bad to exaggerate the virtues of folklore as to minimize them. Much of the rich variety of folksong—Blue Grass, Purist, Protest, Folk-Rock, or just miscellaneous—is a craze based on material pointedly created for a commercial market, a mass medium. By definition in America a commercial market is far from the home-made products of the folk, whether they are moonshiners, lumber-men, sailors, or cowboys. This disparity has led some students to speak with perhaps more asperity than was really needed about "fakelore," and to deplore everything which gets into television or the newspapers as *unauthentic.*

Even our young men who grow beards and learn the folk guitar in ten easy lessons have learned something about this word "authentic" from their hopelessly academic teachers. They have adopted it for their own purposes, purposes occasionally hard for their teachers to comprehend. One young man told me, with considerable sincerity and weight, that Dave Van Ronk sings "Mack the Knife" more authentically than Louis Armstrong does. Dave Van Ronk, a skillful young commercial folksinger, in one of his phases made it his special task to re-create the work of the Negro blues singers. His own race and skin color were white, but like many of his generation he believed that a tribute to Negro genius was one contribution to the civil rights move-ment. Armstrong, on the other hand, though a Negro jazzman and perhaps conscious that the lyrics of "Mack the Knife" might imply to his listeners that the underworld and the underdog can talk back, surely recorded the song for the same commercial reasons he recorded "Blueberry Hill." The song itself, of course, is no folksong at all but an aria from *The Three-Penny Opera,* the product of the combined talents of Bertolt Brecht, Kurt Weill, and the eighteenth-century playwright John Gay. Its tre-mendous popularity since the 1930's was certainly due more to its lush and sentimental melody than to its story of the viciousness of men:

> *Und der Haifisch, der hat Zähne*
> *Und die trägt er im Gesicht*
> *Und Macheath, der hat ein Messer*
> *Doch das Messer sieht man nicht.*

In English:

> And the shark he has his teeth and
> There they are for all to see.
> And Macheath he has his knife but
> No one knows where it may be.

The irony of youth dancing without heeding the words was surely in the mind of both Dave Van Ronk and Louis Armstrong when they sang it to similarly heedless audiences.

No doubt Van Ronk, as a somewhat less successful artist than Armstrong, might appeal more to youthful hipsters. But the joke is that "Mack the Knife" is a highly successful popular song, which transcends Tin Pan Alley and appeals to intellectuals but is anything but a folksong, and that Armstrong, whom he imitates, long ago left the New Orleans haunts which made modern jazz, which certainly had its folk roots. Van Ronk is therefore several removes from folksong *authenticity*, which does not mean that his rendition of "Mack the Knife" is not a very good one. I'm fond of it myself.

I have told this lengthy parable to show something of the problems of a major movement which folklorists ignore at their peril, the so-called folk-derived song revival, survival, or continuing process. There always have been imitators of the folk, and the European romantic movement delighted in collecting folk ballads and rewriting them or newly composing them for sophisticated taste. Sir Walter Scott's "Kinmont Willie" is a new composition, a little more disguised than Coleridge's "The Rime of the Ancient Mariner," Heine's "Die Lorelei" or the songs of Béranger. Scott's "Wife of Usher's Well" and Bishop Percy's "Sir Patrick Spens" are more subtle jobs of rewriting; we cannot tell for certain where the folk genius ends and the editor's begins. German, English, and American composers set songs like "Edward" and "The Foggy Dew" and "The Old Ark's A-Moverin'" to their own version of folk music, as Bach had done with folk music before them. The product was art, and even a theory of art, which asserted that highbrow music became too refined if not perpetually reinspired from lowbrow sources.

To some extent the modern American folk-derived song is like that: an artistic recomposition of songs from hill folk and cowboys and buffalo skinners and lumberjacks and sailors, from the workers and the underprivileged. But like many twentieth-century movements it has become a kind of prestidigitation, crossing and crisscrossing its origins. One youth imitates Negro singers. Another imitates the songs of the tragic Woody Guthrie, who had an authentic folk repertory but who also composed protest songs in New York in the 1930's and 1940's, and now lives with an incurable disease and the sympathy of all who were inspired by both his traditional and his original songs. His admirers often imitate his polemic compositions: Jack Elliott and the earlier Bob Dylan are good cases in point.

Folk-derived music is as worthy of study as the art songs of Schubert or the folksongs recorded by the Englishman Cecil Sharp in the southern Appalachians. But it is quite different: differently inspired, differently heard, and differently composed, with the pen and typewriter. Some true folktale and folksong is also so composed. Perrault's "Little Red Riding Hood" has had a long life in both folk tradition and in print. But the majority of the folktales and folksongs which excited the romantics and still excite us all over the world come from humble, unnamed men, composing orally with the use of common formulas and themes, both verbal and musical, and handing these tales and songs down to active tradition-bearers who re-create them, sometimes for the better and sometimes for the worse. We do not usually know the composers, though Edward Ives has shown us that lumberjack composers are not so anonymous. But we do know the tradition-bearers, the informants, and that is why collectors are so anxious to pin down their names and dates and the time and circumstances of collection. These are the places on the extrapolated graph of process which can be certified. Often, if we are lucky, we may discover a mute inglorious Milton like the Lomaxes' Negro informant Huddie Ledbetter, or Mark Azadovsky's Siberian Vinokurova, or Linda Degh's Frau Palkó, the last from the Hungarian Szekler village of Kakasd. With such artists we approach the realm of true folk creation, not absolutely identical with the *Märchen* and ballad-creating epochs of the Middle Ages, when class structures were hierarchical but entertainment less specialized, before the specializations of the Renaissance, with its printed books and orchestras, set in.

Folklore is, then, in the main oral tradition, transmitted primarily by word of mouth. Only by concentrating on such non-literate composition and recomposition can one study the corpus, a defining body of data worthy of specialized investigation. Such study is not antiquarian but vital, and reveals a segment of human genius often missed by the more formal culture histories. One must not insist that *all* the transmission, or even the composition, be oral. A folktale may come from a Perrault or a Southey and still live in the mouths of men. A folksong may come from an eighteenth-century music hall or a nineteenth-century minstrel show, and yet have a modern life primarily oral. A folktale may be preserved in a Hungarian printed chapbook, read by a literate schoolmaster to a folk audience, and retold as a sequel by an active tradition-bearer. Or a folksong may be written down from oral sources in a West Virginia "ballet" book, or printed in New York or London on a broadside or in a songster. If it gets back into oral tradition it is still a folksong.

But one may insist, I think, that a true folksong or folktale will always have some biography, traceable—or at least hypothetical—as tradition in a non-literate or semi-literate society, or must be preserved orally in a literate society because it is obscene or libelous or otherwise uncomfortable in print. Perhaps, in the last-mentioned circumstances, it may live in the city as its major home. But usually it should have had a home among the same folk who make corn liquor, or rawhide lariats, or wooden plows, or lumberjack coffee, strong enough to counteract lye or sulfuric acid. Thank the Lord we do not spoil it when we borrow it for re-creation or for scholarly record. We can even imitate it, but we should know what we are doing.

And that is the task of the science of folklore, which unless you use the word science is the same in name as the subject it studies. A physiologist studies human life processes; a folklorist studies folklore, or the traditional oral process. The folklorist classifies and defines and probes the many genres: *Märchen*, or popular international tale; ballad; folk lyric; myth; cumulative tale; jest; animal tale. He also studies the categories of folk belief: contagious and imitative magic, witchcraft and weather lore; the crafts of the farmer and the migrant worker; the proverbs and the riddles and the nursery songs which we unconsciously inherit in our infancy. He must study the nature of oral tradition, which has recently been shown by Jan Vansina and others to be an important bearer of law and history, with fully professional and official standing. He will certainly not be uninterested in the evolution of folk narrative into the tales of Chaucer and Boccaccio, the plays of Shakespeare and Molière, the didactic stories of Tolstoy, and the I.W.W. ballads of Joe Hill.

But he will try to keep apart the separate parts of the process, and to study the genesis and structure of a tale or song with full historical and geographical knowledge, as well as with Freudian compassion, Jungian archetypal exhilaration, and Marxian economic sophistication, though perhaps without any school of interpretation taking over. He will never equate folklore with bad science, or brutality, or stupidity, or with any exclusive measure of supernatural inspiration other than that found in all of the arts and crafts of men. He will seek every aid toward definition he can muster, whether of a semantic, a formal, or an operational nature. He may even, as John Stuart Mill said all scientists do, end up with an inductive definition, a mere listing.

But that listing can itself be transcendent. Marius Barbeau, an anthropologist who knew the lore of the Pacific Indian and a folklorist who knew the lore of the French-speaking Canadian, could grow lyrical in the presence of his subject matter. I quote some of his famous definition in Maria Leach's *Dictionary of Folklore, Mythology and Legend*:

> Whenever a lullaby is sung to a child; whenever a ditty, a riddle, a tongue-twister, or a counting-out rime is used in the nursery or at school; whenever sayings, proverbs, fables, noodle-stories, folktales . . . are retold; whenever, out of habit or inclination, the folk indulge in songs and dances, in ancient games, in merry-making, to mark the passing of the year or the usual festivities; whenever a mother shows her daughter how to sew, knit, spin, weave, embroider, make a coverlet, braid a sash, bake an old-fashioned pie; whenever a village craftsman . . . trains his apprentice in the use of tools, shows him how to cut a mortise and peg in a tenon, how to raise a frame house or a barn, how to string a snowshoe . . . then we have folklore in its own perennial domain, at work as ever alive and shifting, always apt to grasp and assimilate new elements on its way. It is old-fashioned . . . fast receding from its former strongholds under the impact of modern progress and industry; it is the born opponent of the serial number, the stamped product, and the patented standard.

Folklore as a whole is not merely "literature transmitted orally," but includes the arts and crafts, beliefs and customs of those who, in American lumber camps, city evangelical storefront churches, back-alley dives, farmers' festivals and fairs, hill frolics, carnivals, firemen's lofts, sailors' cabins, chain gangs and penitentiaries, assemblies of American patriots who are also nostalgic for the Greece, the Serbia, the Scotland, the Polish ghetto, or the remote African jungle from which they come. It may even include city dwellers and college students, who know a lot that they do not get from books. It may appear in print, but it must not freeze into print, on paper or wax or vinyl.

Those of us who know what is written by man know also that it cannot be trusted to reveal the whole of humanity; we need as well the unconscious realms of our minds and souls, which derive from a higher as well as a lower source in their vitality and drive. Sometimes the vitality is best found in folksongs and folktales, which are not impeccable any more than is Shakespeare or Homer, but which often seem to be the best medicine for a lonely crowd of alienated intellectuals who are too much aware of the constant shifting of sophisticated standards and therefore may gain comfort from tradition even when, through revolt, they re-create it. Folklore is oral tradition whenever and wherever you find it; its greatness is that it helps to make the whole man and the whole society both in America and throughout the world.

2

The Men Who Made Folklore a Scholarly Discipline

MacEDWARD LEACH

Folklore in the beginning and for long after was a gentleman's activity. The first requisite was a fixed income, or a government or church sinecure, allowing the gentleman scholar to devote his time to the leisurely pursuit of scholarship for its own sake. There was no worry about making books or making academic way. From a pleasant study overlooking an old English garden or cloistered digs at one of the old universities, the gentleman scholar could indulge in the pleasure of collecting and investigating any odd bits of lore that caught his fancy. If a man was happy in studying the fairy lore of Cornwall, he did that without asking why, or what will it lead to, or is it worth studying. I know only one man today among the some two thousand scholars pursuing knowledge of all kinds at one of our larger universities who is approaching his studies in this unself-conscious, unorganized, but highly enthusiastic spirit. He is studying the wooden toggle fastenings on old Chinese robes. His face glows as he talks about them and with what zeal he shows you fine specimens from his collection.

Such gentlemen scholars were amateurs in the best sense of that term—they loved what they were doing. This does not mean that they were not good at it. Their enthusiasm and industry carried them further than many of their more conventional colleagues ever went in rooting out details, in meticulous concern with data. Most of them died happy in their little world. Of course, they lacked proportion and a sense of relations; these had to wait until the scientific, analytically minded scholar of a later generation came in, scholars who could with a certain amount of condescension use the findings of the amateurs either by refuting them or building on them.

Folklore under various names has been with us ever since man began to take an objective look at his culture. Superstitions, games and pastimes, witchcraft, fairy lore, songs and tales were transmitted orally from generation to generation and as early as the Middle Ages in Europe they were written down and commented on. Strutt's *Games and Pastimes* and Burton's *Anatomy of Melancholy* are examples. Beginning with the eighteenth century, the amateur scholars began to take over as collectors and as investigators of this lore. At first they called it "Popular Antiquities," being impressed with the antique character of it. They also found it fascinating because it was old—the good old days are always better than the here and now. And there was, hovering over, the philosophy that the unspoiled, unselfconscious Eden-like past was perfect—that the road from there is a downward road leading eventually to the prison cell of civilization. The "noble savage" and his close descendants were close to God and to Nature.

It was a bishop and two linguists—brothers—who did much initially to set folklore apart and to make a place for it as a separate field of study. Each was concerned with a single category of folklore, the bishop with the folk ballad and the linguists with tales; but neither saw folk culture as a whole. Bishop Thomas Percy (1729–1811) was more interested in antiquarian things than he was in his bishopric. By chance he discovered a mutilated manuscript in the house of a friend. The maids were using leaves from the manuscript to kindle the fire. When Percy examined it, he found that it contained many old songs, ballads, and many verse tales. Here were songs of witches, fairies, the Devil, tragic stories of unrequited love. Most of the pieces in the manuscript were anonymous, the productions of the folk, sung from generation to generation until they had acquired the fine patina that comes from folk use. Percy published many of the pieces from the manuscript with additions from other sources as *Reliques of Ancient English Poetry* (1765). The book was a sensation in England and eventually on the Continent. Naturally it stimulated men to seek out more such songs and to classify and study them.

Although Percy spent little time in studying the songs, he did try in his way to edit them, to improve on them; in so doing he incurred the wrath of Joseph Ritson, another gentleman scholar interested in ballad and folksong. Ritson declared Percy a fraud, accused him of faking the songs, and even claimed that there was no old manuscript. As a matter of fact, Percy did do a great deal of emendation, rewriting, even perhaps antiquing. The famous ballad, "Edward," which Percy claims was sent to him from Scotland, certainly owes much to Percy's manipulations. Percy and Ritson made England and the Continent aware of folksong and the difference between this kind of song and the sophisticated songs of the time. And Ritson laid the foundation for proper folksong editing and study. Even Sir Walter Scott, one of the greatest antiquarians of them all, one who amassed a great collection of folk ballads, poet that he was, couldn't keep his itching pen away from a ballad fragment, and, like Percy, he added lines, words, and phrases to improve the old pieces that came to him, and, like Percy, by the weight of his authority as an antiquary and as a man of letters did much in Scotland and later in England to cultivate the interest in folksong. His *Minstrelsey of the Scottish Border*—a best-seller through the nineteenth century—kept this interest alive and did much to further the belief that folksongs were likely to need "improving" to prepare them for general acceptance.

The first European scholars to approach folklore as folklore (though they did not call it that) were the brothers Grimm— Wilhelm and Jacob. They have often been referred to as the fathers of folklore because they themselves did systematic collecting and brought their finds to their desks and tried to analyze, classify, and explain them. They did great service to folklore by making it acceptable and available to the public. The scientific scholars may be distressed at their rewriting, editing, and "improving" the folk product, but we must admit that it was this very editing that made them so acceptable and popular. At any rate, the middle-class German and eventually all of Europe came to know something of the charm of folktales. Eventually they became the basic household tales of all Europe and to a certain extent so remain to this day.

Folk theory as worked out by the Grimms was generally subjective. Of the four main ideas promulgated by the Grimms two are today generally discredited; the other two are accepted with some reservation. No longer do we believe that all European folktales are descended from a remote common Indo-European ancestor, as most Indo-European languages are. Nor do we believe that folktales in general are the detritus of ancient myth made more rational. We do accept their third idea that many, not all, folktales in different regions resemble one another closely because they have grown out of similar social mores and cultural situations. Cruel stepparents are found in all cultures; so are cruel-stepparent tales. Belief in the transformation of other animals and men was common; so are tales embodying this belief.

The Grimms also suggested the idea that tales and songs traveled across borders, even across culture and linguistic borders, and that this may account for the similarity of stories among people widely separated. The "Two Brothers" story, originally Egyptian, is now found in every country in Europe and in most Oriental countries. The Grimms had little idea of a science of folklore in the broad meaning of the term, for they were primarily interested in tales only.

English scholars, however, concerned themselves with ancient beliefs, with ancient rituals, with old songs of the folk as well as with the tales. But the approach was always from an antiquarian point of view. In 1846 one of these antiquarians, William Thoms, trying for a name that would be more defining and exclusive, coined the word "folklore." By this term he said he meant man's observances, superstitions, ballads, proverbs—all the lore of ancient times. In other words, Thoms conceived of folklore as culture survival of an earlier day. Thoms was very active in collecting, editing, and publishing folklore. He founded and edited *Notes and Queries* for the exchange of such data and he was founder and first president of the Folklore Society. This society and its journal have been the center of English folklore studies ever since. And Thoms's word "folklore" has been adopted by most of the languages of Europe, suggesting certainly a body of common culture—the lore of all folk transcending language differences, nationalities, political beliefs, and ideologies.

T. Crofton-Croker (1798–1854), an Admiralty clerk, turned to folklore in his spare time. He tapped the rich Irish store of folktales and legends and published them in *Fairy Legends and Traditions of Southern Ireland*. This was a seminal work and a popular one. Crofton-Croker was in advance of his time in providing the tales with scholarly notes discussing the culture matrix out of which the tales came, their sources, comparative data. He stimulated others to produce such works.

Probably the most important of these was his friend Thomas Keightley, also an Irishman. Keightley's important books are *The Fairy Mythology* and *Tales and Popular Fictions*. *The Fairy Mythology* is still unsurpassed as a collection and as a scholarly analysis of the fairy lore of Europe. Oral tradition supplies most of the content but Keightley, after weighing sources, used written collections as well, such as romances and Greek and Norse tales. The revised edition published in the Bohn Library (1860) is still a standard work.

A little later in the century, two scholars, though at first basically interested in other fields, did much to stimulate the scientific study of folklore. The one was Max Müller, philologist, translator, editor, teacher at Oxford; the other, Andrew Lang, journalist, novelist, historian, anthropologist, compiler of folklore and fairy tales, prolific man of letters. Müller was a keen Sanskrit scholar. He edited the *Rig-Veda* and, in fifty-one scholarly volumes, *The Sacred Books of the East*.

These studies in the languages and lore of the East aroused his interest in comparative linguistics and eventually in comparative religions and mythologies. From his cloistered study at Oxford, surrounded by his library of orientalia and philology, by a process of introspection and speculation and using the dubious analogy of the development of language, Müller developed the theory of folklore origins that came to be known as solar mythology or the comparative science of mythology. Myth, he insisted, began when Sanskrit, or later European languages, began to pass into the dialects derived from them, with the result that the original names of the sky gods and their attributes became distorted and corrupted and so ambiguous that new interpretations were made. Through such "disease of language," loss of old meanings, figurative use of words, and folk etymology, the original myths of the old gods were enlarged and directed into new stories. The sun god with his darting rays and beams of light, his heat, his vehicle that carries him across the sky, his battling with the opposite gods of darkness and death as he fights his way over insuperable obstacles, clouds, storms, and raging winds, become, in turn, let us say, CúChulainn, the hero of the Celts, raging down the battlefield in his chariot, his sword flashing, his body heat so great that no one can approach him as he puts to rout the forces of evil, the enemies of his people. Müller had little knowledge of peoples other than the Aryan. Had he known the American Indian, for example, he would have discovered that some tribes have no or few myths and that, in general, the non-mythic folktales far exceed the myths. Basically, Müller's theory is unscientific because it is predicated on superficial knowledge of tales and culture and because its method, like that of the myth-ritualists of our own day, is based on speculation and preconception.

Andrew Lang, the man of letters, was a constant critic of Müller and his solar mythology. He attacked it directly, pointing out that no two solar mythologists had the same explanation for the same set of figures or symbols and that consequently the explanation was what any individual wanted to make it; that Müller took little cognizance of ethnology, preferring to float in a cloud of mystic poetizing rather than fastening his data to anthropological fact. Although Lang was not a trained anthropologist (few were in the 1880's), his approach was generally dubbed anthropological and he was saluted as head of the anthropological school. The Müller-Lang controversy did get folklore widely considered and debated and did much to get it accepted as an important scholarly discipline. The reputation of the disputants was enough to see to that. Groups of scholars lined up on both sides; many books were written and many articles published.

Naturally Müller stimulated interest in Indo-European culture as the fount from which all European culture waters flowed. That idea could be entertained whether one believed in a solarist explanation or not. Were not most European languages traceable to Indo-European? Were not many of the stories in Sanskrit, in such books as the *Mahabarata*, also found in European culture?

One does not need disease of language or a mytho-poetic imagination to explain the close parallel of the tales of the East with many of those of Europe says Theodore Benfey, the great Indianist of the end of the century and student of comparative folklore. Many of the European tales are Indian tales Europeanized. When, for example, the Oriental tale—"Matron of Ephesus"—is read along with its European version, the proof is evident. William C. Clouston (1843–1896) made this idea even more plausible by printing texts from Oriental sources and texts from the West, with studies and analogues, in such books as *Popular Tales and Fictions* (1887). Today folklorists readily grant that many European tales do diffuse from the Orient, but now that we have many good collections from non-Indo-European sources we would never think of the Orient as the one center from which all folk cultures emanated.

The Indianists naturally accepted the idea of folklore as survival and by the end of the nineteenth century this idea came more and more to be echoed. Edward Clodd carried it to a degree uncomfortable to the clergy when he expressed the belief that the Bible is no different in kind from other collections of folktales and that Christian ritual is a survival of older pre-Christian rituals and that Christian myth depends in detail on pre-Christian myth. The church and state attacked such ideas (Gladstone resigned from the Folklore Society, of which Clodd was president). The general public became involved, and with involvement came awareness of folklore. Still today, be it noted, there is a tendency in common orthodox circles to think of folklore as a study housing religion with superstition and indeed sending Christmas back to the rites of Woden and Baldr.

With Sir James Frazer we come to one school in the long series which brought folklore and the science of folklore to worldwide acceptance. Frazer (1854–1941) was a Scottish anthropologist, a professor at the University of Liverpool. The work which brought him international recognition is *The Golden Bough* (1890), revised edition, twelve large volumes (1911–1915). This is a vast compendium of savage and primitive cults, rituals, beliefs, magical practices, ancient religions, taboos, myths, and festivals, drawn from hundreds of sources. It is here arranged and discussed, following principles which Frazer developed over the years.

Unfortunately, Frazer was only a desk scholar; he never went into the field to study people other than those of his own culture. His theory that all people pass through the same evolutionary stages and that consequently they will develop the same rituals, myths, songs, and stories is not now tenable as a generalization. He also believed that survivals of lower culture generally persist into a higher culture. Even so, his insistence on factual material and his predications on concrete data set a precedent and established a methodology in folklore and anthropological studies. *The Golden Bough* became almost sacrosanct, one of the "great books," and it did much to establish folklore as a science. Today *The Golden Bough* is still useful, but it should be used in the one-volume revised edition, edited by Theodore Gaster (1959). Gaster's final evaluation of the book is: "It may be said without reasonable fear of contradiction that no other work in the field . . . has contributed so much to the mental and artistic climate of our times."

The new science of folklore occupied the important scholars during the last decades of the nineteenth and the beginning of the twentieth century. The result was the founding of scholarly societies. The most important are the English Folklore Society with its publications, *Folklore, The Folklore Record*; the American Folklore Society (1888) with its journal and its Memoir Series—book-length studies of folklore. Many of the books published during this period reflect this scientific interest: Sir George Laurence Gomme's *Folklore as an Historical Science* and *Handbook of Folklore*; J. H. MacCulloch's *The Childhood of Fiction*; Hartland's *The Science of Fairy Tales*; George Cox's *An Introduction to the Science of Comparative Mythology and Folklore.* Marion Cox's large study of "Cinderella" should be mentioned because it is a kind of forerunner of the historico-geographical method of studying tales later worked out by the Finnish School of Folklorists as set forth in various publications, such as K. Krohn's *Die Folkloristische Arbeitsmethode,* and culminating in Stith Thompson's six-volume *Motif Index of Folk Literature* and *The Types of the Folktale.* Briefly, the historico-geographical method stresses collecting as many versions of a tale over as wide an area as possible and so establishing a time-space relation to determine the original home of the archetype.

At the very end of the century there appeared another great book, one that did much to give the study of folksong scientific recognition. This is Francis J. Child's *The English and Scottish*

Popular Ballads, in five volumes (1892–1898). Child spent a life-time compiling this collection from all known sources except immediate oral tradition. He drew on dozens of manuscripts and hundreds of books. His voluminous notes based on world-wide sources are astonishingly complete and erudite. This book and a similar great study in Denmark by Grundtvig, *Gamle Volk-viser,* turned hundreds of scholars to scientific study of ballads and folksongs, studies continuing to the present day. Cecil Sharp, a British musicologist, was the first important collector to make a systematic attempt to collect ballads and folksongs directly from folksingers. His work in Appalachian music offered a model for the full study of folksong—text and melody—which finally culminated in what is becoming the definitive work: Bertrand Bronson's *Traditional Tunes of the Child Ballads.*

In the twentieth century, folklore as an educational discipline comes finally into its own. More than one hundred colleges and universities give courses in folklore. Some have gone further and developed planned programs to train graduate students and award advanced degrees. Indiana University has had a full folklore program for a long time, first under the direction of Stith Thompson and now under that of Richard M. Dorson. Every four years Indiana holds a Folklore Institute with an enrollment of more than seventy-five students from all over the world. The University of California at Los Angeles presents an interde-partmental program under the direction of Professors Wayland D. Hand and D. K. Wilgus. The University of Pennsylvania administers a large number of undergraduate and graduate courses leading to the Ph.D. in folklore.

Folk and folklore have become "good words" in American cul-ture. The result is that the chauvinistic as well as the radical groups appropriate these words to sell medicine, trade unionism, beatnik ideologies, and to protest anything one wants to protest about. This pseudo-folklore has very aptly been designated by the William Thoms of the twentieth century, Richard Dorson, as "fakelore." But folklore as a scientific discipline is now firmly established with its own methodology, philosophy, and content.

3

Harvesting Folklore

KENNETH S. GOLDSTEIN

Archivists, library researchers, and analysts all have their importance in furthering the aims of folklore scholarship, but most important are the field workers who harvest the crop of folklore materials and data without which the others would be unable to carry on their work. In the not so distant past, library scholars were usually distinct and separate from those hardy souls who ventured into the field to obtain the data for their discipline. With the increase in the number of professionally trained full-time folklorists, this separation is less marked; the folklorist of today is frequently field worker, library researcher, and analyst all rolled into one. And with this increasing dependence of the folklorist on his own collecting experiences for the raw data out of which he builds his models and theories, there are fewer gross misunderstandings of folk tradition and considerably sounder theories upon which to construct the foundations for the developing science of folklore.

If the aim of modern folklore scholarship is to develop the discipline as a science (albeit a social science closely connected with the humanities), then every step along the route must be dealt with in a scientific manner. No longer can folklorists indulge themselves in collecting for the sake of collection alone. Collecting must be more than merely an enjoyable experience that can be pursued during holidays or vacations. There exist tons of data obtained in such a desultory manner—data which are of little use to the professional folklorist. The researcher-analyst may apply the most rigorous methods during the later stages of investigation, but unless the primary data have been properly obtained with a full understanding of context and process, the most scientific of methods may not retrieve the situation later on. *All* stages of inquiry must be pursued with equal rigor.

The first stage of scientific folklore inquiry involves careful formulation and analysis of the specific problem (or problems) on which the field trip will be based. His knowledge of folklore theory will suggest to the collector what problems need solving, and it is this knowledge which will shape the course of his field work. Collecting that is initiated without specific goals will be arbitrary, unorganized, perfunctory, and wasteful of time, money, and energy. Rarely does a collector have enough time in the field even without such waste.

Once the problem has been stated, the collector must analyze it to determine (1) where field work should be done; (2) the time required to do it effectively; (3) the kinds of materials and data that should be obtained in order to solve the problem; (4) the types of methods and techniques to be employed in obtaining the relevant materials and data; and (5) *an assessment of the collector's ability to carry out the necessary work.* This last point is emphasized because field work means dealing with people; it involves the ability of the collector to adjust to new situations and new personalities that express themselves in ways that may be different from those with which he is familiar. Problem statement and analysis, even with such self-evaluation, will not necessarily guarantee the success of the field trip, but it should minimize the possibility of error.

Once the collector is in the field it may be too late for him to catch up with many details and matters which should have been dealt with in his preliminary preparations. These preparations include familiarizing himself with available literature on the area and peoples among whom he will be living, contacting previous collectors who worked the area, corresponding with persons who may help ease his way into the community (the postmaster, doctor, teachers, librarians, ministers, and so on), and preparing adequate supplies and equipment for use during his stay in the field. In addition to notebooks, paper, typewriter, and other writing supplies, the collector must be sure he has the proper equipment for recording and filming informants. Even more important, he should have prepared sufficiently in advance to allow himself adequate time for testing and practicing with the equipment. Machines are no better than the technicians who run them, and once in the field it may be too late to achieve such proficiency. He must also obtain certain technical information regarding the area in which he will be using the equipment. If the area is only partly electrified, two recorders, one operating from batteries and another from a power main, may be necessary.

The story is told of a collector who spent almost an hour erecting a studio-model tape recorder in the modest home of a rural peasant singer only to be told, when he looked for an outlet to plug in the equipment, that the house was not electrified. The situation could still have been saved, however, if the collector had had a battery-operated machine. Where power mains do exist, he must know the type as well as the voltage and frequency of the current available, so that the equipment may be supplied with converters and transformers. Weather conditions may similarly dictate the type of supplies to be used with the equipment. The collector should also be able to make minor mechanical repairs and know where he can find the nearest repair facilities and sources for spare parts in the case of a major breakdown.

One objective should guide the collector once he reaches the region in which his field work is to be done: he must establish rapport with the inhabitants of the community as quickly as possible and maintain it during the duration of his stay. Without rapport, his project cannot be carried out successfully; with it, he is at least certain of being able to work as effectively as his training and his time in the field will permit.

There is, however, no single technique for establishing rapport. No two situations in the field are identical; no collector is like any other collector; no informant or groups of informants react to the collecting situation in the same way. In northeastern Scotland, one potential informant was ready and willing to sing from the moment I mentioned my collecting project to him while waiting in the line to a grocer's shop; he immediately burst into song to the delight of myself and the persons near us. Other singers and storytellers were more reluctant to part with their folklore, and in some cases it took several months to obtain the first few items, after which, however, their entire repertory was mine with little further urging.

The personal factor rules the scene. The intelligent, personable, sociable, and sensitive person will find his own way to establish the relationships essential if he is to achieve his goal. The manner in which he does so will be guided by his problem, by the time he has to spend in the field, by his knowledge of his own personality, and by his ability to recognize clues to the personalities of potential informants. But from the moment he sets foot in the community, his every activity is part of the pattern for establishing rapport.

In seeking living quarters for himself and his family, in making necessary purchases of food, clothing, and fuel, and in arranging for transportation, he should seek help from his new neighbors. By aiding him, the collector's new friends put him in their debt. He must know how to reciprocate, and usually this will involve little more than satisfying their curiosity as to the purpose of his visit. In doing so, however, he must not jeopardize his project. His purpose in collecting folklore materials and data is a scientific one—one that they may neither understand nor appreciate. No informant likes to be placed under a microscope and scrutinized like test-tube bacilli, and yet, in a very real sense, that is the aim of the collector. A field worker is therefore forced to play a role that an informant can understand and appreciate. The roles from which he may choose are limited, first, to those which he is willing and able to play, and second, to the range of roles which the community is willing to allow him to play. The role he finally selects must fit into those areas in which his intentions and abilities overlap the community's expectations of him.

A statement that he is a folklorist will make little or no sense to most of his potential informants. Instead, the collector, avoiding technical jargon, should stress some aspect of his work that will be understandable and familiar to the majority of the community: "I'm interested in writing a book of the beautiful old stories told here," or "I'm putting together an old-fashioned songbook so that our children will be able to sing the old ballads." The combination of a simple statement and flattery may smooth the way to initial acceptance. In a community in which the citizens are aware of the differences between their own traditions and those of others, the collector's statement that he wishes to study those differences may suffice. Or he may indicate that he wishes to learn the local dialect, immediately putting his informants in the position of experts and readily leading to the collection of song and tale texts. Whatever his initial role, he will find that as soon as he has established some degree of rapport with the community in general, he will be able to broaden that role and subsequently make his full plan clear to them. Eventually he will be looked upon as a part of the daily scene, albeit a rather strange part at times.

The collector will find that his best avenue to such generalized acceptance is through participation in the community's activities. Without forcing his way into such activities, he must try to take part in as many of them as possible. His problem will consist not in having to find entree to these activities, but in being able to find the time to accept the many invitations that will be extended to him.

Such participation involves certain limitations and hazards, however. Though he may consort with members of his own age and sex group at a level of equality, he must contend with lesser acceptance from other members of the community. In one Scots village I was told of women's tea-klatches during which, in addition to gossip, many songs and tales were exchanged. I tried to obtain permission to attend such sessions, but was refused on the ground that the stories and songs sometimes were bawdy, and the women did not wish to have a stranger catch them with their hair down. However, the real reason for my exclusion was my sex. This became apparent when, several weeks later, my wife was invited to one of these gatherings, though she was as much a stranger to these women as I was.

In seeking out contacts with members of the community, the collector must be careful not to invade the privacy of his potential informants in personal matters. Nor should he allow himself to be drawn into any factionalism that may exist. To do so will alienate some, and perhaps all, of the many individuals whose good will he needs.

In addition to the limitations and hazards of participation indicated, the collector must face up to the possible cost in personal discomfort to which participation may lead. Under the strain of constantly accommodating himself to others, of living in the public spotlight, of having his good nature taken advantage of, of playing a role and living up to the status it carries, of not being able to indulge in his own idiosyncrasies while forced to tolerate those of others, of continually being careful to avoid untoward incidents and then having to deal with them as they inevitably arise—under the strain of all these and more, the collector's patience is sure to be tried. The personal discomfort resulting therefrom must eventually affect his field work. Then, too, if the collector overidentifies with his informants, his scientific observation, evaluation, and analysis may be impaired. Aware of this possibility from his training, he must guard against such impairment. But just being on guard can itself result in considerable discomfort.

He may remedy such participation-fatigue by periodically reviewing his role in the community and, from his knowledge of his physical and psychological endurance limits, deciding to what extent he will continue to participate in its activities. Or he may simply remove himself from the field situation, taking a vacation whenever he recognizes the symptoms of participation-fatigue and returning only when he feels refreshed. In determining the degree to which he will participate in the community's activities, the collector must keep two sets of factors in mind: (1) active participation enables him to reduce suspicion, establish rapport, and enhance the naturalness of his position in the community, and (2) participation opens new avenues to understanding his informants and the community, and should lead to collecting more and better data to be used in problem solution. Thus, in a very real sense, participation may be the key to successful field work.

Before proceeding to a discussion of actual collecting methods, the potential field worker should be aware of the kinds of folklore field data which it is possible to collect:

1. *Folklore Materials*: These consist of the folktales, songs, rhymes, games, proverbs, riddles, customs, beliefs, and so on, which are part of the traditional knowledge of the collector's informants. In the past, such folklore materials, with a bare minimum of data concerning from whom, when, and where the materials were collected, were the total data usually reported from field trips. Modern folklore theory and practice requires that the following additional data also be obtained.

2. *Folklore Processes*: These consist of the actual manner in which folklore is transmitted, the social and physical contexts

involved in such transmission, and the specific oral performance styles of folklore informants.

3. *Folklore Ideas*: This category concerns the concepts tradition-bearers hold about folklore, and includes their attitudes, feelings, themes, taxonomy, and aesthetics, as well as individual and group psychological and social reactions to the materials and processes of folklore.

Of the several methods and techniques which may be used in folklore collecting, two will serve to supply the collector with practically all the data necessary for the solution of most field problems. These two methods are observation and interview. *Observation methods* are used by the collector to obtain data by direct observation, looking from the outside in and describing the situation as he sees it. *Interview methods* are used by the field worker to obtain data about ideas and events outside the context of the interview itself through questioning persons believed or known to have that information. During the interview informants may describe processes, contexts, attitudes, and ideas from the vantage point of the insider, in addition to presenting the actual materials of folklore. A combination of both methods should yield the widest range of data, with the emphasis on one or the other shifting with the frame of reference. The two methods will be described separately.

Interviewing is the most common field method employed by folklore collectors. This method is used to obtain the following kinds of data: (1) personal histories of the informant; (2) aesthetics of the informants; (3) feelings, attitudes, and knowledge of the informants, and the meanings that their folklore has for them; (4) information concerning the transmission processes of folklore, including basic data as to when, where, from whom, and how informants learned the pieces in their repertory; (5) descriptions of folklore contexts which the collector is unable to observe; and (6) the informants' repertory of actual folklore materials.

There are two basic interview techniques. The *non-directive* interview consists of a rather generalized conversation between a collector and his informant in which the latter is allowed almost completely free rein after the collector has suggested a subject. People like to talk about things which interest them, and the field worker must be ready to appear interested in the same things. The technique permits the informant's spontaneous responses to be as full and detailed as he cares to make them. It allows for a wide range of subjects and materials to be covered according to the informant's own manner of ordering them. By eliciting the personal and social context of attitudes and feelings, it serves to reveal value-laden implications of the informant's psychology. It is especially valuable in the earlier stages of rapport establishment because of its seeming casualness and lack of directed probing into the informant's life. It may also serve to extract information that an informant would be unwilling to give in response to direct questions.

Once the collector has achieved some degree of rapport with his informant, the *directive* interview may be employed. By a series of pointed questions, the collector elicits highly specific information on particular subjects, ideas, or materials. The informant should be free to express his own ideas in his own terms and frame of reference, while at the same time the collector discourages irrelevancies and endeavors to confine the conversation to the specific issues about which he seeks knowledge. The task is not an easy one, for the collector must obtain the full cooperation of his subject in an atmosphere considerably less permissive than that of the non-directive interview.

Most interviews consist of a compromise between the two techniques described. A topic will be suggested and at first the informant will be allowed to ramble. At some point of special interest to the collector, the directive approach will be applied so that the conversation and responses may be kept within certain limits. The extent to which the two techniques are combined will depend largely upon the kinds of information being elicited.

Even when he is able to obtain full answers to all his questions, the collector should not delude himself into believing he has obtained wholly truthful or accurate responses in every case. Whatever the social or psychological reasons for an informant's supplying untruthful or inaccurate answers, there are several methods by which the collector can check interview responses. Where the informant has given information relative to observable phenomena, the collector may check those statements by his own observations. He may also conduct interviews with other informants on the same subjects; this precaution affords him an opportunity not only to crosscheck the accuracy of different informants but to gain additional information. The third method is to conduct several interviews on the same subject with the same informant. These re-interviews will serve to reveal inconsistencies, enable the collector to obtain a clearer impression of the matters being discussed, and help to develop different aspects of the same subject.

The collector should be aware that statements made and material supplied by an informant may be radically affected by the social context of the interview. When alone with the collector an informant may be willing to discuss things he would never reveal in the company of neighbors or relatives. More than one of my informants in North Carolina, when in the company of his neighbors, denied that he believed in superstitions, but readily admitted it when alone with me. Conversely, the informant may supply certain information only when he has the support of the company, especially if he feels it may otherwise be disbelieved or made fun of by the collector. One of my Scots informants denied ever having heard of ghosts until he heard some of his neighbors tell me stories about them. Then, fortified by the knowledge that such beliefs were not peculiar to him and that the collector would not ridicule him for maintaining them, he proceeded to supply me with many hours of legends about local ghosts and other supernatural creatures.

The collector should also be aware that evasiveness or inaccuracy of information will vary inversely with the degree of rapport that has been established. The collector's approach to all data received from his informant must be one of sympathy, respect, and privacy, and in time the informant will relax his guard. In this sense every interview session is an occasion for increasing rapport with one's informants. The interview is not only the best context for obtaining data about the informant's view of things; it is also the context in which the collecting of most of the longer items of folklore—ballads and tales—is done. We would, of course, like to collect all items of folklore in the contexts in which they are normally performed, but to do so might make the informants so self-conscious as to sacrifice naturalness. We thus usually restrict ourselves to observational methods in natural contexts, and collect the materials of folklore in the artificial context of the interview. Since the natural contexts for the performance of folklore are not particularly conducive to asking questions about the histories of specific items in the informant's repertory, these data should be obtained in interview sessions in which such questioning does not interrupt his normal activities.

Recorded interviews should be transcribed as soon as possible. The greater the delay between interview and transcription, the less keen the memory of what was said or performed. Immediate transcription will enable relatively full recall of the interview to be utilized in deciphering dialect and pronunciation. Where obscure words or localisms exist, the collector can read the transcribed texts to his informants to check the accuracy of his transcription and obtain explanations of any matters not within his ken. Extra copies of all notes and recordings made in the field should be arranged for, and these duplicate sets of data should then be sent to an archive or to the collector's home so that copies will be available if he should lose his original records.

The second major field method—observation—though utilized to a lesser degree than interviewing, is the best means of collecting certain folklore data. It is, for example, the only method which permits the collector to obtain objective empirical data on the intricate workings of the actual physical contexts in which folklore is normally performed and transmitted.

Observations may be made from the vantage point of the collector's role both as an active participant in an event and as an onlooker. If he can arrange to be accepted as an equal in the situation, as a participant-observer, he will be able to study the context objectively, while achieving at least partial identification with other participants and thereby obtaining information on both internal content of the situation and its mechanics. The major disadvantage of assuming the role of participant-observer is the necessary delay in putting one's impressions on paper. If the event is a long one, has many participants or a large number of separate activities, it will be possible for the collector to retain only a portion of the details that need to be remembered and later recorded. It must also be recognized that the ability of the collector to become a participant-observer will depend upon the degree to which he has achieved generalized acceptance in the community. Anything less than a high degree of acceptance may result in his presence continually being noted by other participants, thereby making them so self-conscious that the naturalness of the context is destroyed.

At folklore affairs that involve many participants and large audiences, the collector may make his observations as an onlooker, remaining on the fringe of the activity or mingling with the audience. As a non-participant he may be able to view the entire kaleidoscope rather than merely one or two segments of it. Removed from the center of the action, he should be able to take notes and perhaps even use a tape recorder or a camera to record the event.

Collecting observational data in the natural contexts in which folklore is performed is usually a matter of being in the right place at the right time. By observing these natural contexts, the field worker can learn a great deal about folklore processes. He will be able to record behavior simultaneously with its spontaneous occurrence, thereby noting what people actually do rather than what they say they do. Activities may be observed which informants take so much for granted that they would be unlikely to comment on them in interview sessions. Although certain formal folklore contexts present little difficulty in making observations (for example, those for which there is a large audience), some may never occur when the collector is in the community. Burial and wedding customs may be observed only at funerals and marriages, and if these do not occur during the collector's stay, he must obtain data about them from interviews. Certain semi-formal contexts (the singing of songs and the telling of tales while at work or on occasions of neighborly socializing) present only the problem of arranging to be present when they take place. Because such events are usually unscheduled, this may not always be possible. Many of these semi-formal contexts, however, can be artificially induced by the collector. The collector can invite a number of informants to his home for a social evening and then lead the activities around to storytelling or riddling. While playing the role of participant-observer, he makes mental notes of the context, to be recorded on paper when the evening is over. This can usually be achieved without his informant-friends knowing the real purpose of the evening, thus assuring the unself-consciousness found in natural folklore contexts.

The question is not so much *how* to observe as it is *what* to observe. This will depend, of course, upon the specific problem the collector has set for himself. Of the many details which make up a folklore context only certain ones will be pertinent to the problem. In making decisions as to what is relevant, the collector should keep the following types of data in mind: (1) descriptions of the physical setting; (2) descriptions of the social setting; (3) the interaction between participants; (4) factors in the actual performance of folklore materials; (5) time and duration data; (6) sentiments and reactions of performers and audience; and (7) data describing the collector himself (his role, state of mind, physical condition, and so on, any of which may affect his observations).

In addition to the methods of interview and observation, the collector can utilize certain supplementary field methods to obtain folklore data in the community he is studying. He may make use of available mass communications media in the community to obtain leads to informants. He can utilize school-children to direct him to the major tradition-bearers in their families, as well as collecting from the children themselves through school-sponsored projects. And he may use questionnaires to obtain data from people whom he is unable to meet because of factors of time or distance.

Whatever methods the collector uses to obtain folklore data from the citizens of a community, he should not delude himself into thinking that a mechanical knowledge of field methodology will ensure the success of his project. The most important factor in successful collecting is his ability to persuade informants to search their memories and reveal the folklore texts that are so intricately and personally woven into their lives. While many collectors use such material inducements as monetary payments, gifts, or liquor, the psychological gratification which the informant receives from his relationship to his collector-friend is the determining factor. By participating as fully and naturally as possible in the activities of the community, and by a consistent pattern of socializing with informants, the collector is able to work toward creating the kind of deep relationship which will permit him to obtain the full confidence of his informants. What motivates an informant to allow the collector to probe deeply is the mutual regard which the two eventually develop. There is no question of rewarding the informant at this level because the relationship is rewarding in itself. The informant comes to feel valued as a person, not just as a source of data, to know that he is talking to someone who is sympathetic as well as curious.

The collector who wishes to come to grips with the essence of the folklore process, with its meaning and motivation, must know the inner man behind it. He can know the inner man only by becoming deeply involved with him. In doing so, he sets up a reciprocity of exchange based on rapport and empathy. And it is upon such rapport and empathy with our informants, more than anything else, that our success in the field depends.

4

Ways of Studying Folklore

ALAN DUNDES

There are many ways of studying folklore. The literary scholar treats folklore as literature or as source material for literary masterworks. The historian regards folklore as data supplying folk attitudes toward historical events and figures. The anthropologist sees folklore as a people's autobiographical description of themselves, a description which helps the inquiring ethnographer to see the culture he is studying from the inside out rather than from the outside in. The psychologist considers much of folklore to be collective fantasy with important clues for the analysis of both social and individual psychology. The educator thinks of folklore as part of the treasured heritage of national and ethnic groups which can be used to enrich and enliven otherwise routine curricular offerings. And so the members of different disciplines come to the materials of folklore with different interests and with different ideas as to how folklore should be understood and utilized. This variety of approaches to the study of folklore is healthy and it attests to the inherent value of folkloristic data. However, there are a number of distinct approaches to the study of folklore in the United States.

One of the principal approaches to folklore concerns the question of origin. Where and when did a particular ballad or folktale first arise? Unfortunately, the origins of most folklore are difficult to determine. Still, it is possible to make an educated guess in some instances. For example, suppose someone collected a story from a Creek Indian in which a rabbit trickster challenges first a sea cow and then an elephant to a test of strength in which he and his opponent are to pull on a long piece of vine. The rabbit gives one end to the sea cow and the other to the elephant and tells each to pull as soon as he feels a tug. Then the rabbit jerks the middle of the line which rests on a hill separating the sea cow in the water and the elephant on land. Both the victims pull until they are tired. They are, needless to say, astonished by the apparent strength of the rabbit. What is the origin of this tale? Is it an indigenous aboriginal American Indian tale? Is it one of the many European folktales borrowed by the American Indians? Could it be an African folktale borrowed by the Indians? In order to tackle the problem, the folklorist would consult Stith Thompson's six-volume *Motif-Index of Folk Literature: A Classification of Narrative Elements in Folktales, Ballads, Myths, Fables, Mediaeval Romances, Exempla, Fabliaux, Jest-Books and Local Legends.* A motif is a unit of folk narrative which may be a distinctive actor (e.g., a witch), an item (e.g., a magic wand), or an incident (e.g., a deceptive tug-of-war). In Thompson's *Motif-Index*, which came out in revised form in 1955–1958, folktales, legends, and myths from all over the world have been broken down into their constituent motifs and these motifs are assigned an appropriate alphabetical and numerical designation. Folklorists normally identify narrative folklore with reference to these motif numbers. Looking in Volume Six, the alphabetically arranged index volume, the folklorist must try to determine what the key identifying word in the one or more motifs might be. In the Creek Indian story summarized, the key phrase is "tug-of-war," which is a traditional game in which two individuals or two teams pull against each other. In Volume Six of the *Motif-Index* one finds following "Tug-of-war" the symbol K22. The folklorist would then turn to the fourth volume of the *Motif-Index* (which contains all J–K motif numbers) to K22, where he would find the following:

K22. Deceptive tug-of-war. Small animal challenges two large animals to a tug-of-war. Arranges it so that they unwittingly pull against each other.

This seems to be the Creek story all right, but what about its origin? Underneath the synopsis of the motif are listed bibliographical references indicating where this motif may be found. In this case, there are references to Mpongwe, Ibo, and Ila versions, which reveal that the story is found among these peoples in Africa. (As a matter of fact, the story is widely reported throughout Africa.) Other versions listed in the *Motif-Index* include one in Joel Chandler Harris' famous collection of American Negro "Uncle Remus" stories and several West Indies Negro and South American Negro versions. Of equal importance and relevance is the fact that *no* references are made to collections of European or American Indian tales. Clearly, the tale is popular in African and New World Negro groups and thus one could logically assume that the Creek Indians probably borrowed the tale from American Negro tradition. Since the Creeks formerly lived in the southeastern portion of the United States (especially in Georgia), this hypothesis sounds reasonable. Of course, this explains only the immediate historical origin of the Creek tale. The ultimate origin explanation would have to show when and where the tale first was told in Africa and ideally why the tale was made up in the first place.

There are other folklore indexes besides the *Motif-Index*. For example, there are indexes of American ballads, standard collections of English riddles, and international folklore indexes, all of which are extremely useful to the folklorist. Such indexes enable him to establish in a matter of moments that a given item collected from the folk is in fact a traditional item, and they also provide some hint of the item's distribution and popularity. For example, suppose an American folklorist collected the following joke:

At a wedding, the groom asked his father-in-law for the secret of his marital success. How was it that he had been happily married all these years? His father-in-law replied that he would be glad to explain his secret. On his wedding day, he and his new bride had ridden off on horseback. Along the way, his bride's horse had stumbled and this frightened her. He immediately dismounted and, approaching her horse, he struck it sharply on its snout, saying,

"That's once." They rode on until the woman's horse shied again, causing her to cry out once more. This time he found a stout stick which he used to clout the recalcitrant beast, saying as he did so, "That's twice." After continuing on for some time, the bride's horse, startled by a breaking twig, started to bolt which almost unseated the young bride. At this point, the man took out a pistol, walked over to his bride's horse, and shot it right between the eyes, exclaiming, "That's three times." Watching this, the bride became almost hysterical and she began to berate her husband, telling him that he must be some kind of heartless brute to kill a poor dumb defenseless animal. He suddenly approached her, cuffed her gently on the cheek, and said, "That's once!"

Is this a traditional story? Is it peculiar to the United States or is it found in other parts of the world? The folklorist could look up this story using the *Motif-Index*, but in this instance he might elect to use a folktale index. In 1910, the Finnish folklorist Antti Aarne published his *Verzeichnis der Marchentypen*, an index of folktale types. This index, twice revised by Stith Thompson (in 1928 and again in 1961), contains synopses of most of the traditional folktales of the Indo-European world. Looking in the index section of the 1961 edition of *The Types of the Folktale: A Classification and Bibliography* under the entry "Shrewish wife reformed," one finds a reference to Tale Type, Number 901. Turning to Type 901 in the *Index*, the folklorist would find the following:

901. Taming of the Shrew. The youngest of three sisters is a shrew. For their disobedience the husband shoots his dog and his horse. Brings his wife to submission.

This is the same story as the "That's once" joke, but is it an exclusively American item? Definitely not. Beneath the synopsis are references to versions from Estonia, Finland, Sweden, Denmark, Iceland, Lithuania, Germany, Ireland, Scotland, France, Spain, Austria, Yugoslavia, Russia, and India. And, incidentally, it is also noted that this folktale plot is the basis of Shakespeare's *The Taming of the Shrew*. (One could have found the appropriate tale type if one had looked in the *Motif-Index* under motif T 251.2, Taming the Shrew. Happily, the tale type and motif-indexes are cross-referenced. The *Motif-Index* is worldwide in coverage, whereas the tale type index covers only Indo-European materials and only folktales, not legends and myths.)

A more sophisticated type of origin study involves the tracking down of literally hundreds of versions of the same proverb, ballad, or folktale. This gathering of versions is the first step in what folklorists call the "historic-geographic" method, which is basically the same as the comparative method employed in many other disciplines. It is called historic-geographic because the dimensions of *time* and *place* are both taken into account in trying to reconstruct the original basic or *ur-form* of a folktale or ballad. Generally speaking, the older the version and the more widely it is geographically spread, the more likely it is that some if not all of its elements were contained in the hypothetical original form from which all other (cognate) versions are assumed to derive. The historic-geographic method is sometimes termed the Finnish method in honor of the Finnish folklorist who helped to devise and refine it. (The standard treatise on the method is Kaarle Krohn's *Die Folkloristiche Arbeitsmethode*, which was published in Oslo in 1926. For a sample historic-geographic study in which this essentially European method is applied to an American Indian tale, see Stith Thompson's "The Star Husband Tale," in *The Study of Folklore*, edited by Alan Dundes, in 1965.

One interesting facet of the comparative method concerns the dependence upon international cooperation for a successful study. Most of the folktales and many of the ballads which have been studied have international distribution. The *Taming of the Shrew* tale is a typical example. For this reason, the American folklorist who wants to undertake a comparative study of a particular folktale or game must locate all available versions of his tale or game from all over the world. Some versions will be in published collections, but as many or more will be found in the various folklore archives which exist in many different countries. Folklore archives are essentially repositories of unpublished manuscript and tape-recorded collections of folklore made by professional and amateur folklorists. The folklore archive is so arranged that if a folklorist in one country writes to the archive concerning a particular folktale, the folklore archivist can easily find the appropriate versions in his archive and send copies of them to the folklorist conducting the research.

The point is that since so much of folklore is international in distribution, the study of it must be of equal scope. Since no one folklorist knows all languages, he must depend upon his colleagues in different countries for assistance. (It is a great pity that most of the peoples of the world do not realize how much folklore they have in common; it could be an important unifying force. Unfortunately, folklore sometimes is exploited to promote nationalism rather than internationalism. For example, the Grimms, Jacob and Wilhelm, in the beginning of the nineteenth century were stimulated to collect folklore in part because they wanted to preserve something essentially Teutonic in character. The fact of the matter is that most of the Grimm tales are found throughout Europe, Asia, and North and South America. Thus, strictly speaking, they are not purely "German" tales at all.)

Although the internationally oriented comparative method is probably the most traditional way of studying folklore, it has several serious weaknesses. For one thing, it tends to concentrate on "lore" while ignoring "folk." Folktales and ballads are often tracked down around the world with little or no attention paid to the people who tell and listen to these marvelous forms of oral art. Another problem is that even with as many as a thousand or more versions of a single folktale or ballad, it may not be possible to determine with exactitude the probable origin of that folktale or ballad. And so the historic-geographic method, with its basically romantic nineteenth-century philosophy of trying to reconstruct historically the original form of the past, has tended to yield to a new method of analysis.

In this newer, anthropologically oriented method, the folk as well as the lore are treated. For instance, the act of performance, with its necessary relationship between the raconteur and his audience, is taken into account. The abiding concern with origin has been largely replaced by a concern for function—that is, what does the folktale mean and do for the members of the society among whom the tale is found, and when it is told? In this anthropological-functional approach, the study is not of the international distribution of a single tale so much as the intensive study of the folklore of a single culture.

It was Franz Boas, one of the founders of anthropology in the United States, and his students who encouraged the anthropological-functional approach to folklore. Boas believed that folklore reflected culture and thus one could by examining the folklore of a group glean much of the significant ethnographic data about that group. One of the earliest examples of this "culture-reflector" approach to folklore was Boas' own *Tsimshian Mythology*, which was published in 1916. In this thousand-page monograph, Boas reports the myths of the Tsimshian Indians (who live on the northwest Pacific coast in what is now British Columbia, Canada) after which he presents a lengthy "Description of the Tsimshian, based on their mythology." In other words, in the myths, Boas found details of household goods, family life, religious practices, and the like. In a later study, *Kwakiutl Culture as Reflected in Their Mythology* (1935), Boas even attempted to compare two Indian groups (the Tsimshian and the Kwakiutl) on the basis of their mythologically derived ethnographic pictures. In the culture-reflector approach, the emphasis is clearly upon what the lore can tell the investigator about the folk. Thus while the practitioners of the comparative method are more or less interested in the lore for its own intrinsic sake (without much reference to the folk), the advocates of the culture-reflector approach are more concerned with folk than with lore and they regard the lore simply as a useful tool that enables them to understand the folk better.

Actually, the comparative and culture-reflector approaches to folklore are not mutually exclusive. The use of one does not rule out the use of the other. In fact, ideally, both methods should be employed. For in order to determine what elements in the folklore of a group are peculiar to that group, one must have comparative data. One must know what the normal or typical form of a folktale or a ballad is before one can identify and interpret the significance of the localizations and particularizations of that tale or ballad in a single cultural context. After a comparative study, one can see more easily how a local group or perhaps how a single individual has altered the tale to fit its or his own needs.

There are still other ways of studying folklore besides the comparative and culture-reflector methods. One of these is concerned with the structure or formal organization of various genres of folklore. There can be no doubt that most forms of folklore—for example, fairy tales, children's games, or riddles —are highly patterned. Precisely what these patterns are and what their over-all importance is has only recently been the subject of serious inquiry. For instance, the structure of superstitions seems to be along the lines of a conditional formula: "If A, then B, unless C." An example would be: "If you break a mirror, you will have seven years' bad luck unless you throw the broken pieces of glass into a moving stream of water (such as in a river or a brook). Of course, superstitions, like most folklore, tend to cluster around the dangerous and anxiety-producing portions of both the calendrical (seasonal) cycle and the life cycle of the individual. In an agricultural society, there will be many superstitions concerning the planting of crops; for a professional athlete or a gambler, there will be many superstitions bearing on the success or failure of his efforts. Superstitions, by making the unknowable knowable, help reduce tension. The structure of superstition might be relevant if, for example, the final segment "unless C" were omitted. The presence or absence of this structural segment could be related to a concept of fate. If individuals believe that they can control their destiny through their own efforts, then there would presumably be "unless C" segments which serve to provide a magical means of avoiding misfortune. (If you boast of your good health, you must knock on wood to avoid a punishment for making such a statement of hubris.) If, on the other hand, individuals believe that they can but yield to the dictates of destiny, then perhaps the final counteractant "unless C" segment will not occur as frequently if at all. The idea would be that it is beyond an individual's control to avert misfortune. In similar fashion, the structure of children's games may be related to the philosophy or "world view" of the culture in which they are found. Games appear to be folk models of both adult and child life. In American society, for example, the majority of games are competitive games in which there is a winner and a loser. This is in contrast to other parts of the world in which games may be played without definite winners and losers.

Other ways of studying folklore include investigating the symbolism of folklore (and the extent to which the symbols found in folksong and folk narrative are also found in individual dreams and in sophisticated literature). In general, folklore provides a socially sanctioned means of expressing one's anxiety. Frequently the means are sanctioned only because they involve symbolic disguise. One can joke where one cannot speak directly. In the United States, there are many jokes about sex, religion, and politics. If one realizes that a cluster of jokes (like the clusters of superstitions discussed previously) can reveal a source of anxiety, one can see that an analysis of the symbolic content of jokes may provide important insights into the nature of a society. Perhaps the following discussion centering on a typical example of modern American urban folklore may serve to illustrate the nature of the tradition and methods of study required.

One rich vein of modern American folklore concerns folk stereotypes. Each people has a definite image of itself *vis-à-vis* other peoples and it has equally definite impressions of the supposed national characteristics of these other peoples. One way in which a group defines itself and attempts to establish a sense of group identity is by means of folklore about itself with reference to "others." This is true at the subcultural level, as ethnic folklore abundantly attests, but it is also true at the national and international level. Americans have stereotypes of the peoples of other nations just as peoples of these nations have stereotyped notions of what Americans are like. These folk stereotypes pass unchallenged from one generation to another like other elements of folklore, and all too often they add fuel to the fire of prejudice. It is theoretically possible, of course, that some parts of the stereotype may be accurate, but the student of folklore is in a position to see that frequently one finds standard stereotypes in local dress. For example, most people have an idea that people A are thieves, people B are treacherous, and people C are miserly. And this kind of folklore is found in urban society; in fact the international examples are probably more common in urban than in rural society. Consider the following anecdote.

There is an international conference devoted to the elephant. Scholars from different countries present learned papers on different aspects of elephant life. The Frenchman gives his on "Les Amours des Éléphants" (or "L'Éléphant dans la Cuisine"); the German gives his on "The Military Use of the Elephant" (or "The Elephant and the Re-Nazification of Germany"); and so it goes for each country represented until finally the American rises to deliver his paper, entitled "How to Build a Bigger and Better Elephant." This is surely an international joke and no doubt different stereotypes are employed in each country where it is found. In this case, Americans seem to be aware of their own alleged propensity for size and for commercial enterprises. It would be most interesting to compare the stereotypes in different countries. Are the French regarded as great lovers or expert cooks in other parts of the world, as they are in the United States? In any case, this kind of international urban folklore has important implications for world unity. People's actions are based upon their beliefs and often their beliefs are based upon folk stereotypes. At their worst, folk stereotypes can be the tool of the most terrible kind of racism and intolerance. For this reason, if no other, they should be held up to the light of analysis.

These are but a few of the ways of studying folklore. Whether one employs a comparative approach in a search for origins, a culture-reflector approach to study individual cultures, a structural approach to define the formal features of folklore, or a psychological-sociological approach to illuminate symbols and attitudes, there remain a large number of specialized techniques of analysis one may employ. The complexity and sophistication of some of these techniques are such as to demand serious study on the part of folklore students. One consequence of increased interest in the ways and means of studying folklore has been the development of courses and programs in folklore studies at leading universities in the United States. At such institutions there are not only opportunities to learn the old ways of studying folklore but, more importantly, there are opportunities to develop new ones.

Folklife

DON YODER

"Folklife" is a relatively new word in the English language, which has not yet appeared in American dictionaries. It is an English adaptation, by scholars, of the Swedish *folkliv*, which in turn seems to have been patterned on the German *Volksleben*. The term "folklife research" or "folklife studies" is the English rendering of the Swedish *folklivsforskning*, which is the equivalent of the German *Volkskunde*.

"Folklife studies" or "folklife research"—which is shaping up as an academic discipline in the United States in the 1960's—is a total scholarly concentration on the folk levels of a national or regional culture. In brief, folklife studies involve the analysis of a folk culture in its entirety. Folk culture is traditional culture, bound by tradition and transmitted by tradition, and is basically (although not exclusively) rural and pre-industrial. It exists in tension with other aspects of culture in the civilization. Obviously it is the opposite of the mass-produced, mechanized, popular culture of the twentieth century.

To those who are beginning to use it in Britain and the United States, the term "folklife" is intended to include the total range of folk-cultural phenomena, material as well as oral and spiritual. It is consciously intended to be a term of broader range than the older English word "folklore." In a sense folklore and the folklore movement represent a nineteenth-century discovery, in the English-speaking lands, of a partially conceived folk culture, basically oral tradition. In working on his specialties, whether they were folksongs, folktales, or "superstitions," the folklorist did discover the folk level of his culture, but only part of it. The folklife movement is the twentieth-century rediscovery of the total range of the folk culture.

The exciting thing about folklife is precisely this, that it covers everything. Every phase of life in traditional or folk society can be studied, with the interrelationships and functions of part to whole. Not only does the researcher study the verbal acts of folksong, folktale, riddle, etc.—which the folklorist has long ago made his province—but also agriculture and agrarian history, settlement patterns, dialectology or folk speech, folk architecture, folk cookery, folk costume, the folk year, folk religion, folk medicine, folk recreation, folk literature, and the folk arts and crafts. It is this exciting totality of the verbal, spiritual, and material aspects of a culture that we mean by the term "folklife."

As Europe is the basic source of American culture, so it was European scholarship that preceded and inspired American folklife scholarship. We Americans are just now beginning to create a discipline of folklife studies in our universities that is based upon the European precedent.

American scholars visiting Europe are impressed with what has been done in the study of the indigenous folk cultures of Europe. European scholarship is in fact far ahead of American scholarship in the systematic collecting and archiving of folk-cultural data. Great institutions such as the Nordiska Museet in Stockholm and the numerous folk-cultural and ethnographic institutes in Western and Eastern Europe have been looking at folklife in their geographical and cultural areas since the nineteenth century. In some instances the motivation was that of cultural nationalism—the small nation wishing to defend its language and traditional culture against the onslaughts of a contemporary civilization that insists on conformity. In all cases, European study of European folklife was part of Europe's continuing discovery of itself, for folklife studies are also concerned with folk psychology and folk mentality. Even the most sophisticated urbanite of the twentieth century has some aspects of his way of life that can be explained only by reference to the folk culture in which his own roots lie. As E. Estyn Evans of Queens University puts it, "Nothing less than the whole of the past is needed to explain the present." And Sigurd Erixon, dean of folklife scholars in Europe, has always insisted that the focus of folklife studies is man himself, "in the first place . . . man on Nordic or European soil, but in the long run . . . man in general." There are two basic orientations of folklore studies as they have shaped up in European scholarship: the contemporary and the historical, or the horizontal and the vertical approaches. In Europe, institute after institute has begun an archive of folklife materials from the area which it studies. The horizontal approach involves the use of a network of informants who furnish materials from their own memory, either directly through interviews or indirectly through written questionnaires. The vertical approach is to trace folk-cultural items back through regional history, abstracting and archiving past references to customs, beliefs, and other folklore items from every available historical source, from laws to personal memoirs.

In addition to the archive with its special techniques, the most distinctive institution for the study and teaching of folklife that the Europeans have developed is the open-air folk museum, where entire buildings are preserved in their cultural context, either on their original sites or on a central site to which they have been moved, for comparative study. The first of these, of course, was the great Swedish Open Air Museum at Skansen in Stockholm, founded by Artur Hazelius in 1891. This idea has caught on in America in recent decades, and such open-air museums as the Farmers' Museum at Cooperstown, New York; Old Sturbridge Village at Sturbridge, Massachusetts; Old Shelburne at Shelburne, Vermont; the Pennsylvania Farm Museum at Landis Valley; and the Upper Canada Museum in Ontario have been founded on the Skansen principle. Here students as well as the general public can study the setting of early American life and sense something of its spirit.

So much for Europe and its influence on the American folklife studies movement. America, like all countries and peoples, needs constantly to rediscover itself. At this point in the development of American civilization, amid the rapid social and cultural changes of the mid-twentieth century, it is time to take a long look back, over the ground covered. America—urban and industrial as it is today—can see its earlier self in the rural and pre-industrial America of the pioneer. The pioneer age, which is glorified in the TV "western," deserves authentic documentation and appreciation. The influence of the rural past upon the present moment—in our regional speech and accents, our regional cookery, our regional differences in general—deserves full study.

The hopeful note is that there is so much of our rural folklife left to study. European scholars are constantly amazed at the abundance of log architecture—houses, barns, and meeting-houses—available for study in Appalachia, for one example. Our older people—we call them "senior citizens" now—whose memories go back to the 1880's and 1890's, to that pre-automobile age when rural American life was still intact, can be the most valuable resource, not only for the folklorist's collections of songs and verbal lore, but for the folklife scholar's archives of questionnaire materials on every phase of the rural past.

Hopeful, too, is the fact that museums, universities, state and local historical societies, small towns, and even large cities have begun preservation movements to preserve, or restore, the key examples of colonial and nineteenth-century architecture. And on the popular level, informed tourism is beginning to use folklife data, and folk festivals have arisen in various parts of the country to display the living folk cultures of the area—the Pennsylvania Dutch Folk Festival in July which attracts 100,000 visitors annually, the "Plattdeutsch" Festival in Kansas, the Holland Dutch Festivals in Michigan, the Buckwheat Festival in West Virginia, the Crafts Festival in North Carolina, the Ozark Festival, and others.

We used to think of America as the "melting pot" which unified and homogenized the European stocks who settled here, dissolving their cultural baggage into something uniquely and uniformly American. Today we speak of America as a "pluralistic" society. Basically this concept grew out of our religious pluralism—the stubborn fact that history and emigration have given us more than one basic religion, and religions have a stubborn way of not melting down, of remaining separate. But the pluralism is equally true in folk culture too.

Naturally we cannot, unlike some smaller European countries, study a national folklife. While there may be, in some sense of the word, an American folklore, there just is no American folk culture as a whole, in the sense that one can speak of Swedish folk culture, Welsh folk culture, Burmese folk culture, Japanese folk culture. Even Americans forget how large geographically their country is—that it takes as long to fly the 3,000 miles from

Los Angeles to New York as it does the 3,000 miles across the Atlantic to London.

While American culture is not so old as the European cultures, it has achieved great variety folk-culturally. Into the vast space that is America there came a great variety of peoples, who, bringing what was transportable of their folk, popular, and higher cultures from Europe, settled here, and through acculturation with their neighbors produced new American regional cultures. It is these that we can study, in the twentieth century, horizontally and vertically, using the European folklife methodology.

What are some of these American regional cultures? New England with its Puritan-Yankee culture—its native types of farmhouse, barns, and meetinghouses, its baked beans and its boiled dinners, its accent and folk speech—is one of these, and it has influenced many other American areas, through migration. The area of Holland Dutch settlement in the Middle Atlantic states can still offer certain visible signs of a Netherlands-American folk culture—again house and barn types are the best specific examples. Southern culture has several folk-cultural variants. Because of its geographical isolation, Appalachia has much to offer the folklife scholar, but the other areas of Tidewater, Piedmont, Bluegrass, and Deep South also have distinctive folklife patterns, and the great state of Texas and the Ozark area in Missouri-Arkansas, where Southern and Western folk cultures meet and mingle, are equally important.

French-speaking folk cultures are found in two areas of the United States—in the "Cajun" (Acadian) country of Louisiana, where French farmers from Nova Scotia were resettled by Britain in the eighteenth century, and in New England, where a large French-Canadian population makes it possible to study French-Canadian customs, beliefs, and practices within the borders of the United States. The Southwest was colonized and missionized by Spain. Its historic folk culture is a combination of Spanish, Mexican, and native Indian elements, and has left many material elements for study by folklife scholars—colonial baroque church architecture, a strong native folk-art tradition of carved wooden saints, or "santos," rites which mingle Mediterranean Catholic and American Indian piety, an attractive native cookery, and the strongest folk-drama tradition in the United States.

Two other aspects are major: the influence of the two racial minorities, the Indian and the Negro. The Negro's influence on American culture is increasingly studied, from spirituals to jazz and gospel music. Indian influences must be studied too, and it is significant that recently at an American university a doctoral dissertation was written entitled "The Indianization of the Mountain Men."

These American regional folk cultures are the product of European ethnic heritage, geographical settlement patterns, and acculturation. The example that I wish to use to illustrate what can be done by application of the European folklife methodology to the American scene is the Pennsylvania folk culture of the ethnic group known as the Pennsylvania Germans.

The population of the Pennsylvania German settlements came from Central Europe—from various German states, from the German-speaking cantons of Switzerland, and from the adjoining parts of France (Alsace-Lorraine). The heavy emigration of German-speaking colonists took place before the Revolutionary War. Settling down together in the unbroken wilderness, the colonists were able to transplant some aspects of their European folk cultures to American soil. Because of their geographical concentration they were able to preserve their German dialect into the twentieth century. Language is the matrix of folk culture and this is certainly one reason why so much of Pennsylvania German folklife is still available for study.

Religiously, the Pennsylvania Germans were a mixture. They were basically Protestant, but sharply divided into Protestant "churches" and "sects." The majority of them were "church" people—Lutheran and Reformed. A strong minority was formed by the "plain" sectarian groups—Mennonites, Dunkards, and Amish—who drew a line of separation against the "world" and lived their peaceful, "plain," non-ornamented lives on their side of the line. These "plain" sects are still very much alive in Pennsylvania and add much color to the American cultural picture. Their symbol is the bearded Old Order Amishman, who is known America over for his nonconformity and whose resistance to "worldly" modernity is being studied by anthropologists, sociologists, social psychologists, and others. In his struggle with the world the Amishman rejects state schools, insurance, social security, electricity—and the automobile. Where else but in the "Old Order" settlements of Pennsylvania, Ohio, Indiana, Iowa, and Ontario can Americans see, functionally intact, the "horse and buggy" culture of their own grandparents in the nineteenth century?

The German-speaking population of Pennsylvania did not, however, remain in complete isolation from the outside English-speaking world. Intermarriage was common, for there were English and Irish and Welsh neighbors everywhere. Accultura-tion was the rule in almost every phase of Pennsylvania German life. English words and expressions entered the dialect, so that it became an American dialect of High German rather than just a combination of seventeenth-century Rhineland dialects with an infusion of Swiss German.

While there was unity in language, there was disunity in religion. Hence the Pennsylvania Germans, with a few excep-tions in the nineteenth century, have been content with a gradual Americanization of their way of life. They have not become a political force, like the French Canadians, our nearest example of a unified ethnic culture based on religious unity. The Penn-sylvania Germans were so divided among the varieties of Protes-tantism that they simply could not agree on anything, except perhaps on contributing to Pennsylvania's proverbial conserva-tism. "Dumb Dutch," "Stubborn Dutchmen," and "Sauerkraut Yankees" their neighbors called them, but the Dutchman went his own way, voting now with one party and now with another, speaking English to his neighbors at market, singing High Ger-man in church, but speaking the dialect at his own fireside.

Out of this curious mixture of European cultures were pro-duced several major Pennsylvania gifts to American life as a whole, all at the folk-cultural level:

(1) log architecture, which appears to have spread principally from Pennsylvania and the other Middle Atlantic states to the frontier; (2) the Conestoga wagon, a combination of English and German wagon-building techniques, which became the principal freight wagon on the early frontier, the "prairie schooner" of the Western settlers; and (3) the richest body of folk art produced in any of the colonies. Every major museum in the United States has an interest in Pennsylvania German "fraktur," which is the generic name for the decorated "illuminated" manuscripts done in broken calligraphy that were produced in Pennsylvania and the regions settled by Pennsylvanians, roughly from the 1760's to the 1830's.

One of the large tasks awaiting American folklife scholarship is the mapping of the diffusion of folk-cultural traits. For language patterns this is already well started, with the linguistic atlas programs of Brown, Michigan, and other university centers. When the Pennsylvania German folk culture is competely analyzed, it will be interesting to map its influence on other American areas, through migration, such as Appalachia, the Midwest, and Ontario, to which large migrations of Pennsylvanians trekked in the eighteenth and nineteenth centuries.

As we have said before, the exciting thing about folklife is that it covers everything. Let us take two aspects of folk culture, costume and cookery, and analyze their study in one American regional folk culture, again that of the Pennsylvania Germans. In any culture, costume and cookery are at least as basic as folksong and folktale.

There are more living folk costumes in Pennsylvania German country today than in any other part of America, indeed, than in many parts of Europe. These are the costumes of "Plain" Pennsylvania—the "plain" costumes of the German and Swiss sects, the Mennonites, Brethren (Dunkards), and Amish. The men dress in drab colors, lapel-less jackets (lapels are "worldly"), and broad-brimmed hats, and several conservative sects insist on beards for the married man. The women wear longer skirts than most other American women, wear the apron as part of their public dress, wear a "cape" or kerchief over the shoulders and breast, and many of them wear a small white (or black) close-fitting cap, called the "covering" or the "prayer covering," over the head. A great variety in the over-all look of this basic "plain" costume is achieved from sect to sect by changes of color, cut, style, and the like. These costumes are folk in that they are traditional. They are also different from most European folk costumes, for they are religious costumes and are worn every day rather than just on holidays. Basically they are worn to de-individualize the wearer, to mark visibly his connection with the holy community represented by his sect—which is "in the world but not of it." From our study of religious folk costume among the Pennsylvania German sects we can learn a great deal about their deeply ingrained religion, and sense something of the tensions involved in dressing differently from the "world" and the "world's people," as they call outsiders.

In addition to religious or sectarian folk costume, one can study rural dress in general in America—from the various secular folk costumes of the colonial period to the present generation of American farmers, whose dress, proletarianized and industrialized, is increasingly marked by the mechanic's shirt and trousers and the engineer's boots. Dress, like other aspects of culture, is a significant index of culture.

The folk cookery of the Pennsylvania Germans is, like everything else in that folk culture, a mixture. The core of the cuisine is Continental European. Certain basic—and favorite—foods were brought by the seventeenth- and eighteenth-century emigrants from the Rhineland and Switzerland. There was a great variety of dough dishes—a veritable "dough" culture, if I may be permitted the term—ranking in functional importance with the "pasta" culture of Italy. Dumplings (*Gnepp*) were served with many dishes and in many ways—steamed, baked, boiled; noodles were a favorite dish. The three all-time Germanic favorites in Pennsylvania were *Sauerkraut, Panhaas,* and *Schnitz un Gnepp.* Sauerkraut needs no introduction. *Panhaas,* which English neighbors called "scrapple," is a mixture of meat and cornmeal and buckwheat flour, a favorite breakfast dish. *Schnitz un Gnepp* —dried apples (*Schnitz*) boiled with ham and served with dumplings (*Gnepp*)—is still a favorite dish on Pennsylvania tables. Other dishes were brought from Europe and modified here under local conditions: for example, the thick fruit paste made of plums, which in Pennsylvania, because of the greater availability of apples, became the staple "apple butter." Certain foods were borrowed from their ethnic neighbors from the British Isles: for instance, there is no Pennsylvania German word for "pie" as such—the dialect has borrowed the English word "pie," to be sure, in its dialect pronunciation "poy," suggesting that the concept was borrowed too. And speaking of borrowings, a favorite dish among Pennsylvania Germans from pioneer days down to the twentieth century is homely old boiled corn-meal "mush," an American Indian dish, which, like maize itself, was borrowed by the whites from the Indians.

While these examples are from one geographically limited ethnic culture in America, they suggest that the entire range of folklife lies ready for serious study—both horizontally and vertically—in all the American regional subcultures and ethnic enclaves.

What, then, is the value of folklife studies?

I see three major values in looking at American regional folklife. First, folklife research, introduced into the university level of study, can tie together here, as it has done in Europe, the related work of folklorists and cultural anthropologists, of agrarian historians and dialectologists, of regional historians and cultural geographers, in an interdisciplinary study of the neglected folk aspects of American life.

Second, folklife research can enrich the study and teaching of early American history. As taught in the public schools, American history has too often been linear—1775 to 1865 to 1918 to 1941—with heavy emphasis on military and political phases. Our study of history, like our study of literature, has concentrated on the "great men" approach to the past. It has concentrated on the few creative individuals—the Lincolns in history, the Hawthornes in literature. Their lives have of course influenced others and have symbolic value for mankind. Folklife studies—an across-the-board approach to the folk culture of a region—can form a healthy supplement to the older emphasis on straight American history and literature. Once we get over the initial embarrassment at finding worthy of study those cultural goods which everyone had or made instead of the unique products of the few creative geniuses of our culture, we can at last study our American farmhouses and barns, our country churches and meetinghouses, along with the Greek temples and the Gothic cathedrals of the high cultural past. We can at last look at the "whole" past of America, the total way of life of our ancestors, and instead of overstressing politics and wars, emphasize the long building of American life with the plow and the flail, the husking peg and the hominy block, the schoolhouse and the meetinghouse.

Lastly, the chief value of folklife studies is that their data show us the range of human thought, more basically perhaps than history, literature, and other already accepted subjects. In showing us what life was like before urbanization and industrialization, we are shown the long roots of the life that we share. Again the word of E. Estyn Evans: "Nothing less than the whole of the past is needed to explain the present." And Ruth Benedict, speaking of folk belief and folk custom, makes clear the value of our investigation of it in these words: "More than any other body of material it makes vivid the recency and the precarious-

ness of those rationalistic attitudes of the modern urban educated groups which are often identified with human nature."

Perhaps a flail or a plow can teach us more about man than
a Civil War sword.

6

Where the Workers of the World Unite: The American Occupations

HORACE P. BECK

Three European nations originally occupied North America: Spain, France, and England. At the beginning, the major part of what is now the United States was under English control. As a result, the folklore of this country was, from the first, English in background but modified and adapted to fit the new region.

As time went on, peoples from other areas of Europe came to this country. The early migrations seem to have been mostly from northern Europe, but in the nineteenth century vast numbers of southern Europeans arrived. Many migrated for economic reasons—people who came to escape starvation and disease in their own land and who had heard that the streets of New York were paved in gold. Because of linguistic, cultural, and religious traits peculiar to their nationality, the vast majority of these immigrants tended to congregate in separate communities—at least for the first generation—and kept alive their folk customs, modifying them, as did the English, to adapt to local situations. As they began to be absorbed into the larger cultural pattern of the nation these immigrants came into contact with other ethnic groups and various aspects of folk culture passed from one group to another.

These newcomers tended to congregate in little communities for cultural as well as for economic and occupational reasons. Being poor, they were forced to live in areas in which housing was cheap; thus the isolation brought on by poverty kept them together. More important than the economic aspect was the occupational one. Most of the early immigrants to this country sought certain kinds of work in our economic world. (Indeed many peoples were actually imported to perform specific manual duties.) Hence we find the Scandinavians moving to the Midwest to become farmers and lumbermen, the Greeks to restaurants, the Portuguese to fishing, the Slavs to mining, the Italians and the French to garment work, the Irish and the Chinese to manual labor on canals, railroads, and in the forests. The list could be continued indefinitely.

When a person prospered in one group or another he tended to give up the hard living and move on to other things—again along specialized lines. The more prosperous Chinese moved toward laundries and restaurants, the Italian to certain aspects of farming, the Irish to the police force, the Negro to railroading.

From the outset the American people have lived a nomadic kind of life. They moved from the seacoast inland across the mountains, ranging ever westward. Even today comparatively few Americans live and die in the towns where they were born. Such constant movement has a strong effect upon folklore, for the word "folk" connotes isolation and a sense of permanence. Because of this movement, traditions in the orthodox sense were hard to form. Greeks, Italians, Swedes, and Germans were constantly being exposed to one another to a greater or lesser degree, but always to a greater extent than in Europe, and at the same time this experience was taking place in a predominantly English-speaking country. Such a situation is not conducive to folklore in the traditional sense. However, in the United States there was one circumstance that tended to take all these divergent cultures, movements, and currents and make a new folklore from them.

From the beginning the United States has been a nation of varied occupations—of specialization—whereas in Europe the folk have been thought to be a self-sufficient group working together to produce the necessities of life. Whatever surplus they enjoyed was sold to the markets to provide those small items they could not themselves produce because of their particular environment. In America people depended on an occupation to provide the wherewithal to purchase the major portion of those things needed to keep body and soul together. Surplus time was spent at home producing certain items for which funds were lacking or which the whim of the individual prompted him to grow or make. Were he a fisherman in New England, a trapper in the Midwest, a jing-sing runner and a bee-liner in the South or a prospector in the West, it was the profits derived from the fish, the fur, the herb and honey, or the gold that sustained him and his family. This type of specialization has spread and intensified until today we find farmers, for example, producing only one crop, be it wheat, cattle, or potatoes.

These various occupations were engaged in from generation to generation and folk groups developed. Also, as time went on, two things were happening. First, people tended to drift slowly from one occupation to another. Hence a man whose family had been sailors for generations might become a lumberjack. Second, the immigrant, as already mentioned, tended to gravitate to certain kinds of work.

To cover all the occupations in America would be a tremendous task. Rather I should like to point out a number of ways of earning a livelihood that have gathered about them a corpus of folklore. Let us examine a few of these and try to show the various kinds of oral material each produced, why some of it is peculiarly American, and how the folk culture expressed in one trade or occupation is carried over to another related field.

Chief among the occupations are seafaring, lumbering, cattle ranching, farming, trapping, riverboating, railroading, mining, oil drilling, steel making, and the automotive industry. These categories may be subdivided numerous times. Seafaring could be divided into coasting, whaling, fishing, and clipper-shipping. Riverboating could be divided into flatboating, steamboating, and canalling. Mining could be divided into bituminous, anthracite, gold, silver, copper, and so forth. The other occupations can be stratified in the same way. Each would have its own peculiarities based partly upon the background of the people initially employed and partly on those who came into it from a related field.

Each occupation has its own lore, which would include songs, stories, superstitions, customs, and beliefs pertaining to the particular kind of work. Unfortunately, in the United States, all types of folklore have not received the same attention, nor have the occupations themselves been uniformly studied. Folksongs have received close scrutiny, as have tales; custom, belief, and superstition have not been so widely collected or investigated. Seafaring, lumbering, ranching, mining, and railroading have received great emphasis; others, like farming, have been largely neglected.

In the formation of a corpus of American lore, seafaring has been the most important occupation. Not only was it one of the earliest means of livelihood, but for many years it was the largest, employing thousands of seamen from all over the world—especially from Ireland, where, because of the potato famine in the middle of the last century, thousands of starving Irishmen migrated to America, many finding employment aboard ships. Since seafaring, especially among smaller craft like coasting and fishing vessels, was a seasonal occupation not generally pursued in the stormy, cold, winter months, and since shipping often languished during periods of economic depression and war, many seamen moved ashore to find work at tasks for which seafaring had prepared them. One of these was lumbering, another canalling.

At first the lumber industry was conducted along the coast and the sailor worked in the woods during the winter, returning to the sea in the spring. Before long, however, the timber along the shore was exhausted and the ring of the ax was heard farther and farther inland; now a return to the sea in the spring became less practical. At the same time, as the population increased and business grew, the demand for lumber exceeded the supply until what had once been a seasonal trade became a year-around occupation. Thus lumbering began in New England and moved westward into New York, Pennsylvania, Michigan, and Minnesota until eventually the lumbermen came to the great treeless plains of the Midwest. Here, faced with a dearth of trees, the woodsman was forced to seek new employment. He found it in the hunting of buffalo—a job that paid well for a short period during the 1870's. When the buffaloes were slain the sailor, turned logger and then buffalo hunter, became a cowboy tending the great herds of cattle that covered the Western plains.

Far from the sea, according to legend, two eighteenth-century trappers built a campfire in the mountains of Pennsylvania. They surrounded their fire with rocks and were amazed to see the stones burst into flame. They returned to civilization, told their experience, and anthracite mining, which drew thousands of Europeans to this country, began. First the Welsh, then the Slavs, became the predominant coal miners. From Pennsylvania and the hard-rock tunnel mines used for anthracite, people moved into West Virginia, where they began open-pit mining for bituminous coal.

In 1849 gold was discovered in California. With the promise of riches in the air, a mad scramble to reach the gold fields began. Three ways were open: to go across the Great Plains by caravan; to sail to Panama, cross that land strip, and proceed up the Pacific coast by boat; or to go by ship around Cape Horn. To reach California quickly was of the utmost importance, and to meet this demand, hundreds of great clipper ships raced with incredible speed and at great hazard around Cape Horn. In California the crews often deserted and rushed to the gold fields along with the passengers.

Unfortunately, gold was not so easily found as dreamed about, with the result that many sailors, out of money and recovered from gold fever, moved on to seek work on the cattle ranches. Meanwhile, miners from the coal fields had also sought riches in the West. Thus the lore of the sea and the lore of the coal mines met in California. However, the coal miners were also to be disappointed in their search for gold and turned to copper mining, bringing their tales of the coal mines with them. In this way the folklore of one occupation has modified that of another and the lore of the ethnic groups involved has mingled. Out of these modifications and minglings two areas that bear examination emerge. One involves the occupational heroes and their tall tales; the other, folksongs.

Nearly every occupation seems to have a folk hero. Among the better known are the sailor's Old Stormalong; the river boatman's Mike Fink; the cowboy's Pecos Bill; the Midwestern farmer's Febold Feboldson; the steel worker's Joe Magarac; the lumberman's Paul Bunyan; and the railroader's John Henry and Casey Jones. There is continual dispute whether these characters are creations of the folk or inventions of literary hacks. For instance, we know little of Paul Bunyan before he appeared in advertising copy promoted by the Red River Logging Company in 1914. However, such disputes need not concern us here, for the heroes, whatever their origins, are of folk stuff and have not only been accepted by those whom they are supposed to represent but have become national symbols of their occupations.

All of these heroes are, in large measure, comic characters. They tend to blend the characteristics of the culture hero with the components of the tall tale. All of them, with the possible exception of Casey Jones, are giants, and all are benevolent. Their activities are usually bumbling but beneficial. The good they do is most often accidental and is usually attended by an unexpected calamity which the giant is forced to rectify with as much or more difficulty than he encountered in his initial effort. Often the giants are accompanied by a small helper who, although feeble in physical powers, is titanic in mental ability. The small one's brains complement the muscular prowess of his huge friend.

One of the things that Americans are famous for is the tall tale. This sort of story operates on a very simple principle: it starts with a plausible premise and exaggerates until a ridiculous result emerges. The humor often lies more in the effect of the story upon the listener than in the story itself. For example, a trapper carrying his canoe across a portage sees a partridge on the ground and throws his skillet at it with deadly aim. Seeing the bird and the skillet on the ground together he plans to pick them up when he comes back for the rest of his gear. On his return both are gone. The next spring when he returns to the spot on his way to civilization, he sees the bird with the skillet stuck to her leg dragging it along with nine little ones in the pan. Or a great hunter sees a bear. He also sees a jumping trout, a squirrel, a deer, and a honey tree. He bides his time and when all are lined up, he fires and kills them all with one shot, the bullet puncturing the honey tree and letting the honey run out.

These are the materials with which the American occupational heroes are concerned. Old Stormalong runs his great white ship between England and France. The passage is too narrow and the paint is scraped off on England, forming the white cliffs of Dover. Pecos Bill likes to pick up rattlesnakes by the tail and snap their heads off, and when the streams are frozen and no snakes are around he does the same thing to rivers—straightening them out or making them more crooked. Febold Feboldson changes the weather and Paul Bunyan cuts down a petrified forest. Stormalong has a huge ship. Paul Bunyan has a blue ox named Babe, so large that it takes a sparrow six months to fly from one horn to the other. Pecos Bill rides upon a cross between a mountain lion, a mustang, a streak of lightning, and a tornado. Paul Bunyan can denude a forest in one day and Joe Magarac, who claims to be made of steel, can operate a steel mill by himself, lift a ton of steel with one hand, or swim in a ladle of molten metal.

But the best-studied, best-recorded aspect of occupational folklore in the United States is the folksong. Indeed the folksong has been given more attention than all other forms of folklore combined. Further a close study of these songs often reveals a great deal about the entire cultural matrix of a group and about the interrelationships of one occupational group and another. Although all occupations have a core of folksongs evolved from their particular kind of work, they also have songs from other occupations, as well as traditional ballads, broadsides (often adapted to the occupation), and popular songs. Of all the occupations, seafaring has the greatest number of songs. Moreover, many of the sea songs moved inland into other occupations and even became part of the general body of American folksong. Let us examine these songs for a moment.

Shipboard life was admirably suited to all forms of folklore, and songs in particular. Voyages lasted for months, even years. During that time the crews were relatively isolated and depended upon themselves for entertainment. Since the crews were largely non-literate men, their pleasure had to be achieved orally or physically. Because they often came from different backgrounds, they tended to mix their folklore into a common body. Finally, their work necessitated gang labor, where a high degree of coordination was demanded. To satisfy the requirements of shipboard life, two types of songs became prevalent: chanties, or work songs, and forecastle songs for entertainment.

Of the two, the chanties were the simplest and fell into two groups, short-haul and long-haul chanties. Both depended heavily upon a refrain to sustain them and emphasized a rhythm that was easy to work by. The long-haul chanty was used for lengthy jobs such as hauling up the anchor, setting a topmast, or

manning the pumps; the short-haul chanty had a faster tempo
and was used chiefly to "brace around" a yard, hoist or trim a
sail, or some other task that required a bit of short, united effort.

The chanties did not survive the sailing-ship era chiefly because they did not seem to fit into other occupations where
coordinated group exertions were less important. Forecastle songs
were a different matter. These were songs from varied sources
sung as entertainment in the off watch and intended to ease the
tedium of a long voyage. Some were old traditional ballads,
others were broadsides, and others were popular music-hall ditties
of the day. A considerable number grew directly out of the seafaring experience and these should be considered briefly.

The seaman's life was a hard one. Life was cheap and the
sailor lived in constant danger of death from many causes. Wages
were low, food bad, and living quarters abominable. To survive
in such an environment, the sailor had to be insensible to much
of the trivia of life. But he had one deep emotion—a strong
feeling for his ship. His songs therefore were about vessels—
about shipwreck, about fast passages, and about conditions at
sea. Also in his make-up was a strong sense of superstition and
a large amount of sentimentality. In his song bag there would
be ballads like "The Flying Cloud," telling of the supposed
activity of a slaver turned pirate; "The Flying Dutchman," about
the ghost ship that hovered off Cape Horn; "The Greenland
Whale Fishery," about a whale that drowned four men; "The
Shannon and the Peacock," describing a naval battle; and "The
Scilly Rocks," the story of a vessel that was driven ashore with
the loss of fifty men out of a crew of fifty-four. Interspersed with
these ballads were bawdy songs: "Ramble Away" recounted the
amorous excesses of sailors; sentimental broadsides like "The Unfortunate Rake" described the death of a soldier from venereal
disease in Dublin; "The Ocean Burial" was about a sailor who
did not want to be buried at sea; and "The Jacket So Blue"
told of a sailor who was faithful to his sweetheart at home.

Singing was only a part of the sailor's life. He told stories
similar to his songs. He dabbled in art—fancy knot-work and
ivory carving called scrimshaw. He had his own customs, beliefs,
and superstitions. Because his life depended on his ability to
judge the weather, he became a skilled interpreter of weather
signs and was careful to heed them. Sometimes he made little

rhymes about these things, like "Wild geese, wild geese ganging out to sea / All clear weather it will be," or "Red in the morning, sailors take warning / Red at night, sailors' delight."

Over the years, as has been mentioned, the sailor gave up his occupation and moved inland. Into the lumber camps he took much of the material that had been his at sea. Many of his skills —for example, his ability with rigging—many of his beliefs, stories, songs, and superstitions went with him. In fact we are informed that at one time the only way a man could get a job in the woods was to be able to sing the thirty-two stanzas of "The Flying Cloud." Sometimes the occupation would color these songs, and what had once been a song about a sailor would become one about a lumberman and then one about a cowboy.

The lumber camps, too, had their own lore, just as did the ships, and when the logger moved or went into another occupation, he took his material with him. Often songs and stories would be changed to fit location after location. In fact one song, "Canaday-I-O," is often used to trace the lumbermen's migration westward from Maine to Pennsylvania to Michigan. When the loggers went into the business of hunting buffalo on the plains in the 1870's, the song became "The Buffalo Skinners," describing the buffalo drives instead of the felling of trees.

So far we have talked almost exclusively of the earlier occupations. Save for Joe Magarac, we have scarcely mentioned industrial folklore. Although almost every occupation has its own lore, the automotive industry, being one of the largest, deserves special consideration. What can be said of this industry applies to a greater or lesser extent to the others—to coal mining, to the garment business, for instance.

The lumber industry recruited from the sea, and the automobile industry, with its center in Detroit, recruited largely from the rural areas of the South. Lured by higher wages, thousands of people who had lived for generations in isolation came out of the hills. They brought with them their own folklore, much of it imported from Europe centuries ago. This material was adapted to fit the new environment and, using the older folklore as a model, fresh folk material was produced. At first glance one would not see much in an assembly line to promote folklore, unless it were in the realm of superstition. There is little leisure time for tales or songs, and the people engaged in the work are together for but part of the day. However, there was a powerful force that encouraged the production of folklore—the union.

Shortly before World War I, long hours, low pay, and poor working conditions caused some of the workers to band together into unions. In order to make their resistance effective, these unions strove to enroll all the workers in their ranks, and the best way to do this, it was felt, was to provide entertainment. Accordingly, halls were hired and the entertainment took the form of folksinging, which was already popular among the people. The workers came to be amused, stayed to listen, and departed as members of some labor organization.

It soon became apparent that folksinging could be a most successful device to arouse the workers, and gradually the union leaders rewrote the old folksongs to give them new meanings. Under the influence of such songs the workers began to distinguish between themselves and their employers and became eager to strike and better their position. A song like "Casey Jones" (originally about the death of a brave railroad engineer) was transformed into a song of protest wherein Casey was killed because he wouldn't complain about unsafe working conditions. What was done to "Casey Jones" was done to hundreds of other songs.

As a result of these songs, there was an increase in strikes against management and a certain amount of bloodshed. This violence was tailor-made for the folksinger, and a new genre of folksong was born—songs of social protest. Whereas in the past a factory fire, a riot, or a mine disaster was recorded factually and objectively in folksongs, the new songs were often biased in their narration and purposeful in their approach. The union and, indeed, all the employees began to suggest that any disaster or any riot was the fault of management. As such suggestions hardened into beliefs, workers once disorganized found reason to band together against their employers.

This entire movement met with such success that the union organizers decided to pick a scapegoat. They chose the image of "the boss." Formerly a paternal character, he was now depicted as fat, bald, greedy, and wholly out of sympathy with his employees. The boss soon became another giant like Paul Bunyan, Stormalong, or Pecos Bill. But he was not a benevolent giant; he was an ogre. Very often the ogre was given the name of a captain of industry, like Dodge, Ford, Hill, or Sloane. With songs to arouse them and with a figure against whom their displeasure could be directed, the solidarity of the workers grew apace. Violence increased, but the result was that more and more employees joined unions and helped to harass management until it was forced to give in and sign contracts that raised pay and improved working conditions.

What happened in the automotive industry also occurred in anthracite mining, with one notable difference. That old and hazardous industry had an indigenous folklore much resembling sailor lore. In the case of mining, the unions simply redirected existing material against the owners, creating a new lore with a new direction. Instead of a company "boss," they made the "company store," where the miner bought all the necessities of life, the ogre. As in the automotive industry, the result was greater safety precautions, shorter hours, and higher pay. While these gains were being won, oil was becoming a major competing fuel. The consequence of this, plus the increased cost of mining, was to force many anthracite operations to shut down. In order to survive, the miners began to work for themselves and mine "bootleg" coal. Lacking sufficient funds to install proper safety devices or to purchase the needed equipment, the miners found themselves working under far more unpleasant conditions than before. If folklore had been used successfully in one occupation to improve the plight of the worker, in this instance, at least, it worked the other way.

This, then, is a summary of some of the chief themes and ideas embodied in occupational folklore. So wide and varied are the occupations, so interlocking in structure and so diverse are the skills, that the best one can do in a short space is to indicate trends in representative areas. Yet one dare not close without a word about the broad-ranging effect of this lore. As the songs of the sailors changed and were adopted by the lumber camps, so were the tales and ideas embodied in occupational lore integrated into the folk culture of the nation. To many who never heard the ring of an ax, the shadow of Paul Bunyan dominates their picture of lumbering's early days. To many, far from the smell of salt water, Old Stormalong represents the spirit of seafaring. Songs once used while men were driving steel spikes on the railroad or sweating out a sail home are now performed on the stage as intrinsic parts of American musical expression. The

banker on his way to the subway glances at the sky and mur-
murs, "Mackerel skies and mares' tails make tall ships carry low
sails," and predicts an impending storm. Thus it is that far
from the scene and away from the occupation the songs men
sang and the beliefs they held live on and help to give the
United States the semblance of a national culture.

7

Tributaries to the Mainstream: The Ethnic Groups

AMÉRICO PAREDES

Folklorists in many parts of the world regard their discipline as the study of peasant groups, a viewpoint that few folklorists in the United States would be willing to accept. We cannot go into the reasons for their difference of opinion; suffice it to say that American folklorists think of their discipline chiefly as the study of "special groups"—age groups, occupational groups, groups living in certain regions of the country. One of the most common and significant ways of identifying the special group is by national or ethnic origin—that is to say, by identifying it with one of the minorities that make up the population of the United States.

It is the variety of ethnic minorities that gives a young country like the United States the kind of cultural diversity produced in Europe by a centuries-long overlay of cultures and represented in regional or peasant groups. Like the metropolitan culture of the European upper classes, the majority culture of the United States is equated with prestige and material rewards, and thus is something to be attained. On the other hand, the minority cultures, like the peasantry of Europe, may be regarded by their

70

more ambitious members merely as obstacles on the pathway to success, but to the majority they afford strong emotional ties and deep spiritual satisfactions. Furthermore, there is a trend in the United States away from the uncompromising 100 per cent Americanism of earlier times when the country was younger and less sure of itself. There is a tendency to admire the values of minorities and to recognize their role in the enrichment of the majority culture, especially in the contributions made to it from the folklore of diverse ethnic groups.

One way of looking at the folklore of American ethnic groups is to think of it as survivals, not of a dim Stone Age past but of the Old Country, whence the immigrant ancestors came. But the folklore of ethnic groups is made up of more than survivals. It develops in the new environment, taking new forms and receiving new emphases that make it different. This is mainly so because it fulfills an important function for the people who cultivate it: that of helping them as individuals and as a group to cope with the conflicts and tensions arising from their position as minority groups. Among other things, folklore helps create a feeling of unity and homogeneity that enhances the dignity of the group and helps them face with greater confidence the challenges of what to them is a hostile world. All this contributes to the well-observed fact that the least acculturated individual often has the best-integrated personality, while the member of an ethnic group who appears eager to attain acculturation in the most complete and rapid way possible often suffers from all kinds of internalized conflicts and feelings of inferiority. One can only generalize, though, and in an extremely tentative way, when one speaks of "the ethnic groups of the United States." They are so many and so varied. Some have old roots in the soil of America; others are but recently arrived. Some, like the groups living in the Ozarks and the Appalachians, have close affinities with the majority culture; others seem quite exotic to the majority—for example, the Japanese-Americans on the West Coast.

Let us take the Mexican-Americans by way of illustration, since they are representative. They are not really outsiders to the average American, yet their culture is substantially different from that of the majority. They cover a wide geographical area in the United States, significant numbers of them being found from the Southwest to the Great Lakes and westward to the Pacific Coast. Some are descendants of people who settled in what is now the southwestern United States in the late sixteenth century, and thus may look on the Pilgrims as relative newcomers. Others arrived as immigrants yesterday or the day before. Their history amply illustrates the conflicts and tensions and the ups and downs of majority-minority relations: few minorities in the United States have been looked upon with so much hostility at some times, or been so romanticized and sentimentalized at others. Lastly, they are representative because they share a number of characteristics with other minorities that we consider folk.

Ethnic groups are recognizable because they are in some way different from the majority. The difference may be mainly the result of geographical isolation, as with the groups from the Appalachian and Ozark regions. Others who have the same language and general culture as the majority may be separated from them by barriers of prejudice against their physical differences, so that they live in a kind of cultural rather than geographical isolation, as has been the case with the Negro. In other groups the essential difference may be linguistic, though other cultural variations would be present as well, while physical differentiation from the majority would be negligible. The Pennsylvania Dutch—the German-speaking groups in Pennsylvania and neighboring areas—are a good example. Other groups may seem like the majority in almost all respects, except for one important cultural difference significant enough to affect the whole cultural pattern—religion, as is the case with the Mormons and the Jews.

All of the above categories are shared by the Mexican-American. In a country until recently strongly Protestant and still ruled by Protestant values, he is a Catholic who considers his Catholicism less a faith than a way of life. He is distinguished by his use of a language other than English, to which he clings with as much tenacity as he does to his religion. Though there is no physical type one could identify as "Mexican," the majority of Mexicans and Mexican-Americans are of Indian ancestry and thus often as identifiable by physical type as is the Negro. The Mexican-American, furthermore, is closely identified with one special area of the United States, the Southwest, so that he also has developed peculiarities attributable to geographic isolation.

A common mistake, however, has been to consider Mexican-American folk groups as being exclusively restricted to the geographical area of the southwestern United States. In reality Mexican-American groups fall into three categories: the regional, the rural immigrant, or *bracero*, and the urban. But the best known to collectors as well as the oldest Mexican-American folk groups are indeed the regional ones found in the Southwest. They answer well to Richard M. Dorson's definition of regional folk cultures in his book *American Folklore*: "In the folk region, people are wedded to the land, and the land holds memories. The people themselves possess identity and ancestry, through continuous occupation of the same soil." In this respect the Mexican-American is like other regional minorities in the United States such as the Pennsylvania Germans, the Louisiana French, and the Anglo-Saxon mountaineers. One could also include as regional many Negro groups with strong attachment to rural areas in the United States, and some Indians as well.

The ancestors of the regional Mexican-American groups came into the Southwest as colonists from Mexico and thus originally were "regional" in respect to Mexico rather than to the United States. After 1848 they became Mexican-Americans and were immediately involved in conflict with the English-speaking majority. In the former province of Texas (what is now the state of Texas north and east of the Nueces River) they were dispossessed by English-speaking settlers and driven south of the Nueces. In California they were engulfed in the wave of immigration following the discovery of gold in 1849. Only in two regions did Mexican culture make a successful stand: in the area of the old province of New Mexico (embracing the present state of New Mexico, parts of Texas, Arizona, Colorado, and the Mexican state of Chihuahua) and in what had been the province of Nuevo Santander (what is now south Texas, the Mexican state of Tamaulipas, and adjoining areas of Coahuila and Nuevo Leon).

The Mexican-American regional groups felt themselves assailed by the English-speaking invaders of their homeland; their whole structure of life was threatened. Their reaction was inward, in search of greater cohesion and homogeneity within their inherited traditions. This is reflected in their folklore, which includes ancient folk beliefs, old European ballads, archaic wonder tales, historical legends, and legends of the supernatural. Theirs is a strong tendency to hold on to the old forms of folklore handed down to them from the happier past, before the Americans came.

Thus New Mexican groups, and to a less extent the Border Mexican descendants of the old Nuevo Santander settlers, have retained folkloric items no longer found among regional groups in Mexico with similar ethnic backgrounds and degree of isolation. New Mexican groups still retain fragments of *romances*—old ballads telling about the legendary Spanish warrior, the Cid—while both in South Texas and New Mexico may be found other *romances* such as "La Bella Dama y el Pastor," no longer collected in Mexico proper.

The need to hold on to one's own not only preserved but reinvigorated ancient folk traditions, creating new ones as well. Along the Texas-Mexican border, for example, a whole tradition of border balladry emphasizing the theme of border conflict developed from 1850 to 1930, using as a vehicle the Mexican *corrido*, itself a variation of the Spanish *romance*. Stories about Mexican-Americans who took the law into their hands during this period of violence became legendary; the initial facts surrounding the hero's actions attracted motifs from universal folklore. These legends and ballads, in which Mexican-American heroes like Elfego Baca of New Mexico and Gregorio Cortez of Texas perform all kinds of heroic deeds, played an important part in maintaining pride and self-respect among the Mexican-American groups when living conditions for many individuals had become almost intolerable. They also intensified the feeling of unity that characterized the regional groups even as they slowly changed under the impact of the majority culture.

Another means of achieving a feeling of belonging was through the use of the Spanish language in and out of folklore. But even more important in creating a feeling of particularity is the use of bilingualism in jokes, puns, and songs. Spanish is something that even the most newly arrived immigrant or visitor from Mexico knows, while English is the common language of the rival culture. But bilingualism is another matter; a joke that depends on the knowledge of both languages, and even more on some turn of phrase that has a purely local currency, belongs only to the Mexican-American and presumably may be enjoyed only by him. There is no better way of reaffirming kinship with one's fellows while shutting out the rest of the world. Jokes satirizing the member of the majority culture as a greenhorn or as a stupid tourist visiting the area are part of this way of achieving a feeling of homogeneity.

Much the same evidence is available as to the folklore of regional groups other than the Mexican-American. The same desire to hold on to traditional lore as a mark of individuality and the same adaptation of European folklore to American environments has been noted, for example, among the Pennsylvania Germans and the Louisiana French. There is also the same use of the language to define the exclusive character of the group, especially the use of bilingualism for purposes of humor. Macaronic songs and verses that attain their comic effects by mixing German and English seem to be as popular among the Pennsylvania Germans as are songs mixing Spanish and English in the Southwest. Outlaw heroes and ballads of cultural violence seem to be absent among other regional groups in the United States. We should note, however, that the Negro does have his family legends about heroic ancestors who flouted the white man back in the slave days, and the Negro also admires modern heroes of violent action such as Shine and Stackolee.

Only a border line separates the southwestern United States from Mexico, and there has been traffic of persons and things across that border since it was established in 1848; but large-scale immigration from Mexico into the United States did not occur until about 1890. At this time economic conditions in Mexico were worsening under the Díaz regime, causing Mexican farm workers to seek better conditions farther and farther away from home. At the same time increasing industrialization in the United States and the movement of the population from the farms to the cities created a demand for agricultural workers and other unskilled laborers. In the Southwest and the South the demand was for cotton pickers and workers on the railroads. It was filled by Mexican farm workers, who began to come across the border into the United States in great numbers. Some of them crossed legally, many others did not. At first they moved into established Mexican-American regional areas, where they glutted the labor market, forcing a migration north in search of better-paying jobs. Then they moved into California and into Texas beyond the Nueces, reoccupying areas that once had been Mexican in culture. Finally they spread out into other parts of the United States where Mexicans and their culture had never been before. These *braceros*, or agricultural workers, are vulnerable to harassment by immigration authorities because they prefer to think of themselves as being in the United States "just for a little while" and often neglect to legalize their immigrant status. Their difficulty in adapting to American life, their humble economic status and low educational level, and finally their Indian ancestry make them the target of discrimination.

In the face of all this the *bracero* seeks refuge in his own little circle and his own traditions, much as does the member of the regional group, but with some significant differences. Though closely associated with the land, the immigrant has no real attachment to it or historical roots within it, most often being a migrant besides. His older traditions are of course recent importations from Mexico and in any given group may be an amalgamation representing several Mexican subcultures instead of one. The lore he develops in the United States is chiefly occupational lore. And while the member of the regional group assumes the stance of one who defends his own against intruders, the *bracero* is full of the typical wonder of the immigrant taking in the new land.

The hardships of this new land are one of the major themes expressing the feelings and attitudes of the *bracero* and making him one of his fellows. There are many songs on this theme, either songs of serious protest or satirical compositions about the adopted country. Some are similar in tone and intent to the lumbermen's mock complaint "Canaday-I-O." Others are full-blown songs of social protest complaining of working conditions and racial discrimination. Still others, resembling the Scandinavian-American "Oleana," adapt songs inherited from medieval Europe to satirize the supposed abundance of the new land, an abundance in which they do not seem to share, and they sing of lands where roast geese fly about asking to be eaten, streets are paved with tamales, and trees bear tortillas. The member of the majority culture appears in different aspects in the folklore of the immigrant and that of the regional groups. The member of the regional group, wrapping his assaulted culture about him, assumes a somewhat superior attitude toward the outsider who intrudes into his way of life. His jokes and humorous anecdotes show the member of the dominant majority in the role of the stupid, bumbling greenhorn newly arrived in the area.

The immigrant, however, is in a much more defenseless state in respect to the majority culture. Torn from his own roots, he finds himself in a foreign land and among a foreign people, to

whom he must look for all his wants. In his folklore the member
of the dominant majority is more likely to appear as The Boss,
both in serious and in comic narratives and songs. In some ways
the immigrant is likely to take an apologetic attitude toward
himself and his culture, where the member of the regional
group is fiercely defensive. The immigrant is more apt to admit
that "Americans do things better than we do" or that "Americans are very smart." After all, just look at those combines and
the mechanical cotton pickers. But he will go on to point out
a hundred weaknesses in the way of life of the American, accus-
ing him especially of all kinds of moral faults. The immigrant
is very likely to sum the whole thing up with a proverb, *"Cada
oveja con su pareja"*: To each his own. So he holds fast to the
folk culture he brought with him from Mexico with a patient,
resigned amazement at the things that happen in this world.

In general the Mexican *braceros'* problems are those of other
ethnic groups that have come as immigrants to the United States.
They bring with them a little part of home in their customs, their
beliefs, their songs and legends and other folklore, to sustain
them in their role of aliens in a confusingly new environment.
Their children or grandchildren, given the opportunity, will
reject it all for entrance into the majority culture. But not all
of them will follow that road. The less successful and the more
traditionally minded will retain the old lore in a spirit not
unlike that of antiquarianism. This is scarcely true of Mexican-
American immigrant folklore, but it is due to special factors: on
the one hand the close cultural and geographic bonds with the
people of neighboring Mexico, on the other the barriers faced
by the *bracero* in his attempts at acculturation.

When the immigrant farm worker and the displaced member
from the regional group move into town, we have the Mexican-
American urban groups. These are immigrants, but of another
kind; the focus of their life is the big-city ghetto, in the case
of the Mexican-American the "Mexiquitos," or Little Mexicos, in
cities like Los Angeles, San Antonio, and East Chicago. Some
members of these urban groups are former agricultural workers
from the regional areas, displaced by *bracero* labor. Others are
the more ambitious migrant workers from Mexico, who came to
labor in the fields and stayed to work in the factories. The
children and grandchildren of political refugees who left Mexico

during the Revolution are most often found in the cities too. Of the three kinds of groups the *braceros* obviously are the least acculturated; but it is hard to decide which of the other two possesses the higher degree of acculturation, the regional or the urban. Like the regional groups, the urban groups are bilingual and bicultural to greater or lesser degree. If anything, one would expect the city to work its way upon the member of the urban group, so that he would be quickly assimilated. But while the member of the urban group is more greatly affected by influences outside his cultural orbit, he is also the object of greater hostility in the complexities and pressures of urban life. He is likely to feel much more insecure than the members of either the regional or the *bracero* groups; and this, coupled with the threat of urban depersonalization, impels him to seek a sense of identity within his own group, laying claim to an ethnic culture that is still his only in fitful glimpses.

For the city has left its mark upon him, and his lore is less Mexican (or Italian or Polish or Jewish or what have you) and more the kind of lore found among urban groups everywhere. One certainly would not look for Mexican forms of the wonder tale among the urban groups, or for the legends of cultural conflict that stiffened the pride of the regional groups. Gone also are the field workers' songs of protest and the ballads about border outlaws. The songs making macaronic fun of bilingualism are absent, too; they are highly prized where one recognizes the differences between two languages, but they cannot be very funny to people who unconsciously talk in the same macaronic fashion. But argot, the ethnic slur, the jest, and verbal play are very important, which is true of most ethnic groups in the cities, as one may see in such studies of urban lore as Roger Abrahams' *Deep Down in the Jungle* concerning the Philadelphia Negro.

While much of the folk literature disappears, there is a tendency to emphasize the importance of more tangible forms. Thus, one hears few Mexican folksongs in East Chicago, Indiana, though folksongs may still be collected aplenty along the lower Texas-Mexican border. But the Mexican food is superior in East Chicago in quality, variety, and traditional character. East Chicagoans until recently flew in from Mexico regular shipments of *cilantro*, an herb traditionally used to give a delicious flavor to salads, soups, and sauces. Now *cilantro* is no longer imported;

the Mexicans of East Chicago have learned to grow their own. In Austin, Texas, where I live, *cilantro* is not to be had at any price; and I am told it sometimes is hard to get even on the border. Other items of Mexican material culture crop up unexpectedly in contexts involving a good degree of acculturation. Among Mexican-American urban groups, for example, the American custom of passing the hat for worthy causes or to help a friend in need has become firmly established. But in many cases the act is given special dignity and formality by passing around a silver-braided Mexican sombrero of the *charro* type.

Here are three ways in which ethnic groups may react to the majority culture, using their inherited lore as a means of security and self-identification. The regional groups, with their roots in the land, enjoy the feeling of permanence and depth one associates with peasant groups. When their values are challenged, when their coherent world is attacked from the outside by the majority culture, they try to shut out the disturbing elements, making of their lore a stable little tradition to be set against the majority culture. The *bracero* groups, agricultural migrants, are in a state of permanent transition—always moving and arriving nowhere. They come from Mexico into an alien world to which they must adjust if this world is to become meaningful to them. Some *braceros* become attached to regional or urban groups. A very few become acculturated and cease to be "ethnics."

The great majority drift along at the edges of a society to which they would like to belong but that never quite accepts them. With the urban groups the idea of a coherent, meaningful world seems to fade away—whether it is one's own world, to be defended at all costs, or that of the majority, which one is seeking to understand in order to enter into it. The member of the urban group is a splinter from a shattered society, one of a mass of anonymous fragments. He seeks to give some meaning to existence, some dignity and individuality to himself, by shoring up his ruins with the bits and pieces of his ethnic past. In every case, however, folklore performs the function of giving to an ethnic group, if not actual homogeneity, at least the feeling of it.

The Mexican-Americans are but one of the many peoples that go into the making of the variegated web that is American culture. All of these ethnic groups exist in the character of folk groups in respect to the majority, emphasizing their uniqueness and individuality, but in the end contributing to the enrichment of the whole culture of the United States. In fine detail the cultural history of the Mexican-Americans may differ from that of other ethnic minorities, but in broad outline it exemplifies the experience of all ethnic groups in this country, and the place occupied by folklore in that experience.

II

AREAS
OF
FOCUS

8

Stories Told in Song: The Ballads of America

G . M A L C O L M   L A W S ,   J R .

Before I discuss the American traditional ballad, I think I should explain the meaning of the word "ballad" as I am using it. This is a word of various meanings, and even ballad scholars may disagree with each other in defining it. First of all, I will be dealing with a kind of narrative folksong. The story element is vital. If the folksong does not actually tell a story from beginning to end, I do not call it a ballad. If we find a poem that tells a story but is never sung, again I would not call it a ballad. And I am limiting the term in still another way. To be called a ballad, the song must have a traditional life; that is, it must live primarily in the memories of the people and be passed by word of mouth from one singer to another. Finally, I want to point out that I will not be discussing ballads which have passed out of tradition but only those which have been collected from singers in this century.

Three main groups of ballads are traditional in the United States. The oldest of these are the so-called Child ballads, which were named in honor of Francis J. Child of Harvard. In the 1880's and 1890's he edited a great collection in five large volumes called *The English and Scottish Popular Ballads*. Most of these old stories of border warfare and violence and the supernatural date from the sixteenth and seventeenth centuries, though a few come down from the late Middle Ages. More than sixty of Child's 305 ballads have a vigorous traditional life in America. The second group consists of ballads which originated in the British Isles as poems composed for sale on printed sheets, called broadsides. Many became popular with singers and passed into tradition; some 275 ballads of broadside origin, most of them composed in the eighteenth and the early nineteenth century, have been collected in North America. The third group consists of ballads composed here in America and circulated by singing and by print. The more than 250 native American ballads date from the second half of the last century, although some are older and some more recent. Of course the folksingers do not distinguish among their ballads by origin as I am doing. They sing pieces from all three groups and they ask only for ballad stories that are meaningful to them and worth retelling.

We owe our huge store of ballad texts to the work of collectors during the past half-century. Schoolteachers and college professors and their students, musicologists, amateur and professional singers, all have helped gather traditional songs. Ballads have been found in large numbers in the Appalachian Mountains (from Pennsylvania south to Alabama), in rural New England, in the Middle West, and in the Far West. And new books of folksongs keep appearing. We now have at least one collection from most of the states. Anyone interested in such a collection from a particular state might want to look at Volume II of the Frank C. Brown Collection of North Carolina Folklore. A good general anthology is Alan Lomax's *The Folk Songs of North America*. Both of these books contain many ballads from the three main groups.

Before I discuss specific ballads, I should say a word about the folksingers and the composers of the songs. There has never been one spot in America where a large part of the population could sing ballads in public. Usually each rural community had one or two men or women who were famous as singers, and sometimes these men (less frequently the women) also composed ballads. The broadside ballads in the British Isles were largely the work of hack writers or journalists. And the Child ballads were probably composed by minstrels and minor poets. In America, folksingers were much in demand as amateur entertainers, but they were not alone in spreading balladry, for those who heard them would often remember some of their songs and pass them along within the family. Thus a fishing village in Maine, or a farming community in Indiana, or a prison in the South, or a remote mountain settlement might be the scene of a lively ballad tradition as well as the place of origin of new ballad texts. While city people may never hear a ballad sung by a real amateur folksinger, more isolated people enjoy folksong as an important part of life. But the movies, the radio, and television are undoubtedly making amateur community entertainment increasingly rare.

If there is such a thing as a typical ballad, we might say that it contains from ten to twenty short rhymed stanzas or half as many longer ones. The diction is simple and straightforward, but the grammar is uncertain. The ballad is likely to contain characters, situations, and expressions familiar from other similar pieces. The story is told with much dramatic detail, considerable dialogue, and little if any comment from the author. None of the traditional texts are identical, mainly because of the forgetfulness of singers. The longer the ballad is sung, the more likely it is to acquire the style and the language of the people who sing it. Anyone who studies balladry can soon recognize its distinctive qualities.

Among the most popular Child ballads in America are the stories of love and domestic tragedy which are understandable to everyone. These ballads usually deal with characters of wealth and high rank in a feudalistic society. Gold and silver, servants, and fine houses are emphasized. The stories often tell of murder and other crimes resulting from such basic emotions as hatred and jealousy. Although the supernatural frequently appears in the older British texts, it is rare in the modern American ones, but ghosts are not unknown in texts collected here.

One of the most widely distributed stories of jealousy and murder is "The Two Sisters," a ballad which exists in various forms and in different languages throughout Europe and the British Isles. Tristram P. Coffin's book *The British Traditional*

Ballad in North America refers to dozens of texts collected from singers. The story is of two sisters—princesses in the older versions—of whom the younger is the more beautiful. She is wooed by a young man who gives her valuable presents. The jealous older sister lures the younger one to the water's edge and then drowns her. In some texts the murder is revealed by supernatural means after a miller has pulled the girl's body from the water. A harpist strings his harp with her hair, and the harp speaks and accuses the older sister. According to Coffin, this ballad "has more American story variations than any other song."

Here is the full text of "The Two Sisters" from the version sung by Horton Barker of Virginia to Herbert Halpert for the Library of Congress collection.

> There was an old woman lived on the sea shore,
>   Bow and balance to me;
> There was an old woman lived on the sea shore,
> Her number of daughters, one, two, three, four;
>   And I'll be true to my love if my love'll be true to me.

From here on, I am omitting the repeated lines and refrains.

> There was a young man came there to see them,
> And the oldest one got struck on him.

"Got struck on him" means "fell in love with him."

> He bought the youngest a beaver hat,
> And the oldest she got mad at that.
>
> "O sister, O sister, let's walk the sea shore,
> And see the ships as they sail o'er."

You will notice that the dialogue is introduced without explanation.

> While these two sisters were walking the shore,
> The oldest pushed the youngest o'er.
>
> "O sister, O sister, please lend me your hand,
> And you may have Willie and all of his land."
>
> "I never, I never will lend you my hand,
> But I'll have Willie and all of his land."

Notice how various phrases are repeated in advancing the story.

> Sometimes she sank and sometimes she swam,
> Until she came to the old mill dam.

> The miller he got his fishing hook,
> And fished the maiden out of the brook.

In this version, the girl is still alive. The ballad continues:

> "O miller, O miller, here's five gold rings,
> To push the maiden in again."

> The miller received those five gold rings,
> And pushed the maiden in again.

> The miller was hung at his own mill gate,
> For drownding little sister Kate.

And that's the end of the story. You will observe that in this American text the girls are no longer princesses. But some of their wealth remains in the five gold rings with which the older sister bribes the miller. The gift of a beaver hat is typical of frontier America; in the British texts the girl is given jewelry. The supernatural element has entirely disappeared, and the miller becomes the actual murderer. Although the victim is pushed into the sea, her body is taken from a stream with a mill dam; the inconsistency also appears in the British texts, but it does not seem to bother the singers. This version leaves certain questions unanswered, particularly the fate of the older sister. Such a compressed and abrupt ending is a feature of many of the older ballads, possibly because some of the verses have been lost. The refrain—which helps remind us that ballads are songs —is found frequently, but is just as likely to be missing.

Perhaps the best-known Child ballad in America is "Barbara Allen," in which a trivial misunderstanding between two lovers results in the death of both. The young man pines away because Barbara is annoyed with him, and she in turn must die from grief. Her last words are addressed to her mother:

> O, mother, mother, make my bed,
> O make it soft and narrow;
> Since my love died for me today,
> I'll die for him tomorrow.

We aren't always told why the ballad characters act the way they do. In "Lord Randal," which sometimes becomes simply "Johnny Randall" in America, we have a dialogue between mother and son. The son has been to see his true love, has been poisoned by her, and has returned home to die. We never learn why the crime was committed. The last stanza of a text received by Ruth Ann Musick in West Virginia is quite effective:

> "What do you will to your sweetheart,
>   Johnny Randall, my son?
> What do you will to your sweetheart,
>   my own dearest one?"
> "I will her hell's fire, and it will
>   scorch her heart brown;
> I've a pain in my head, and I fain
>   would lie down."

A well-known ghost ballad among the Child pieces traditional in America is "Fair Margaret and Sweet William." In this Margaret dies of grief after her lover falsely marries someone else. Her ghost appears at the foot of William's bed to remind him of their love. Thinking he has had a dream, he goes seeking Margaret, discovers her corpse, kisses her clay-cold lips, and dies. In the world of balladry, there is no worse crime than disloyalty in love. Its usual punishment is death.

Far more numerous in America than the Child ballads are the traditional broadsides, those journalistic narratives once sold in street and tavern and from the peddler's pack. While the Child ballads are aristocratic, the broadsides are plebeian and deal not with royalty and nobility but with soldiers and sailors, milkmaids and merchants. These ballads were extremely popular in Britain; they were brought to America, as the Child ballads were, in the memories of the English and Scottish immigrants. From the middle of the nineteenth century on, tens of thousands of Irish people came to this country, and they, too, remembered many broadside ballads. Additional printed ballads were exported to the United States or were reprinted here in songbooks and on broadside sheets.

Many of the broadsides deal with the problems of young lovers who had to contend with the opposition of their families. A rich man's daughter may fall in love with a poor plowboy or a sailor and risk her family's wrath to elope with him. Or a girl may disguise herself as a man and enlist in the army or the navy to be near her lover. In "Jack Monroe," for example, the girl follows her true love to the wars in Germany and cares for him after he is wounded. In "The Golden Glove" a rich lady prefers a poor farmer to a wealthy squire and cleverly arranges to marry the one she loves. No doubt such stories reflect some wishful thinking on the part of poor soldiers and farmers. Another very popular type tells of the lover who returns in disguise after a long absence and tests the loyalty of his girl. Such a ballad is "The Banks of Claudy," which begins like this:

> It was on a summer's morning all in the month of May,
> Down by yon flowery garden where Betsy did stray;
> I overheard a damsel in sorrow to complain,
> All for her absent lover that plows the raging main.

When the girl says that she is searching for Johnny, the narrator tells her that Johnny's ship has been wrecked and he is lost. She begins to tear her hair and vows never to marry anyone else. Only then does he reveal his identity. He says:

> I am the faithless young man whom you thought was slain,
> And since we are met on Claudy's banks we'll never part again.

Other broadside subjects include war and its results, murder and other crimes, disasters on land and sea, sentimental incidents and farcical ones. Marital conflicts appear, too, as in the humorous ballad "Johnny Sands." In this, Johnny says he is tired of life and plans to drown himself. His wife agrees to push him into the water with his hands tied behind him. When she comes rushing down the hill, he steps aside and she plunges into the water instead. She calls for help, but he reminds her that she has tied his hands. The number of traditional comic pieces is not great, but those that do appear are very popular. Far more common are songs with a gloomy tone like "The Butcher Boy," the sad tale of a girl whose unrequited love leads her to suicide. All over the country people know the ballad which begins:

> In Jersey City where I did dwell
> A butcher boy I loved so well;
> He courted me my heart away,
> And then with me he would not stay.

When the American composers began to write ballads, they imitated the style and substance of the broadsides rather than that of the older Child ballads. The broadsides were more up to date, more democratic in content, and less demanding artistically. Also being more sentimental and less imaginative, they were better suited to the talents and inclinations of the folk composers.

Native American balladry, which is crude in technique but delicate and sincere in feeling, originated to meet needs which the imported ballads did not satisfy. This was especially true of sensational news events, which usually inspired ballad composition. "Springfield Mountain," one of the oldest native ballads, tells of a young man who is fatally bitten by a rattlesnake while mowing his father's field. When the father, who had not understood that the boy was calling for help, finds his son's body, the scene is described as follows:

> He took him up and he carried him home
> And on the way did lament and mourn,
> Saying, "I heard but did not come
> And now I'm left alone to mourn."

This stanza, from a text collected in Vermont by Helen H. Flanders, shows the sensitivity and tenderness typical of native balladry. This eighteenth-century ballad was followed in the nineteenth and twentieth centuries by dozens of versified accounts of the sad accidents of peace and war. In fact, native balladry is based largely upon actual events, and whatever it lacks in smoothness is made up for by the sense of reality it conveys. No American ballad, for example, is better known than "Casey Jones," the story of a railroad engineer who is killed in a collision. And this is but one of many ballads about railroad accidents. Other factual ballads tell of a mine disaster, a flood, a fire, a tornado, and one widely known piece, "Young Charlotte," is the story of a girl who freezes to death in a sleigh while riding with a young man to a ball.

Broadside ballads of murder have long been popular in Britain. A number of these were sung here from early days, and some of them became the models for new murder ballads. The favorite plot goes like this: to avoid marrying a girl who has grown burdensome to him, a young man lures her away from home on the pretext of discussing wedding plans. He then says he will kill her, and does so despite her pleas, by beating, stabbing, or drowning her. Eventually the crime comes to light and the murderer is punished. Most American texts give the names of both the murderer and his victim and include various specific details about the crime. Pearl Bryan, Ellen Smith, Naomi Wise, Lula Viers, and Mary Phagan are some of the unfortunate American girls whose stories are told in murder ballads.

Most native ballads arose from occupations and situations which made nineteenth-century American life distinctive. The vast plains of the American West produced the cattle industry and the cowboy, and naturally the cowboys composed and sang ballads about their life. These range from the satiric to the sentimental and tragic, from a comic tale like "The Strawberry Roan," which tells of an unsuccessful attempt to ride a bucking horse, to "Little Joe the Wrangler," the tale of a cowboy who dies under his horse in a cattle stampede. There was danger in the great Northern forests, too, as the men who worked in the lumber industry knew. The lumbermen would listen to ballad singing at the end of the day or on Sundays, and the songs would often tell the tragedies of the woods, of the men killed by falling limbs, or cut by the great saws, or drowned in the rushing rivers. "The Jam on Gerry's Rock" is such a ballad. It tells of Young Monroe, the foreman of a crew, who volunteers to help break a huge log jam and dies when the jam suddenly gives way and he is crushed beneath the logs. Great disasters are remembered, too, as in "The Avondale Disaster," a lament for the coal miners killed underground in Pennsylvania in 1869. The composer of this ballad must have felt the tragedy deeply. The ballad ends as follows in a Library of Congress text collected by George Korson:

> Now to conclude and make an end,
> Their number I'll pen down—
> A hundred and ten of brave strong men
> Were smothered underground!
> They're in their graves till this last day,
> Their widows may bewail
> And the orphans' cries they rend the skies
> All round through Avondale.

The colorful criminal or outlaw has appealed to the folk imagination since the Robin Hood ballads became popular centuries ago. The best-known American ballad outlaw is Jesse James, whose exploits as a bank and train robber and whose murder by one of his own gang have often been told in song. Just before he was killed, Jesse was living under the assumed name of Howard. In a version from Henry M. Belden's Missouri collection, it is obvious where the ballad-maker's sympathies lay:

> Jesse James was a lad that killed many a man
> He robbed the Danville train.
> But that dirty little coward that shot Mr. Howard
> Has laid poor Jesse in the grave.
> It was Robert Ford, that dirty little coward,
> I wonder how he does feel;
> For he ate of Jesse's bread and slept in Jesse's bed
> And laid poor Jesse in the grave.

Among the most direct and vivid American ballads are those of the Negro. The stories are likely to be full of violence and its consequences. Often the main character is described as a bad man—that is, one whose illegal activities have earned him a reputation. Among the Negroes he is both admired and feared, and the white sheriffs are wary of him. But the superior power of the law usually triumphs, and the bad man is captured and jailed. John Hardy is such a character. He carries out his threat to kill the first man who wins his money in a gambling game. He escapes briefly but later is hanged for his crime. It is the woman who kills in "Frankie and Albert," when she finds her lover visiting another woman. There is no more familiar line in American balladry than the refrain which gives her motive for the murder: "He was her man, but he done her wrong." But the best-known character in Negro balladry is a proud and noble hero. John Henry works on the railroad, driving steel spikes with his ten-pound hammer. When he hears that a steam drill is to be tried on the job, John Henry offers to compete with it. His statement to the captain, in a version collected by John A. Lomax, shows some of his character:

> John Henry told his old captain
> That a man ain't nothing but a man;
> Before I let that steel gang down,
> I'll die with my hammer in my hand.

And John Henry does beat the steam drill, though the exertion costs him his life, and he is given a hero's burial. No native ballad is more memorable.

A folk ballad has great powers of endurance in its own environment, especially if flagging memories have been aided by occasional reprinted texts. But it has little power to survive in uncorrupted form in the alien world of professional entertainment. The successful ballad composer, who understands the mind of the folk, tells his story so as to appeal to their tastes, their ethical sense, and their hearts. And it is a rare audience indeed that does not fall under the spell of a ballad well sung by a genuine folksinger. By a genuine singer, I mean one who has learned his ballads from other folksingers in a folk community, rather than one who creates an artificial repertory from the music book and the printed page. The more closely the audience can identify with the singer and his material, the more meaningful the ballad will be. In the folk community the ballad serves the universal need for story and song by providing both together in one moving work of folk art. It offers the excitement of vicarious experience and frequently conveys some of the pity and terror of tragedy. To the outsider it gives a deeper understanding of ways of life different from his own. And to everyone who reads them or listens to them, the simple ballad stories offer memorable scenes from the ever-changing drama of human life.

9

"Just Sing It Yourself": The American Lyric Tradition

W. EDSON RICHMOND

A number of years ago, according to Howard W. Odum in *The Negro and His Songs*, a university dean sat on the stone wall in front of his house and took down the words to a song being sung by a road gang. Suddenly he became aware of what he was writing:

> White man settin' on wall,
> White man settin' on wall,
> White man settin' on wall all day long,
> Wastin' his time, wastin' his time.

These nonce words were obviously composed at that moment. Perhaps they would never be sung again. But at that time and place they came to life and were an appropriate comment on an immediate situation, preserved by the same accident which created them.

94

A very large number, perhaps the bulk, of lyric folksongs found in America lend themselves to this sort of immediate variation. Lacking the conservative force of a specific narrative, expressive of a mood rather than a story, lyric folksongs are amorphous. They adapt to particular situations, changing form and shape according to the demands of both singer and audience. Unlike ballads, which appear slowly to shorten, to lose incidental stanzas, and to drop all except the essential narrative elements, lyric folksongs expand at one moment, contract at another. Stanzas are improvised, never to be sung again; stanzas disappear only to crop up again; stanzas migrate from song to song: the only constancy lies in theme. As a result, it is nearly impossible to estimate the number of folk lyrics known and sung in America. For folk lyrics are, to use James Reeves's expression, "the idiom of the people."

It could not be otherwise. Lyric folksongs, like all other folksongs, are a product of oral tradition. Composed originally by an individual, folksongs are remodeled and reworked by singer after singer until the impress and significance of the original composer disappear. To say this in another way, only constant resinging by people unconcerned with the preservation of specific words makes a song into a folksong. This process of communal re-creation depends, however, upon the accepted cliché. Precise repetition of a particular set of words is neither demanded nor valued, but neither can the singer of folksongs stray from the common way of saying things. Thus, no matter how a particular song originated, whether it was the inspiration of an inglorious but not so mute Milton, as a popular song, as a broadside, or in any of a myriad ways, once it is accepted in a culture it is recast in terms familiar to that culture. In extreme cases this process can turn a song into something unrecognizable as itself. More commonly, however, it simply results in the substitution of a well-worn phrase or stanza for the less familiar, and thus less easily remembered, wording of the original composition.

It is not easy to generalize about songs of this sort. Much less is it easy to classify them, for lyric folksongs are a compendium of human experience. Moreover, the passage of time and shifting attitudes can turn a serious lament into a richly humorous satire with the change of hardly a word. Nevertheless, it is safe to say that American folk-lyric tradition is basically British in its origins and that in the country as a whole only an evolved and ever-changing Anglo-American tradition is alive. In the Southwest, a Spanish-language tradition thrives, but it has had virtually no effect upon the English-language folksong tradition in its own area and absolutely none upon the tradition in the rest of America. Similarly, French-language songs can be found in Louisiana and in the Northeast, German-language songs in Pennsylvania and the Middle West, and Scandinavian-language songs in Michigan, Minnesota, Wisconsin, the Dakotas, Nebraska, and in a few isolated areas. But in all of these instances the tradition is dying. The songs are neither translated into English nor do their styles affect the English-language tradition. Even more remote are the songs of the American Indian. Indeed, only the Negro has made any significant contribution to the traditional Anglo-American heritage, and his has been in the manner of rhythmical modification and the addition of a rather special idiom that has had a greater effect upon popular song than upon folksong. That is, the Negro has borrowed folksongs and recast them, but his adaptations have not been perpetuated as folksongs by non-Negroes.

What has been said about the textual tradition of American lyric folksongs is also true about the musical tradition—it is basically British in origin. Moreover, although there are many indigenous American folksong texts, there seem to be relatively few indigenous American folksong tunes, for the folk do not appear to compose tunes so freely or so easily as they compose texts. Thus new words are frequently developed for old tunes, but almost never does one find a completely new tune either for an old text or for a new one.

But tunes, like texts, do change. It is generally agreed that British folksongs, in addition to the now conventional seven-tone major and minor scales, employed scales of fewer tones, frequently five rather than seven, with the half tones appearing in various places within the scale. Such pentatonic, modal scales can still be found in certain isolated American areas such as the southern Appalachians, the Northeast, and the Ozarks, but they are rare. The increased use of conventionally scaled instruments to accompany folksinging tends to restrict singers to standardized scales. In addition, the older styles of singing have not been able to resist the influence of radio, television, and gramophone records. The result is the occasional transmogrification of a pentatonic tune into a heptatonic minor (since it, too, somehow sounds "different"), or, more commonly, the simple shift to an ordinary major scale based on the same tonic as the original.

Perhaps the most peculiarly American of all of the folksongs sung in this country are those which evolved on the Western frontier. They are distinguished, however, by an individuality of scene rather than by any oddity of theme or style. With very few exceptions, each is a modification, a relocation in space and spirit, of an older song. One of the most widely known of such songs is "The Girl I Left Behind Me." The following stanzas are taken from a version printed in *Cowboy Songs and Other Frontier Ballads*. It was collected by the late John A. Lomax sometime before 1910, presumably in Texas:

> I struck the trail in seventy-nine,
> The herd strung out behind me;
> As I jogged along my mind ran back
> For the gal I left behind me.
>> That sweet little gal, that true little gal,
>> The gal I left behind me.

> If ever I get off the trail
> And the Indians they don't find me,
> I'll make my way straight back again
> To the gal I left behind me.
>> That sweet little gal, that true little gal,
>> The gal I left behind me.

Truly traditional, though its medium of transmission was sometimes the popular songster as well as word-of-mouth, the song is found in a mid-nineteenth-century British publication, William Chappell's *Popular Music of Olden Times*, where it is described as a march and where the words are dated 1758. American versions vary widely in title, but in nearly every instance, as in the Western stanzas just quoted, the song is Americanized only in locale, and stanzas such as:

> She wrote ahead to the place I said,
> I was always glad to find it.
> She says, "I am true, when you get through
> Right back here you will find me."
>> That sweet little gal, that true little gal,
>> The gal I left behind me.

exactly parallel the older form and clearly reveal its conversion from the British soldier's farewell song.

The most popular of such relocalized songs is, of course, the now famous "Streets of Laredo" or "Cowboy's Lament." First collected in this country by a self-styled cowboy poet, N. Howard "Jack" Thorpe in 1886, this song has been traced back to an eighteenth-century Irish original called "The Unfortunate Rake." It subsequently passed into English tradition and described the final words of a British soldier dying, like his Irish progenitor, of venereal disease. The American versions, though substituting a gunshot wound for the less acceptable syphilis, kept the impress of the English version by retaining the description of a military funeral in such stanzas as:

> Oh beat the drum slowly and play the fife lowly,
> Play the Dead March as you carry me along;
> Take me to the green valley, there lay the sod o'er me
> For I'm a young cowboy and I know I've done wrong.

and

> Oh, muffle your drums, then play your fifes merrily,
> Play the Dead March as you go along.
> And fire your guns right over my coffin,
> There goes an unfortunate boy to his home.

In a similar manner, "Bury Me Not on the Lone Prairie" evolved from the British "Bury Me Not in the Deep, Deep Sea," and one suspects that many Western songs now thought to be purely American will ultimately be traced to British originals. Yet songs descriptive of the cowboy's life and its appendages, songs like "Little Joe the Wrangler," "The Zebra Dun," and "Git Along Little Dogies" with its refrain stanza:

> Whoopee ti yi yo, git along little dogies,
> It's your misfortune and none of my own.
> Whoopee ti yi yo, git along little dogies,
> For you know that Wyomin' will be your new home.

have, no matter what their origin, been so thoroughly imbued with the Western scene that they have become as American as the grandchildren of the immigrants who originally brought similar songs to the plains and mountains of the West. Moreover, the most popular Western song of all, a song which today is heard in Oslo and in Rome almost as frequently as in Fort Worth and Phoenix, has defied even legal attempts to prove it to be anything other than a truly American folksong. One suspects that this song, "Home on the Range," has its roots in the nine-teenth-century music halls. Brought to the attention of the literate world by John A. Lomax in 1910, the song's lyrics are nostalgic and overly sentimental:

> Oh, give me a home where the buffalo roam,
> Where the deer and the antelope play,
> Where seldom is heard a discouraging word
> And the skies are not cloudy all day.

> Home, home on the range,
> Where the deer and the antelope play,
> Where seldom is heard a discouraging word,
> And the skies are not cloudy all day.

These words are a far cry from the naturalistic lyrics of "The Chisholm Trail," and they ring especially false in stanzas such as the following:

> The red man was pressed from this part of the West,
> He's likely no more to return
> To the banks of Red River where seldom if ever
> Their flickering camp fires burn.

for the situation is more realistically depicted in a stanza from "The Dreary Black Hills":

> Don't go away, stay at home if you can,
> Stay away from that city, they call it Cheyenne,
> For old Sitting Bull or Comanche Bills
> They will take off your scalp on the dreary
>   Black Hills.

Yet the sentiments of "Home on the Range," whether emotions recollected in tranquillity or imagined by a romantic tenderfoot, captured the public fancy, so much so that in the 1930's Tin Pan Alley claimed the song for its own. The resultant legal investigation brought to light a folk version known as early as 1874, and subsequently Lomax found a record of its being sung in Texas in 1867. The song is probably not much older. Though it once lived in popular tradition, it no longer does so. Today it is a fossil, a magnificent specimen to be studied and exhibited but, like all fossils, a mere shell of its former self.

Despite their popularity, however, there is really very little that distinguishes the songs of the American West from the rest of America's folksongs. Though often modified to fit the local scene, American folksongs appear to be unhampered by geographical boundaries. The same types of songs—indeed, the same songs— are sung throughout the country. Consequently, it is more satisfactory to discuss songs in terms of functional categories than in terms of geographical areas, to speak of lullabies and nursery songs, love lyrics, work songs, protest songs, game and dance songs, and religious songs, instead of Western songs, Appalachian songs, or songs from New England.

American lullabies, like those of most of the rest of the world, tend to be soporific in tune and repetitious in text. Indeed, any song, even the most incongruous, may serve as a lullaby if it meets these two requirements. Thus one of the best-known lullabies found in America is a three-stanza fragment often encountered in an eighteenth-century British riddle ballad, "Captain Wedderburn's Courtship." The ballad depicts a contest between a man and a maid: she asks difficult questions which he must answer if he will bed her. The lullaby omits a number of the questions and all references to their significance; it consists solely of:

> I gave my love a cherry without a stone,
> I gave my love a chicken without a bone,
> I gave my love a ring without an end,
> I gave my love a baby, there's no cryin'.
>
> How can there be a cherry without a stone,
> How can there be a chicken without a bone,
> How can there be a ring without an end,
> How can there be a baby, there's no cryin'?
>
> A cherry when it's blooming, it has no stone,
> A chicken when it's pippin, it has no bone,
> A ring when it's rolling, it has no end,
> A baby when it's sleeping, there's no cryin'.

In addition, America has borrowed innumerable British lullabies such as "Rock-a-Bye Baby in the Treetop," "Bye Baby Bunting," and "Taffy Is a Welshman," but there also seem to be some distinct American contributions to the genre such as "All the Pretty Little Horses":

> Hush a by an' don't you cry,
> An' go to sleep, little baby;
> When you wake you shall have some cake
> An' ride a pretty little horsey.

> You shall have a little canoe
> An' a little bit of a paddle;
> You shall have a little red mule
> An' a little bitty saddle.

> The black an' the bay, the sorrel an' the grey
> All belong to you, my baby.
> So hush a by an' don't you cry
> An' go to sleep little baby.

Love songs, of course, run the gamut from comments upon the appearance and abilities of the beloved—songs such as "Black Is the Color of My True Love's Hair" and "Gently Johnny My Jingle-O"—through courtship propaganda, such as "Locks and Bolts," to the lament found in "The Rejected Lover":

> I wish I'd adied when I was young
> Or never been born,
> For I never would have met her rosy cheeks
> Nor heard her flattering tongue.

and the even more poignant comment in "I Wish I Was Single Again":

> I married a wife, oh then,
> I married a wife, she's the plague of my life,
> And I wish I was single again.

A number of songs fall between these extremes, perhaps as many as five hundred, but emotionally they are summed up in the most famous of all, "On Top of Old Smokey," a song which has incorporated verses from at least three others: "The Wagoner's

Lad," "The Inconstant Lover," and "Courting Too Slow." One of its North Carolina variants is as well constructed as a poem by Robert Burns:

> On the top of Old Smokey,
> All covered in snow,
> I lost my true lover
> By courting too slow.
>
> Courting was pleasure,
> But parting was grief.
> A false-hearted lover
> Is worse than a thief.
>
> A thief he will rob you
> And take what you save,
> But a false-hearted lover
> Place you in the grave.
>
> The grave will decay you
> And turn you to dust.
> Not a boy in a thousand
> That a poor girl can trust.
>
> They will tell you they love you
> To give your heart ease,
> And when your back's turned upon them
> They'll court whom they please.
>
> It's raining, it's hailing
> The moon gives no light.
> Your horses can't travel
> This dark stormy night.
>
> So put up your horses
> And feed them some hay.
> Come sit here beside me
> As long as you stay.
>
> My horses ain't hungry,
> They won't eat your hay.
> I'll drive on, my true love,
> And feed on my way.

As sure as the dew drops
Fall on the green corn
My lover was with me;
But now he is gone.

So back to Old Smokey,
Old Smokey so high,
Where the wild birds and turtle doves
Can hear my sad cry.

None of these songs is especially static. As in "On Top of Old Smokey," stanzas are frequently borrowed from similar songs. Moreover, few love songs are so well knit as the foregoing; for the most part each stanza is treated as an independent unit and sung when and if it comes to mind.

This latter characteristic is shared by work songs, which may be roughly divided into songs descriptive of various occupations and occupational heroes and songs employed within the work itself. The former impinge upon balladry, often telling a relatively complete story, but more frequently describing a series of independent scenes which with only a few verbal changes may be shifted from occupation to occupation. Since the middle of the nineteenth century these songs have often taken the form of "Come All Ye's," a genre which has its origin in broadsheets and which takes its name from the opening words as in "Casey Jones":

Come all ye rounders
For I want you to hear
The story of a brave Engineer.
Casey Jones was the rounder's name
On a six-eight wheeler
He won his fame.

Miners, lumberjacks, railroaders, sailors, cowboys—all have their particular songs of this type. Many, indeed, are simply parodies built on parodies until it is difficult to trace their evolution and even more difficult to determine the original.

The songs employed in work are more varied. Almost anything quiet serves the cowboy riding nightherd who needs merely to keep the cattle aware of a human presence and at the same time

needs to thrust away his own loneliness. For his purposes "The
Streets of Laredo," "Bury Me Not on the Lone Prairie," or "The
Cowboy's Dream," with its soporific refrain,

> Roll on, roll on;
> Roll on, little dogies, roll on, roll on,
> Roll on, little dogies, roll on.

serves very well. Moreover, some communal work moves better
simply if accompanied by singing. Thus in the American South
a number of songs have been developed to lighten the hours
spent at cornhusking. The best known of these songs is probably
"Old Bob Ridley," a nonsense song which originated on the
minstrel stage and which has as its chorus:

> Boys, come along and shuck that corn,
> Boys, come along to the rattle of the horn,
> We shuck and sing till the coming of the morn,
> Then we'll have a holiday.

But some communal work songs serve for more than mere entertainment. Sailors, lumberjacks, railroad trackmen, and even
hoers employ rhythmical chants to aid cooperation. Usually such
songs consist of a line or two chanted by a leader followed by a
word or a brief phrase shouted by the group. A fine example of
such a song has recently acquired wide popularity:

> Take this hammer,
> Whuck!
> Take it to the captain,
> Whuck!
> Take this hammer,
> Whuck!
> Show it to the captain,
> Whuck!
> Tell him I'm gone,
> Whuck!
> Tell him I'm gone.

On occasion, of course, laborers object to their lot, sometimes
metaphorically, sometimes directly. Such a protest song is the
double-barreled "The Boll Weevil," which can be taken both
as the description of a normal agricultural situation and as a

reflection of the Southern farmworker's determination to survive
despite abominable living and working conditions. A few stanzas
will serve to illustrate this:

> The first time I seen the boll weevil
> He was settin' on the square;
> The next time I seen the boll weevil
> He had all his family there.

and a chorus after each stanza:

> They's lookin' for a home,
> Just lookin' for a home,
> They's lookin' for a home,
> Just lookin' for a home.

The verses continue:

> The farmer took the boll weevil
> And buried him in the sand;
> The boll weevil say to the farmer,
> "I'll stand it like a man."

> Then the farmer took the boll weevil
> And left him on the ice;
> The boll weevil say to the farmer,
> "This is mighty cool and nice."

> The boll weevil say to the farmer,
> "You better lemme 'lone,
> I et up all your cotton
> An' now I'll begin on the co'n."

with the chorus significantly changing to "I'll have a home" after
this last verse.

The symbolism inherent in "The Boll Weevil" is, of course,
hidden from many singers and audiences, just as the significance
of many of the game songs of children and dance songs of young
adults is unrecognized by their practitioners. These latter songs,
for the most part, are descendants of the songs sung by adults,
and although it is unfair to speak of them as corrupt versions, it
is true that misunderstanding appears to have contributed more
to their present form than did any sort of creative imagination.

Children's game songs are replete with words and phrases created
by a process akin to popular etymology in which the familiar is
substituted for the unfamiliar—as, for example, the "Farmer in
the Dell" becomes the "Farmer in the Well"—and dance songs
have been curtailed and stanzas of dance directions have evolved
from or been substituted for stanzas once an essential part of the
song. Thus the nineteenth-century popular stage song "Captain
Jinks of the Horse Marines" had as an original stanza:

> I'm Captain Jinks of the horse marines,
> I feed my horse on oats and beans,
> I know it is beyond my means,
> But I'm Captain Jinks of the army.

for which the dance song substitutes:

> Captain Jinks came home last night,
> Gentleman passes to the right,
> Swing your lady very polite,
> For that's the style in the army.

Except perhaps among the underprivileged in large cities and in
a few very isolated rural areas, neither of these traditions is alive
today. Planned recreation programs in city parks and schools
have eliminated traditional children's games, and other forms of
recreation have replaced the once familiar play-party and old-
fashioned barn dance. The square dance as it is known today
is an artificial revival, not a survival, as remote from modern culture as the wearing of crinoline dresses or coonskin hats.

The line separating children's game songs from the dance songs
of young adults is difficult to draw. Children borrowed the songs
sung by their parents to accompany their games and continued to
sing many of the same songs into their teens, when dancing
replaced simple play. The origins of many games, such as "The
Melven Vine," "London Bridge," and "Here Comes a Queen
from Dover," are so lost in antiquity as to suggest that they were
once ritualized myth. Others, such as "King William Was King
Jamie's Son," with its initial stanza:

> King William was King Jamie's son,
> Who from the royal race did come.
> Upon his breast he wore a star,
> Like the points of the compass are.

appear to be dramatized history, poorly remembered. Still others, like "It Rains and It Hails," "Miller Boy," and "Hangsaman," are selected stanzas from folksongs, just as the aforementioned "Captain Jinks" as well as "Marching to Quebec," "Old Dan Tucker," "Wait for the Wagon," and "Nora, Darling" are abbreviated forms of minstrel and vaudeville songs. A very few, of which "Skip to My Lou" is a prime example, illustrate the principle of formulaic composition. Customarily, this game or dance is begun by a leader singing a traditional first stanza, usually:

> The cat's in the buttermilk, skip to my Lou
> Cat's in the buttermilk, skip to my Lou,
> Cat's in the buttermilk, skip to my Lou,
> Skip to my Lou, my darling.

and then immediately pointing to a member of the group who is expected to contribute another stanza which may be either traditional or an invention of the moment. Most frequently, like the stanza of the work song with which this chapter begins, such invented verses have but a momentary existence, but on occasion an invented stanza catches the imagination of a community and is perpetuated in tradition. "Pop Goes the Weasel," "All Go Down to Rowser's," "Here We Go 'Round the Mulberry Bush," and "Pig in the Parlor" have developed in a similar manner.

Indeed, American game and dance songs illustrate the hallmark of all American folksongs: inventiveness within a tradition. Nor is this inventiveness confined to the Anglo-American tradition here discussed; it is found also in blues and spirituals. Each song represents a kind of Platonic ideal of which a particular text is but one of an infinite number of possible examples. The spirit of such a tradition is well stated by a commonplace stanza frequently attached as a conclusion to nonsense songs:

> Girls in the parlor, hat on the shelf,
> If you want any more, just sing it yourself.

10

The Glory Songs of the Lord

BRUCE JACKSON

The term "spiritual song" was in use as early as the middle of the sixteenth century, when it meant, simply, a song that was not secular. It wasn't until the camp-meeting phase of the Great Revival, shortly after 1800, that the term took on the meaning we understand: a body of folksongs of a more or less religious nature, fairly loose in structure, generally designed for group responsive singing.

There are three main types of spirituals: those sung by the Pennsylvania Dutch, the newest and least known; those sung by the whites, the oldest; and those sung by the Negroes, the best known. The three types are intimately related yet are different enough to have caused violent disagreements that have lasted for three quarters of a century. Arguments have ranged over what belongs to whom, over whether or not the Negro created his spirituals, over how much borrowing went on from whom. Some have insisted that the promised land in the Negro spirituals was the traditional Christian afterlife, others insisted the slaves meant freedom from physical slavery; some said the spirituals' reports of battling against sin *really* meant warfare against the slave-holders, others say the spirituals meant just what they said, nothing more. On one side are those who have seen the spirituals as a sung code language through which the slaves, on their own initiative, managed to express political and sociological notions they were otherwise prohibited from expressing; on the other side are those who have seen the spirituals as religious activities, exactly the same in content, if not in style, as what certain whites were doing.

One of the reasons for the confusion is that the two contributing folklore contexts—African and early American—were not studied until long after the more didactic works on Negro spiritual singing had been completed and accepted. Another reason is that few of the early students were adequately equipped or sufficiently interested to relate the spirituals to the historical context in which they arose, a context quite distinct from the institution of slavery.

The religious roots go back to the middle of the eighteenth century, when John Wesley and his followers, reacting against the formalism characterizing permissible religious expression, preached of faith through inner emotional conviction. His followers were called the Methodists and their numbers grew rapidly as the century drew to a close. Compared with the rigorous and austere formalism of the Church of England, Wesley's mode offered an excitement that appealed to the lower and middle classes. Music was an important part of Wesley's approach; his brother Charles composed about sixty-five hundred hymns. Racially mixed services were not uncommon in the early nineteenth century, especially among the dissenter groups. Bishop Francis Asbury, leader of the Methodist missionaries to America, and Lorenzo Dow, who was also instrumental in the spread of Methodism in this country, both preached to mixed audiences.

Early in the nineteenth century there began a large-scale religious revival in America that has been called the "Second Awakening." According to folklorist Don Yoder, the "Second Awakening, using in part the materials created through the Great Awakening—the Evangelical Hymn, the new lighter tunes—but originating the 'chorus' which became the distinctive mark of its songs, created the camp-meeting spiritual. By the addition of the chorus to the Evangelical hymn-texts, through the use of folk and popular melodies rather than the antiquated psalm-tunes and chorales of New England and the Middle Colonies, a new genre of religious folksong was created which was to hold its own into the 20th Century." Yoder sees the spirituals as having a natural appeal to the camp-meeting crowds. "The spirituals," he says, "were live, rather than literary. They were folk-dominated rather than clergy-dominated. Hymnbooks were discarded. Many of the frontiersmen were illiterate; besides, it was difficult to read the words of a hymn by a flickering torchlight at a night-session of the camp-meeting—or when one had one's arms around a fellow 'mourner.' "

Because many of the whites could not read, the practice of "lining out" hymns was often adopted: the leader of the session, sometimes a minister and sometimes just a member of the congregation who had the "call," would read or call out two lines to be sung, then the congregation would sing them back to him; then he would call out the next two lines and they would sing those back. There were variations: he might sing or speak, he might do one or two lines at a time; interspersed might be a chorus that all knew, and sometimes the leader would sing out a verse line and the congregation would sing a burden, or chorus line, and the effect would be conversational or antiphonal. In the more formal expressions, the group only repeated after the leader or sang back a regular chorus, but in those situations that have been described as "wilder," there was much more freedom for everyone. Those who wanted to sing harmony could do so, those who wanted to shout could do that, too, because there were plenty of other people to carry the words; the preacher himself could vary both melody and text considerably if there were a chorus, because the audience knew the tune and acted as a sort of guide. This dovetailed nicely with the already existing Negro call-and-response tradition which may have been in religious singing and which certainly was in such secular traditions as the work songs. The wilder songs in white tradition rarely found their way into print, but they continued to exist in the more isolated church groups. As the other church groups became more literate and middle class—in orientation if not in means—they more and more used hymnbooks into which the more presentable of these songs found their way. These books were often titled or sub-titled "Hymns and Spiritual Songs."

It was the proselytizing of the Methodists and Baptists that caught the Negro spirit, but they did not work virgin soil. Almost from the beginning of slave-importing to this country there were attempts at religious instruction for the slaves. In the seventeenth century slaves were baptized and taken into the Anglican Church; in the eighteenth century there was a more serious attempt to recruit the Negroes when the Church of England established its Society of the Propagation of the Gospel in Foreign Parts, an organization that trained Negro preachers and established missions along the Eastern seaboard. During the century Negro religious identification was courted by other groups as well—Moravians, Presbyterians, Quakers, and Catholics among them.

But it was the mass appeal of the Methodists and the Baptists that proved most effective. The ministers and preachers were of the people, not the educated and alien preachers of other sects, and these men had a natural and mutual affinity with and for the people to whom they spoke. In the camp-meeting style of religious expression, simple and direct feeling was negotiable: it certified faith and was more important than textual proficiency, than literacy or formality.

"Beginning in 18th Century New England," says Don Yoder, the spiritual "passed southward through Pennsylvania to the Upland South, where it changed *color*, and the Negro spiritual was born. As the Negro and White spiritual came with the camp-meeting to Pennsylvania at the time of the Second Awakening, the spiritual changed *language*, and the Pennsylvania (Dutch) Spiritual was born." The Dutch spiritual, at least at first, was "a German-language or Dutch-dialect copy of the White spiritual of the Methodists (and others) in early Americana."

Newman I. White, of Duke University, was probably the first serious scholar to establish the intimate relationship of the texts of the white and Negro spirituals. But it was George Pullen Jackson, of Vanderbilt University, who extended White's textual correlations to tunes, and in so doing presented what is still the most coherent picture of the spirituals' genesis and development. Jackson saw the songs others have called spirituals as existing in three categories: religious ballads, hymns, and spiritual songs.

The religious ballads were songs for individual singing. As other ballads, they told a story, often drawing on Biblical sources, but many were also first- or third-person morality or conversion stories. One of the oldest of these is "Romish Lady," which begins:

> There was a Romish lady, brought up on popery
> Her mother always taught her, the priests she must obey.
> "O pardon me, dear mother, I humbly pray thee now,
> But unto these fake idols I can no longer bow."

Then, in what is an Inquisitional context, the girl is questioned and finally burned for her Protestant renunciation of Catholic artifacts and ikons in favor of the Bible itself.

The folk hymns, unlike the religious ballads which were not tied to any particular religious group or movement, were, according to Jackson,

> bound up genetically with the protestant evangelical activity which followed John Wesley's lead in England and then in America. The Wesleyan revival began as an ordered small-group affair and spread and developed ultimately into a movement whose aspects and practices were completely free-affairs of the uninhibited masses. In the same way the songs of that movement, beginning with merely the taste of textual freedom offered by Watts and the Wesleys, and of musical freedom offered by those who furnished the melodies, spread ultimately far beyond the "allowed" tunes and hymn texts of the authorities until religious gatherings were musically completely liberated.

The words to these songs were penned by various eighteenth-century religious poets and song writers—some of them, like Watts, quite well known; the tunes were often lifted directly from traditional secular songs, such as "Barbara Allen," "Lord Lovel," "McAfee's Confession," "Three Ravens," "Wife of Usher's Well," "The Girl I Left Behind Me," and "Pretty Saro." The texts, in this stage—which Jackson dates around the last fifth of the eighteenth century—seem to have been fairly rigid; what varied were the tunes and styles of performance.

The camp meetings that occurred during the first part of the nineteenth century were large, boisterous affairs and the folk hymns didn't quite suffice for the spirit of the crowds. Jackson says,

> At the camp meetings it was not a question of inducing everyone to sing, but of letting everyone sing, of letting them sing songs which were so simple that they became not a hindrance to the general participation but an irresistible temptation to join in. The tunes of the folk-hymns were adequate. But the texts (Watts, Wesley and their schools) still demanded a certain exercise of learning and remembering which excluded many from the singing. The corrective lay in the progressive simplification of the texts; and it was in the main this text simplification which brought about and characterized the type of camp-meeting song which was called, in contradistinction to all other types, the spiritual song.

These songs were not taken seriously by scholars or publishers during the nineteenth century, but a few collections did find their way into print; one of the earliest of these was *The Christian Harmony*, published in 1805.

The Negro spiritual was discovered, for all practical purposes, by the Northern whites who went south in the early years of the Civil War to work with some of the recently freed slaves. Some of these were military officers, like Colonel Thomas Wentworth Higginson, whose 1867 *Atlantic Monthly* article, "Negro Spirituals," was the first such collection ever to see print. Others were involved in religious or educational activities, as were the editors of *Slave Songs of the United States*, published later in 1867, the first volume of real Negro songs published in this country. They presented their discoveries with the feelings of those who have found something new on the face of the earth.

How was it that the early discoverers of the Negro spiritual failed to recognize its relationship to white singing? Newman White says that "The Northern welfare workers who took up the spiritual in the eighteen-sixties as an instrument of propaganda were further away from the White spirituals than Southern White people were. . . . Thus they made the honest, characteristic mistake of assuming the fundamental originality of the Negro spiritual. They had to, or what would have become of their preconceived notion that the Negro spiritual was the 'sorrow-song' of slavery?" "What these sympathetic interpreters overlook," White says, "is that precisely the same imagery was common in the religious songs of White people during the early nineteenth century and down to the present day. . . ." And, "Whatever they may have come to mean to some Negroes at a later time, they were never originally, or even generally, the expression of the Negro's longing for physical freedom."

Only one of the songs in *Slave Songs of the United States* can be taken as a direct reaction to slavery: "Many Thousand Go." The words are simple and striking:

> No more peck o' corn for me, no more, no more
> No more peck o' corn for me, many thousand go
> No more driver's lash for me
> No more pint o' salt for me
> No more hundred lash for me
> No more mistress' call for me

One of the very first Negro spirituals to reach white Yankees was "Roll, Jordan, Roll," which Lucy McKim, one of the editors of *Slave Songs*, included in an 1862 letter to the Boston publication, *Dwight's Journal of Music*. In that letter, she said the songs expressed the character and life of the Negro race: they were wild and sad and reflected the misery of the slaves' current situation and faith in the future; she said also that the songs were adaptable to a variety of functions. Ironically, the song she picked to illustrate her theme was one that has a long and demonstrable existence in white tradition. At one time, the song celebrated an admiral's mid-eighteenth-century return to England in victory:

> He comes! He comes! The hero comes!
> Sound your trumpets, beat your drums!
> From port to port let cannons roar
> His welcome to the British shore.

Charles Wesley changed it to its spiritual form:

> He comes, he comes, the Judge severe, Roll, Jordan, roll.
> The seventh trumpet speaks him near, Roll, Jordan, roll.
> I want to go to heav'n, I do, Hallelujah, Lord
> We'll praise the Lord in heav'n above, Roll, Jordan, roll.
>
> His lightnings flash, his thunders roll,
> Roll, Jordan, roll;
> How welcome to the faithful soul, Roll, Jordan, roll.

When the song passed into Negro spiritual tradition it changed again. In *Slave Songs of the United States* it appears this way:

> My brudder sittin' on de tree of life
> And he yearde when Jordan roll
> Roll, Jordan, Roll, Jordan, Roll, Jordan, roll!
>
> O march de angel march, o march de angel march
> O my soul arise in heaven, Lord
> For to yearde when Jordan roll.
>
> Little chil'en, learn to fear de Lord,
> And let your days be long;
> Roll, Jordan, etc.

O let no false nor spiteful word
Be found upon your tongue;
Roll, Jordan, etc.

For "My brudder" in the first stanza, other nouns could be substituted, expanding the singing time indefinitely. The editors of
that early collection said: "This spiritual probably extends from
South Carolina to Florida, and is one of the best known and
noblest of the songs."

Publications such as *Slave Songs* and the Higginson article
created so much interest that some Negroes decided to take
practical advantage of the situation. Fisk University, a Negro
college under white control, organized a choir called the Jubilee
Singers, who sang the slave songs. They quickly adapted the
rough and enthusiastic singing style of traditional singing to
the tastes of the white music-hall audiences, still keeping some
part of the original drive. They were enormously successful,
and they raised a considerable amount of money for the school
and sang to audiences on two continents. Hampton Institute,
Tuskegee Institute, and other Negro colleges soon had choral
groups out on tour, raising money for their schools. One of the
accidental side effects of this was that it took nearly fifty years
for anyone to notice that Negroes sang anything *but* spirituals;
folklore collectors didn't notice secular singing among Negroes
for quite some time.

In the spirituals, the Negro ones especially, Biblical figures are
seen as persona in a stanzaically intermittent sequence of dramatic scenes. These are no vague abstractions or metaphorical
religious actors; they are real people, functioning in a world that
is very much like this one. We find "Paul and Silas bound in
jail," and we learn that "Fisherman Peter out at sea," though
"he cast all night and he cast all day / he catch no fish but he
catch some soul." Satan and Jesus have a horse race that one
could hardly call other-worldly:

> I an' Satan had a race, Halelu, halelu
> I an' Satan had a race, Halelu, halelu
>
> Win de race agin de course . . .
> Satan tell me to my face . . .
> He will break my kingdom down . . .
> Jesus whisper in my heart . . .
> He will build 'em up again . . .

Satan mount de iron grey . . .
Ride halfway to Pilot-Bar . . .
Jesus mount de milk-white horse . . .
Say you cheat my fader children . . .
Say you cheat 'em out of glory . . .

And the kingdom of the afterlife is seen in terms of the pains and trials of this world that will be absent:

No more rain fall for wet you, Halelu, halelu
No more rain fall for wet you, Halelujah

No more sun shine for burn you . . .
No more parting in de kingdom . . .
No more backbiting in de kingdom . . .
Every day shall be Sunday . . .

The themes of the spiritual may be other-worldly, but the referents are of this life. Trains, wheels, rivers, all figure prominently in the imagery; major Biblical figures are encountered in *vis-à-vis* situations; when death approaches, Jesus doesn't hover in some abstract theological background but instead prepares a bed that is quite corporeal:

Oh, well, well, don't be uneasy
Well, don't be uneasy
Well, well, don't be uneasy
Jesus gonna make up the dyin' bed.

Oh, well, he's a dyin' bed maker
Well, he's a dyin' bed maker
Well, well, he's a dyin' bed maker
Jesus gonna make up the dyin' bed.
Oh, well.

Well, in my time of dyin',
I don't want my friends around
Well, it's all I want my mother to do
Is just to ease that pillow from under my dyin' head.

Well, well, I'll be dyin' easy
Well, I be dyin' easy
Jesus gonna make up the dyin' bed
Oh, well.

He's a dyin' bed maker
Well, he's a dyin' bed maker
Jesus gonna make up the dyin' bed.

Devices familiar from other genres of folksong, such as the
catalogue of relatives, are frequently employed. The loose style
permits considerable play here. A one- or two- or three-verse sequence may be repeated over and over again, with the only change
being the relation named, as in "Way Over in the Promised
Land," which an informant of mine learned as a boy from his
grandmother in Apaloosas, Louisiana:

O lord, I wonder where is my mother
Wonder where is my mother
I wonder where is my mother
Way over in the promised land.

She sittin' down in God's kingdom . . .
She's tellin' God 'bout her trials . . .
Lord, one a these mornin's I'm goin' meet her . . .
Oh bye and bye I'm goin' meet her . . .

Then he sings,

Lord, I wonder where is my father. . . .

and goes through the entire sequence again. Then the same for
"auntie," etc. The problem of sin is seen as traditional combat,
not as a theoretical rule violation; Satan becomes as corporeal
as the bedmaking Jesus:

I shall not, I shall not be moved
I shall not, I shall not be moved
Just like a tree that's planted by the water
I shall not be moved.

On my way to heaven . . .
Fightin' sinnin' Satan . . .
Jesus is my captain . . .

For the island boatman, his craft becomes a metaphor for the
transport to the promised land, a metaphor that retains all its
realistic characteristics:

Michael row de boat ashore, Hallelujah!
Michael boat a gospel boat, Hallelujah!
I wonder where my mudder deh . . .
See my mudder on de rock gwine home . . .
On de rock gwine home in Jesus' name . . .
Michael boat a music boat . . .
Gabriel blow de trumpet horn . . .
O you mind your boastin' talk . . .
Boastin' talk will sink your soul . . .
Brudder, lend a helpin' hand . . .
Sister, help for trim dat boat . . .
Jordan stream is wide and deep . . .
Jesus stand on t' oder side . . .
I wonder if my maussa deh . . .
My fader gone to unknown land . . .
O de Lord he plant his garden deh . . .
He raise de fruit for you to eat . . .
He dat eat shall never die . . .
When de river overflow . . .
O poor sinner, how you land?
Riber run and darkness comin' . . .
Sinner, row to save your soul . . .

Because of their moving quality and broad applicability, the
spirituals have produced an excess of sentimentality from both
Negro and white observers. James Weldon Johnson, in his *Book
of American Negro Spirituals* (1925), manages to say that in the
songs "you catch a spirit that is a little more than mere nobility;
it is something akin to majestic grandeur. The music of these
songs is always noble and their sentiment is always exalted.
Never does their philosophy fall below the highest and purest
motives of the heart." And, "The White people among whom
the slaves lived did not originate anything comparable even to
the mere titles of the Spirituals." And, "The Spirituals are purely
and solely the creation of the American Negro . . ." Miles Mark
Fisher, displaying the same kind of sentimentality but a less
excusable degree of ignorance, defines a spiritual broadly "as the
utterance of an individual Negro about an experience that had
universal application at whatever time that song was popular,"
then, relying on internal evidence entirely, manages to infer that
the songs were a kind of mystic musical cryptography: Biblical
nouns are taken by him as code names for current socio-political
figures; the journeys are into and out of slavery; sin and spiritual

questions, with which the songs are so much concerned, play hardly any role at all in his elaborate structures.

Even at the present time there is a tendency to confuse, as ballad scholar D. K. Wilgus has said, "origin and essence. Early evidence is scanty and confused; the authority of print has been opposed to internal evidence; and both sources have been variously interpreted. In fact, the same evidence has nourished both sides."

Although these are a number of comments about *how* Negroes sang in the early nineteenth century, there is almost nothing to tell us *what* they sang. About the whites we know a great deal more, and what we do know suggests that what happened was, to quote Professor Wilgus again, "To America from Africa the Negro brought a song tradition differing from and yet in some respects resembling the European folk tradition (with which, in fact, it had some historic connections). From the songs of the Whites, the Negro borrowed what was congenial to him, and the Whites were debtors as well as creditors. The resulting hybrid [and in this we must include Don Yoder's Pennsylvania Dutch] is a folk music which sounds African in the Negro tradition and European in the White tradition."

11

The Music of the Songs

B R U N O   N E T T L

Folk music in the United States has a paradoxical existence. America is tremendously rich in folk music; if one were able to make a count of the folk music of the world, and to compare countries on the basis of such quantification, America would surely emerge as one of those with the largest bodies of music. On the other hand, students of folk music in the United States often come to ask themselves, just what, really, is American folk music? Is there actually such a thing? Can one distinguish it from the folk music of other nations? Does it have a distinctive sound?

If we believe that the folk music of a nation must be a body of songs and instrumental tunes which is truly indigenous and which has actually been composed in its country, that it must consist of songs which go back far in its history, that it is songs which are unique and could not be mistaken for the product of a neighbor nation, and that its melodies are unrelated to those of other peoples, then it will be difficult to find anything we could call the true folk music of the United States. The only kind of music which could meet those qualifications is that of the American Indians. And while Indian music is of great interest, the vast majority of Americans neither understand it nor feel that it is at all a part of their musical experience. But perhaps we are wrong to expect all folk music to be truly indigenous. After all, even the folk music of some of the more isolated nations of Europe is closely related to that of other European countries. For instance, we know that songs are borrowed by one tradition from another, that they travel easily across national and ethnic boundaries. We still know some tunes that were known throughout all of Europe centuries ago.

Accordingly, I would maintain that there is such a thing as truly American folk music. It is music which, like other kinds of folklore, reflects the history and the composition of American culture. It is a mirror image of a nation which combines attitudes deeply rooted in its European background with the unique mixture of cultures, peoples, and races that are its main characteristics. It represents the Janus-like self-view of the American, a man deeply conscious of his history and background who nevertheless concentrates on the present and the future.

Folk music in America has many manifestations. In the more isolated parts of the rural South, the Midwest, and New England, old English songs are sung for entertainment by a few people who learn them from parents and older relatives and who continue to teach them to their children, maintaining family traditions that have preserved a great many songs in forms which are older than those now being sung in England and Scotland. But these same songs, in different versions and accompanied by ensembles or orchestras, are now also sung by professional entertainers in concert halls and on university campuses. On Midwestern farms the Old Order Amish sing folk hymns in German, in a musical style that probably goes back to medieval Europe. In our cities, Polish, Italian, Armenian, Hungarian, and other non-English-speaking groups are more interested in their folksongs now than they were in the Old Country, hoping that these songs will help them to become established in their new, American way of life while still retaining some of their cherished traditions. Negroes and labor groups have used folksongs as a way of protesting intolerable living and working conditions. Sailors have sung songs of courage and tragedy to accompany their rhythmic work and to entertain themselves when work is done. Children still sing traditional songs to accompany games in both city and country, and mothers still sing them traditional lullabies.

Until quite recently, songs were made up to describe current events, and especially tragedies, such as railroad wrecks and murders, and they spread with the speed of rumor. And although even backwoodsmen now have access to other music through radio, television, and phonograph, it was only a short time ago that they were entirely dependent on music passed on by word of mouth and learned by listening, in an existence which made much use of music as simple entertainment, for marching, dancing, playing, work, and worship.

As I have implied, each of the national groups which immigrated to America brought its own folk music, and many continue to use it. But since American culture is mainly English-speaking, and since the British element has been the dominant one, we will concentrate here on the music from that tradition.

The number of songs in this British tradition is vast, but the tunes which are used come from a relatively small stock of materials. The process of oral tradition makes it necessary for a tune to be rather widely accepted if it is to remain alive. If the poet of a folksong sets his words to a tune that is not liked, the song will not be picked up by the tradition. People will not learn it, sing it, and teach it. They may just abandon the song, or they may find other tunes, tunes which they already know, and set the words to these. According to Samuel Bayard, one of the scholars of American folksong, the vast majority of tunes belong to about forty tune families. This means that each of the tunes from this vast majority goes back to one of about forty parent tunes. Now, of course, we cannot be sure just what each of these parent tunes was actually like. The parent tune may not be in existence any more. We can only say that a particular group of tunes in use today, or collected and written down at some point in the past, have sufficient points of similarity to allow us to believe that they go back to a single parent tune—that they are, as we say, genetically related. We could perhaps, in the manner of linguists who reconstruct extinct languages from the languages that are presumably derived from them, reconstruct parent tunes by comparing the songs. But we have never had much luck with this procedure. Now, according to Professor Bayard, of these forty tune families there are seven which account for the largest and most widely used group. I would like to reproduce one tune from each of these seven families. These are not parent tunes, nor would I claim that they are particularly close to the presumed parent tunes. They are simply representatives of their families, chosen more or less at random. But, if I were asked to give one or two minute samples of the most typical musical materials in Anglo-American folk music, I would probably choose those shown on pages 123–125, which are taken from Volumes I and II of Bertrand H. Bronson's monumental compendium, *The Traditional Tunes of the Child Ballads*, which the Princeton University Press began publishing in 1958.

(1) Lord Randal

(2) Child I II

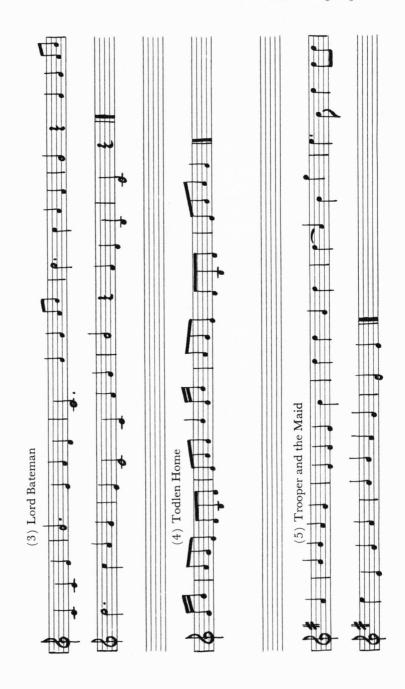

(3) Lord Bateman

(4) Todlen Home

(5) Trooper and the Maid

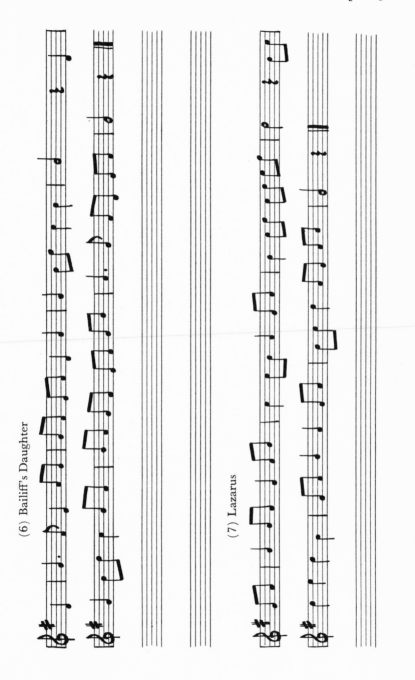

(6) Bailiff's Daughter

(7) Lazarus

One of the important characteristics of a folksong is that it changes, or rather that singers change it. Some singers are creative, they like to improve and elaborate a tune. More frequently, singers are forgetful and delete material from a song. Again, because a folksinger has no standard version that he can look up in a book, he may combine material from two songs. Or he may change a song so that it will conform more closely to the style of other music which he has learned and with which he feels familiar. When a tune is passed from one country—say, Poland—to another—say, Slovakia—it is likely to take on, in its new country, Slovakia, the characteristics of other Slovak folksongs. And there are other reasons for a tune's changes. At any rate, we know that some tunes can be collected in dozens or even hundreds of different variants and versions.

Just what happens to one tune in the course of its history is hard to trace, but we can at least tentatively guess what must have happened from a comparison of variants. Again, let me refer to a study by Samuel Bayard, "Two Representative Tune Families of British Tradition," published in 1954 in *Midwest Folklore*. Bayard studied the tunes comprising a family which he calls, for convenience, after one of the sets of words used with it, "The Job of Journeywork." At one point, the tune evidently had a good many variants, all of which resembled the form shown on the following page.

This form of the song we will call simply the long form. Later someone, as it were, chopped off the first half of the tune, and another set of variants, based on the second half of the tune, was created. At the same time, variants from the long form continued to be sung. But later, again, the short form underwent change. Some, perhaps thinking that it sounded incomplete, added material at the end of the short form, making what Bayard called the "extended short form," which again proliferated in several variants. The short and the extended short forms are shown on page 128.

Curiously, what was the second half of the original long form became the beginning of the third extended short form. And variants of all three of these forms of the tune continued to be sung into the twentieth century in both Britain and America.

The American singer of folksongs normally regards the words as somewhat more important than the music. But text and tune usually form an inseparable unit in his mind, to the extent that

Job of Journeywork, long form:

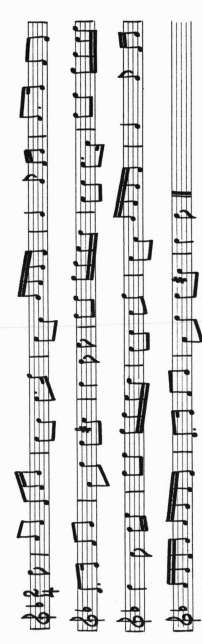

Short form:

Extended short form:

he cannot easily recite the words without singing them. Music
and words are indeed closely related, and nowhere is this more
obvious than in the rhythmic patterns of the songs, for these
seem to be determined largely by the meter of folk poetry.

The most common sort of poetic meter—so important that it
has come to be called "ballad meter"—is a structure that has
four lines of iambic feet in which two lines with four feet alternate with lines having three feet. For example:

> She wet her cheeks with fallen tears
> And then she kissed my hand
> Said, Willie, dear, remember me
> When you're in some distant land.

Musically, this kind of stanza is usually set to one of three
rhythmic patterns:

(1) $\frac{2}{4}$ ♪ | ♫ ♫ | ♫ ♪♪ | ♫ ♫ | ♩· etc.

(2) $\frac{3}{4}$ ♪ | ♫ ♩ ♪ | ♫ ♩ ♪ | ♩ ♪ ♫ | ♩· etc.

(3) $\frac{6}{8}$ ♪ | ♩ ♪ ♩ ♪ | ♩ ♪ ♩ ♪ | ♩ ♪ ♩ ♪ | ♩͡♪ etc.

These three kinds of rhythm account for the vast majority of
Anglo-American folk tunes.

Now, since a fairly small number of rhythmic stanza types is
used, and since the music of the American folksongs also has a
rather small number of rhythmic types, it follows that it would
be rather easy to take a set of words and set it to any of a large
number of tunes. And it would be equally easy to use the same
tune for a large number of different texts. Of course, this is
precisely what was done, and so we find members of one tune
family used for many sets of words completely unrelated to each
other except that they use the same metric patterns; and we find

variants of one text set to a large number of different tunes which, again, have little in common except their rhythmic patterns. In this sense, we may feel that words and music are not so closely related. But the very fact that words and music can be so easily exchanged and interchanged is due to the tremendously high degree of unity in the rhythmic structure of these two components of folk music.

The forms of the folk melodies are also determined to a large extent by the words. Of course, each line of poetry is set to a line of music, and pauses in the phraseology of the text are reflected by pauses in the music. But in other respects we cannot claim that the music expresses the meaning of the words. Composers of English folksongs—and, for that matter, of folksongs elsewhere—hardly ever tried to reflect in their melodies the emotional content, or the ideas, or the actual events described in the text. And folksingers do not reflect in their singing the content of the words. They do not sing sad songs with a sad expression, and the happy songs are sometimes distinguished from others only by a somewhat faster tempo. But the very contrast between a story told vividly though sparely and a dispassionate rendition in music gives these songs a special aesthetic effect. The method of composition in the Anglo-American folksong repertory is rather unexpectedly uniform. Songs are structured in very much the same way. They commonly have four musical lines. The melody moves upward and then gradually descends, making what on music paper looks rather like an arc. In many songs the four musical lines are different, giving us a structure that could be described as ABCD. In many others, the first and last line are identical, as are the two middle lines, giving a form described at ABBA.

The scales—that is, the actual tones used—in Anglo-American folksongs have been widely discussed. Much emphasis has been put on the fact that many of the songs are pentatonic—that is, they use only five different pitches: those which can be produced by playing the black keys of the piano. Actually, the majority of the scales have six or seven tones, and many of the songs are in the major mode, the most familiar kind of tonal arrangement to us. A great many songs, also, are cast in other modes, such as those of medieval church music, which gives the tunes a peculiarly archaic sound that attests to their age. Thus, we have songs not only in major and minor, but also in the Dorian, Phrygian,

Lydian, and Mixolydian modes, which one hears in the Gregorian chants of the Catholic Church.

But perhaps more interesting and more significant than the structure of the folk-tune compositions is the way in which the songs are sung. First, it is important to remember that the Anglo-American folksong repertory is essentially one of solo singing. Group singing was, of course, also found, but most of the songs, and particularly the ballads, which are probably the most significant creations discussed here, are usually sung by one person. Until rather recently, moreover, the singers were not accompanied by instruments, although already around 1825 accompaniment with guitar, banjo, mandolin, and even lute or harp began to be known. Being a soloist and unaccompanied, the singer was free to vary tempo and rhythm, and he frequently did this by adding to the tune all kinds of vocal embellishments, glides, trills, grace notes, which give it a distinctive sound. The way the voice is used is also distinctive. The American folksinger produces a somewhat tense, occasionally nasal, and flat-sounding tone, and he sings with a rather curious lack of expression in his face and sometimes with closed eyes.

Most of the minority groups in the United States have bodies of folk music of their own, but after their arrival, the contact with other groups, especially with the English-speaking majority, inevitably causes them to learn new material and to teach their songs to others. Thus we find Midwestern French-Americans and Pennsylvania Germans occasionally singing their own songs to tunes from England; Slovaks in Pittsburgh making up songs, in their native language, about the solidarity of the labor movement, and setting them to melodies of nineteenth-century American ballads and hymns; and Hungarians in Cleveland making choral arrangements of their folksongs in the style of American choral church music. The United States, where so much that is old survives, serves also as a catalyst for change in the European folk music which it has come to harbor and to nurture.

In all the cases I have mentioned so far, a body of folk music already in existence in Europe has been brought to and developed in America. The largest of our minority groups, the American Negroes, do not fit into this category, because their folk music is much more distinctive. It has some specific elements of African music, and, although it uses the English language and much of the same melodic material found in the songs sung by white

Americans, it is essentially a separate body of folklore. Scholars have frequently debated the degree to which American Negro folk music is related to that of the English-speaking whites. Some believe that the Negro songs are essentially African in character, that their use of European melodies is really incidental and irrelevant. Others maintain that African traditions were forgotten long ago, and that the body of Negro folk music is essentially identical with that of the whites who live in the same area.

I believe the truth is, as usual, somewhere in the middle. It is true that most of the tunes of Negro folk music have analogues in the repertory of the white singers. For example, it has been demonstrated that the music of the spirituals, the most widely acclaimed group of Negro folksongs, was largely taken from the hymn tunes of the nineteenth-century white South, particularly the rural South. On the other hand, there are definitely important remnants of African musical practices still extant; they are shared also with the Negro populations of the Caribbean islands and South America. Most of these musical practices involve not the music itself, as it might be written down on musical paper, but the way the music is performed. For instance, Negroes like singing with the use of call-and-response patterns in which a soloist and a group alternate. They stick strictly to a tempo or beat. They frequently use instrumental accompaniment. All of these characteristics are found in the folk music of the American whites, but they are much more pronounced in Negro folk music and are very highly developed in Africa. The conclusion must be that Negroes, faced with learning a new musical culture and style, selected from it those features which they already were acquainted with in Africa, and developed them, making a sort of specialty out of them. Perhaps most significant, Negroes use the voice differently from whites. They sing in a less restrained manner; they use a more varied tone color; their singing sounds more animated; and again, this singing style is closely related to that of certain African cultures.

We have spoken of folk music as if it were entirely a vocal phenomenon. But there is also, in the United States, a large body of instrumental folk music. Among the English-speaking whites, string instruments have been most widely used. Some of them, such as the violin, are identical with those used in the more sophisticated musical culture of cities by professional musicians. Others, such as the dulcimer, have analogies among the folk instruments of Europe. Others again, such as the banjo, have been developed in America from models brought from various parts of the world. The instrumental music itself consists partly of tunes which are also used in song, and partly independent music. A typical feature of most of it is the use of the drone— that is, of a tone or a chord which is played throughout a piece to accompany the melody. The drone is particularly evident in the music of certain dulcimers, in which two unfretted strings are struck constantly while a third string is used for the melody. Beating two straws on the unused open strings of a fiddle produces a similar effect.

Some people maintain that folk music in the United States is dying. Certainly they are right to some extent, for the isolated, semi-literate, conservative community in which folk music flourished is becoming a phenomenon of the past. But folk music is today fulfilling new functions, such as helping immigrant communities become acculturated to the American way of life and allowing minorities to retain a degree of cultural independence. And folk music has become accepted—in a new way, with new styles, functions, and even with new songs—as part of the sophisticated entertainment of the cities and as the expression of nonconformist students. In these new forms, American folk music is still very much alive.

12

"Honor Your Ladies": *Folk Dance in the United States*

BRUCE R. BUCKLEY

The folk dances of seventeenth- and eighteenth-century America represented the retention or survival of Old World dances, both popular and "country," and were of English, Scottish, Irish, or German origin. Although most of these dances became either modified or lost during the nineteenth century a few may be found today as the folk dances of the communities which have retained their traditional character—in the upland areas of New England, the Catskills of New York, the southern Appalachians, and the Ozarks. The development of dances which might be considered the "true" folk dances of the United States took place during the early part of the nineteenth century. The process of re-creation of Old World material, of course, started in the earlier period as a result of the settlement of many groups in one community and the resulting intermixing of dance traditions into a homogeneous community tradition. This process became the dominant pattern of the nineteenth century with the development of a "national" or "regional" identity which characterized this century. The resulting dances had some European and

African characteristics; they also reflected individual creations of regional groups and the popular dances of the theater, the minstrel show, and the ballroom.

A third phase of folk dance in the United States has been described as the "revival" of interest in the traditions of the past during the twentieth century. This movement might be more properly described as the "discovery" rather than the "revival," since it involves primarily participation by urban groups which have rediscovered the folk dances of their country cousins who have retained the dance tradition of the first half of the nineteenth century. However, this twentieth-century phase also may be viewed as the development of a "national dance" tradition and as a new emphasis on the value of retaining Old World dances in their purest forms.

One international characteristic of folk dance which seems to have been lost in the United States is the use of special dances for the celebration of the critical events in the life cycle of the individual and the marking of the work cycle by particular dances. Although the tradition of special dances of courtship, marriage, or at planting and harvest time, was continued in the earliest period, the dances soon lost their specific use and became a means of socializing which has become the main purpose of folk dance in the United States. One exception to this is found in religious dances such as those practiced historically by the Shaker communities. These communities followed the dance traditions of English Shakers, "singing, shouting, or walking the floor, under the influence of spiritual signs, shoving each other about—or swiftly passing and repassing each other"—and seem at first to be individualistic in their dance patterns. In 1788, the first distinct dance, "the square-order shuffle," was introduced by Father Joseph Meacham. Reflecting the Puritan tradition to which it was heir, the square order was a solemn exercise, a forward-and-backward movement of ranks, with the men and the women in separate groups shuffling toward and away from each other. Different Shaker communities created their own dances, based on European dances of longways and circle types, and always maintaining segregation of the sexes. Other religious dance traditions were part of the first period and continued into the revivalist movements of the nineteenth century and are found in the twentieth century as part of the worship of the Church of the Holy Spirit and the Holy Rollers of the Southern states.

The folk dances reported in the colonial period included the country dances of Europe which were primarily the survival of courtly and popular dance of the previous century. Circle dances, especially English and Irish round dances, the turning movements of the $\frac{2}{4}$ time Irish reel, and the $\frac{6}{8}$ jig group dances were among the most popular of the country types. These dances seemed to have remained regional in the nineteenth century, for they are virtually nonexistent in the West, which was settled during that period. The Western round dance is more closely connected with the ballroom couple dances which attached themselves to the couple section of the traditional round dance in the East. The dancing masters of the period taught the popular quadrille form, and this became both a social and country dance of the period. The roots of the American square dance can be found in country quadrilles of the late eighteenth century.

The three folk dances of the United States which may be called typical American folk dances were prevalent during the first three quarters of the nineteenth century. Two are group dances —the square dance and the play-party—and the third a solo dance which finds its culmination in the tap dance.

The American square dance is usually danced by four couples and shares characteristics of the circle and promenade of the round dance and the form and figures of the quadrille. It developed regional and subregional styles in the East, South, and West, while the Midwest takes qualities from all three. The East developed more set formations, with or without a caller to prompt the movements, and used a shuffling step. The West had a freer form combining new formations and figures, sometimes using a waltz or polka step. The South developed a faster-running set which shared more characteristics with the round dance, using either the square-dance shuffle step or a clogging step.

The "caller" was the name given to the prompter of the dance figures. He also might have been a dancer and would with his partner be considered the head couple of the square. When he was not dancing, the caller often provided the music for the dance, playing the fiddle or violin while calling the directions. If there was a group of musicians, the caller himself did not play or dance but concentrated on calling the sequence and teaching new figures.

The square-dance caller has three types of calls which he can use: the prompt call, the patter call, and the singing call. The prompt calls are brief instructions to the dancers for the next movement to do, and nothing more:

Honor your ladies, Corners address
Head four, circle four
Side four, circle four
Head couple, forward and back
Same couple, Allemande right
Separate, go around alone
Do si do, When you meet your own.

The patter call gives instructions to the dancers and fills in the time while the movement is being executed with rhythmic rhyming verses. It is a half-sung, half-spoken patter:

Head couple eight and circle four
Circle four busy as a bee
Birdie in the center, circle three
Bird hop out and crow hop in
If he won't hop in then kick him on the shin
Crow hop out and circle four
Right and left through—and on to the next.

The singing call, like the patter call, fills in the time with rhyming verse but is sung to a musical accompaniment:

The first couple lead to the couple on the right
Stay there till I find you (balance)
Right straight through, balance too.
Swing with the girl behind you
Swing that girl, that pretty little girl
The girl you left behind you
Then go right back on the same old track
And swing with the girl behind you.

The figures of the square dance were usually performed by couples. Every couple performed in progression or one couple visited each of the other couples in order to perform. The figures had many colorful names—for example, "The Texas Star" and "Dip for the Oyster." Standard figures for every set were "Allemande Left or Right," "Do-Si-Do," "Grand Right and Left," and "Promenade."

The most colorful of the traditional square dances is the

Southern style commonly called the Kentucky running set. This exhausting figure dance of the southern Appalachians combines round and square dance and usually is performed by energetic young couples. The couples begin with a large circle and dance in unison, they then break off into a serpentine pattern and wind themselves up into the figure called a "Ball of Yarn," or perhaps break off into a double line like a Virginia reel or form an arch called the "Open Tunnel." They then divide into odd and even couples; the even couples dance in place and clap their hands, the odd couples perform in turn figures such as "Birdie in the Cage" or "Open and Close the Garden Gate." The young men may come together in the center to show their skill at dancing a rapid "whickerty-whack," or clog step. In the twentieth century this characteristically fast clog has been adopted by professional square-dance groups, but they usually limit the square to four performing couples.

The second traditional folk-dance type of the nineteenth century, the play-party, was actually not defined as a dance by the people who performed it. The play-party was developed by groups who were against dancing because they felt it was irreligious. The result of their compromise was half game, half dance. The local definition of when a dance was not a dance varied from community to community. Usually they agreed that no instruments were to be used to play the accompaniment; only singing by the participants was allowed. Sometimes the interdiction of instruments was automatic—that is, the settlers didn't have any instruments in the frontier communities—but more often the reason was that they considered the traditional dance instrument—the fiddle, or violin—an instrument of the Devil, a belief shared by their European ancestors. The definition of dancing might be further indicated by the way a couple would swing together—whether the man was allowed to swing his partner by her waist, her arm, her hand, or by a handkerchief she held. In some communities the steps performed by passing one foot over the other were called dance steps; if the feet did not cross, one was not dancing.

However, when you describe the figures and forms in the play-party, very little difference between a game and a dance can be discerned. The figures of the Virginia reel longways dance are the same as the Virginia reel longways play-party game. Round-dance, square-dance, line-dance figures were all used in the play-party:

> Circle to the left, Old Brass Wagon,
> Circle to the left, Old Brass Wagon,
> Circle to the left, Old Brass Wagon,
> You're the one, my darling.

or

> First young lady all around in the center
> all around in the center
> all around in the center
> First young lady all around in the center
> And balance to your partner.

> Swing your partner and we'll all run away
> and we'll all run away
> and we'll all run away
> Swing your partner and we'll all run away
> And all chaw hay on the corner.

The play-party outlasted its pseudo-religious beginnings and was still popular in the first quarter of the twentieth century and remains a part of the get-acquainted section, or "ice-breakers," of the modern square-dance gatherings.

The growth and development of traditional dances and play-parties during the early part of this century were tied very closely to a tradition of sharing the work of your neighbors. The philosophy of "more hands make lighter work" was a common one held by the small rural communities, and neighbors would work together and use each of these occasions to play together. These combinations of work and play were called "bees." There were "sugaring-off" bees at maple-sugar time, husking bees after the maize was harvested, and apple bees for peeling apples or making cider. After the work was over, all would have a meal together, clear out the kitchen or the parlor (many times both rooms), and the dance would begin. This was a family affair and old and young alike would participate—an ideal environment for the children to learn the traditional music and dances of their elders. Very little drinking of hard liquor was allowed at these family gatherings—a tradition which holds even today at square dances. Sometimes these affairs were held on the threshing floor of the barn, but the tradition of the large "barn dance" did not become popular until the last half of the nineteenth century.

Negro dance and its music in the United States are now so integrated with the entire dance and popular music tradition that it is difficult to isolate Negro elements or describe their many manifestations. Of major importance are the solo dances, the virtuosity of the footwork, with heel beats and toe beats,, learned in Africa, but which became even more important as a drum substitute when the Slave Laws of 1740 outlawed the drum. These jig- and reel-type dances became popular stage presentations in the latter half of the eighteenth century and the early nineteenth century and were used by both Negroes and blackfaced whites between the acts of the plays. A typical performer in this tradition was Daddy "Jim Crow" Rice, who performed in blackface a jig and shuffle based on a dance he had observed among Negroes—"Spin around and turn around and Jump Jim Crow." From 1840 to 1890 the blackface minstrel show spread the Negro-like dance throughout the nation and the world. Among the Negro performers of the 1840's who met with both national and international acclaim was William Henry Lane, better known as "Master Juba." The juba dance was an African jig-type step with elaborate variations, including stiff-legged shuffles and hops as well as crossing and uncrossing the hands against the kneecaps, which fanned back and forth. One of the significant influences of these dances can be seen in the social dances of the United States in the twentieth century. The Charleston, cakewalk, bunny hug, Lindy hop, big apple; the later boogie-woogie dances, the sand, camel walk; the still later jitterbug steps and the modern twist steps of the monkey, frug, dog, and Watusi find their forms and steps in Negro folk and stage solo dances. However, the folk traditions do remain today in the streets of the cities alongside the tap dances of stage and television and the social dances of the ballroom.

The folk-dance revival of the twentieth century has taken two forms in the United States, the revival of the square dance in an urban setting and the retention of Old World dances by the second- and third-generation offspring of the immigrants of the late nineteenth and early twentieth century. Square dances were rejuvenated by two very different movements that came together in the 1940's. They were introduced into ballroom dancing in the 1920's by Mr. and Mrs. Henry Ford, of automobile fame. These dances, published in a book called *Good Morning*, were danced in formal attire at the great balls and were described as "old-fashioned dancing being revived after a sleep of twenty-five years." At the same time, these dances also were being taught by recreation directors and social workers in the large metropolitan areas to young people as a healthy entertainment and as part of their national heritage. Both of these movements, especially the latter, were successful beyond all expectations. Revived at the time America was most conscious of its identity, the square dance has developed into what could be called the "national dance" of the United States. Regional costumes, either "Western" or "Pioneer," have become associated with it and hundreds of professional and semi-professional groups have been formed to perform the modern as well as the traditional square dance.

During this same period, the young people of various ethnic groups became interested in the dances of their parents—dances which their parents were giving up as they became a part of the "American Way of Life." Encouraged by the square-dance groups and their leaders, these young people began learning, performing, and teaching the Old World dances to others. There was great emphasis on teaching the "right way" or the "old way," and many of these dances have taken fixed forms which would seem archaic to Europeans because they represent a style of seventy-five to a hundred years ago and have not undergone the normal changes a creative folk dance goes through in its natural environment. Many of these modern groups are shocked when they see how the European folk-dance groups have changed the old dances.

Although the traditional forms we call folk dance have difficulty surviving in the twentieth century in a mass-media culture, the folk dance of the United States may still be found as an active part of small-community life around the country. The neighborhood gatherings still occur and are being encouraged now that folk dance is part of our popular national tradition.

13

Magic Folktales in America

LEONARD W. ROBERTS

Folktale collecting in the New World did not yield any appreciable results until the present century. The few volumes that did come into the hands of collectors in the last decade of the nineteenth century did not attract very much attention. The energy and the enthusiasm in the field of folklore from 1875 to 1920 went into the folksong. Ballad study was begun at Harvard by Francis James Child, the great ballad compiler, and was continued by English teachers and anthropologists interested in old folk poetry. Following the lead of European groups well launched in folklore study, they organized the American Folklore Society in 1888 and began to print their collections and papers in their *Journal of American Folklore.* As the circle of folklore students widened into other sections of the United States, the editors of the *Journal* began to receive some quaint and strangely familiar old folktales. A new and fascinating interest opened beyond the study of balladry.

Some of the earliest collectors of folktales and legends went among the American Indians and among the race and color groups of the West Indies. When they returned with their manuscripts, the Society began to print them in a *Memoir* series. Volume I, appearing in 1894, was a small monograph of folktales from Angola. The second *Memoir*, in 1895, contained some Old

World magic tales from the French Creoles of Louisiana; and the third, also issued in 1895, was an anthology of English and African songs and stories from the Bahama Negroes. Among the next dozen *Memoirs*, four were collections of myths, legends, and tales from American Indian tribes, and one was a stout volume of Filipino tales.

The *Memoirs* have continued to appear almost yearly up to the present time, and many independent volumes of tales have been published by university and commercial presses. By 1955 the *Journal* also had printed more than six hundred traditional folktales. With this fairly imposing harvest of folktales on library shelves, we have begun to ask: What are the sources of these tales? What is their value to the New World?

The earliest and perhaps the most important carriers of tales to this hemisphere were the Spanish. Coming in the sixteenth century, they planted colonies in the islands of the West Indies, on the coasts of South America, Central America, and Mexico, and in the states of Florida, Louisiana, Texas, New Mexico, and California. In the course of time, Spanish culture and folkways prevailed in this vast region. The Negroes from Africa, with their own animal tales, assimilated Spanish magic and religious legends and tales with their own. The native Indians added the same Spanish materials to their more primitive myths and legends.

Other important carriers of tales across the Atlantic were the French. They, too, established trade among the peoples of the West Indies and in the Mississippi River Valley. They also entered the continent to the north, along the St. Lawrence River, spreading west to the Great Lakes. The French and the Spanish traded and intermarried with the native Indians. We are not surprised, therefore, to find more than two hundred European folktales among North American Indian tribes. Not many French tales have been preserved in the United States, but wherever found they still retain their zest, their wit and charm, and their inventiveness.

Other carriers of tales to the heart of America were of course the British. The English came across the Atlantic as settlers and planters in the seventeenth century and occupied the coast from Massachusetts to the Carolinas and Georgia. It is difficult today to estimate the number and variety of oral tales carried to America by the English. Perhaps they brought many that later died out at home, as did the ballads. Stories definitely English did come to the New World, such as "Jack the Giant-Killer," "Tom Tit Tot," "Jack and the Bean Stalk," and "Dick Whitting-ton and His Cat." The Scottish and especially the Scotch-Irish came to America in large numbers in the eighteenth century. Since the East Coast was already occupied, they pushed on into the Appalachian range. The Germans came at about the same time and settled in western New York and Pennsylvania. At the close of the Revolutionary War this reservoir of population poured into the Northwest Territory, through the Appalachians, and around their southern foothills into the South. Most of the Irish came to America in the nineteenth century. They lodged in the large growing cities and in the Appalachians. They found jobs with the large crews and gangs digging cross-country canals, laying railroads, and cultivating the plains of the Midwest. These English-speaking peoples gave the new Americans their lan-guage, their love of freedom and liberty, their doughty and silent character traits, and their dominant social traditions and folk-ways.

These British peoples pursued their quiet way of life and passed on their traditions in inland America for a hundred to a hundred and fifty years before they were found by folklorists in the twentieth century. Some small collections of stories from them appeared from time to time in the *Journal*. In the 1930's Elizabeth Gardner published her *Folklore from the Scho-harie Hills, New York*. Then followed Richard Chase's *Jack Tales, Grandfather Tales*, and later volumes from the Appa-lachian folk of North Carolina and Virginia. Vance Randolph has so far presented five volumes of tales from the Ozark mountain people of Missouri and Arkansas. I began to collect tales from the people of Tennessee, Virginia, West Virginia, and, nearer home, in the hills of Kentucky in the 1940's. My collections are titled *South from Hell-fer-Sartin, Tales and Songs of the Couch Family*, and *Old Greasybeard*. Marie Campbell has released *Tales from the Cloud-Walking Country*, one of five volumes also col-lected in eastern Kentucky. Richard M. Dorson has found tra-ditional tales among the Scandinavians of Upper Michigan and among the Negroes of Lower Michigan and Arkansas. Ruth Ann Musick has found many tales among the Hungarian, Italian, and English peoples in Missouri and West Virginia.

Most of these collections contain all types of tales. What are some of these tales like? How well are they told? How alive is the American tradition? To answer these questions I am selecting the *Märchen*, or Old World magic tales, for evaluation. For convenience I shall use the descriptive names given the stories by Antti Aarne and Stith Thompson in their index *The Types of the Folktale*.

In the middle of the German collection by the brothers Grimm is an unpretentious story called simply "The Gnome." A version of Aarne-Thompson's "The Three Stolen Princesses," the plot in its simplest form is as follows: After eating their father's forbidden apples, the king's three daughters fall down a hole into an underworld. Three huntsmen appear at the king's palace, offering to rescue the girls if they can marry them. The offer is accepted. The youths set out. The first two are beaten for no apparent reason by a gnome, who in turn is beaten by the youngest huntsman. The gnome then tells his conqueror how he can rescue the girls. The hero descends to the underworld, kills three many-headed dragons with a magic sword, and sends the girls up in a bucket, though he himself is left below. However, when he takes a magic flute from the wall and blows on it, thousands of gnomes appear and carry him out of the underworld by the hair of his head. He gets to marry the youngest, prettiest princess.

The story in this form is found throughout Europe. It has been carried by the Spanish and the French to the West Indies and to Louisiana. Twenty-two texts have appeared in the *Journal of American Folklore*. In one of my Kentucky versions the gnome becomes the abductor, called Little Black Hunchety Hunch. After killing him in the pit and sending up the girls, the hero, Jack, has to escape on an eagle's back by promising him all the meat he can eat on the way. When Jack runs out of meat, he cuts strips from his own thigh until the eagle deposits him safely on earth. In the *Jack Tales* the abductor is a bearded man, called Old Fire Dragaman, who spits balls of fire at Jack.

The German story lacks the "Strong Man and His Companions" introduction, which is supplied by hundreds of texts in northern Europe, France, and Spain. In it a bear carries off a princess. Their half-bear and half-man offspring is named John the Bear. He tears things to pieces at home and runs away, only to make trouble in another kingdom. The king bribes him with a bag of gold to leave. He meets up with two wonderful companions and they set out on adventures.

The story of "The Gnome" or "The Three Stolen Princesses" reminds us of the fascinating histories that lie behind these tales of magic. The fact that the main incident of the first part of *Beowulf*, the Grendel adventure, appears to be a version of "The Gnome" suggests the great age, and possibly the mythological origins, of some of these stories. Psychologists, anthropologists, and students of literary history, often pursuing Freudian and Jungian themes, have been excited by magic tales and written a great deal about them, much of it fanciful, all of it interesting.

There are thousands of texts of this next story, described in *The Types of the Folktale* as "The Girl as Helper in the Hero's Flight." It is a long, complex story, with six major episodes in three forms. Only two of the six tales in the Grimm collection contain all of the episodes; they are titled "The True Bride" and "The Drummer." The story has been found in profusion in all areas of Europe. In the New World, thirty-four texts have appeared in the *Journal*, twenty-two among the French and English in the Antilles, thirty-nine among the Negroes of the West Indies, and five among the Spanish of Mexico and New Mexico. Some of the best-preserved and most robust versions have been found in Appalachia and in the Ozarks. Most of these feature a spirited horse in the magic flight. One of my stories, with the unique title "Raglif Jaglif Tetartlif Pole," contains all of the episodes. The bare plot is as follows:

Young Jack gambles with an old man and finally wins his daughter. When he finds the old man's wilderness castle, he is given three difficult tasks that he must perform or be beheaded: to clean out the stable that hasn't been cleaned out in seven years; to catch some wild horses, led by old Raglif Jaglif; and to get eagle's eggs from the top of a tree 500 feet high. He is helped by the prettiest daughter and they flee on Raglif Jaglif. They impede the old man's pursuit by throwing down two magic objects: a stick that makes a thicket and a drop of water that turns into the Red Sea and drowns the old man. Jack has been told not to kiss the girl. However, he does kiss her and is punished by forgetting all about her. He plans to wed another. The forgotten girl appears at his wedding with three magic boxes containing roosters and hens. When a rooster pecks a hen, she sings out: "Cack caa, you forgot about me cleaning out the barn, hadn't been cleaned out in seven year or off come your head at night." Jack's memory comes back to him and he and his first love flee again on old Raglif Jaglif.

A difficult task in one of my stories, "Jonis and the Giant," is to thatch a barn with all manner of birds' feathers, no two alike. Also in this story are two somewhat unusual episodes. In one, the girl, forgotten by Jonis, climbs a tree that leans over a spring. Her reflection is cast on the water. An ugly wife comes for water, sees the reflection, and, thinking she is too pretty to carry water, runs away from home. The other episode reveals the cunning of the girl. She has so many suitors after Jonis leaves her that she announces she will marry the one who brings her the most money and jewels. She and the lover she selects run away with all the gifts. In most of the Grimm versions and in those in the Antilles and in New Mexico the couple elude the witch in the magic flight by changing into a rose and a brier, into a church and a priest, and into a pond with a fish in it.

A shorter and less complex story, found throughout Europe and in most American collections, is described by Aarne and Thompson as "The Children and the Ogre." In the Grimm volume this is "Hansel and Gretel," and in the French of Perrault it is "Hop o' My Thumb." The story has come to America but usually in versions close to print. Another form, found thinly scattered over Europe from Russia to England, is described as "The Devil Carries the Hero Home in a Sack." In the third form, "The Dwarf and the Giant," three boys exchange nightcaps with three girls, causing the giant to kill his own children. In America, seventeen texts have been printed in the *Journal*; fifteen texts appear in collections from the Antilles and from the Missouri French. There are some excellent stories in the Appalachian volumes, two in *Grandfather Tales*, and a dozen in my materials. Chase's "Mutsmag" and my "Polly, Nancy, and Muncimeg" neatly blend all three forms:

A mother dies and leaves her three daughters some simple gifts: the youngest receives a magic knife and fork. The girls are captured by a giant, but escape when the youngest has them exchange nightcaps with the giant's children. They flee to the house of a friendly king over the river. The youngest is sent back to steal three objects: a primitive lamp, a bag of gold, and a horse. Caught by the giant on her last trip, she is put in a sack while the giant goes for a club. The girl escapes and puts the giant's dog, cat, plates, cups, and saucers in the sack. The giant returns and beats the objects to pieces. In my tale, called "Nippy," the boy Nippy steals the giant's gold staff and gold lockets, his halfmoon light, and his yankee doodle (a musical instrument).

A story that is good for Halloween, or for any cold night before the hearth fire, is described by Aarne and Thompson as "The Youth Who Wanted to Learn What Fear Is," the same title used in the Grimm stories. An abnormal—or at least a strange—boy cannot shudder and goes into the world to learn how. Returning home disappointed, he marries and finally learns one kind of shuddering when his wife pours a bucket of fish on him in bed. The tale is found throughout most of Europe, but is less well known among the Negroes and French of the West Indies. There are seven texts in the *Journal* and one among the Zuñi Indians. One each appears in the Schoharie hills and in the Ozarks.

A folktale that has had two thousand years of telling is described by Aarne and Thompson as "The Search for the Lost Husband." It is the old "Cupid and Psyche" story, best preserved as the "Singing, Soaring Lark" among the Germans and "Beauty and the Beast" among the French. Found in almost all the collections in Europe, it is only moderately popular in the New World. In the American variants the story is simply and beautifully told. The hero is named Whitebear Whittington in New York, in North Carolina, and in the Ozarks. There are four texts in Miss Campbell's *Tales*, one with the revealing title "The Girl Who Married the Flop-Eared Hound-Dog." One of my six stories, "Bully Bornes," has a prize-fighter hero. Most of the plots start with a wishing chair, brought home by a father or a grateful friend. The youngest daughter wishes for an unusual husband, and when he appears she finds she must go with him. Later, their three children are stolen away, and then the husband also leaves. The wife begins a long search. Finally by means of three magic gifts she finds her lost husband and buys three nights in his bedroom. She chants her story in cante fable verses and wins him back. In the Ozarks story, rather short and realistic as usual, the lover, Mr. Whittington, comes dressed in a white bearskin coat and wears it all the time—even at a dance.

The story in the Grimm collection called "Mother Holle" is described by Aarne and Thompson as "The Spinning-Women by the Spring: The Kind and the Unkind Girls." Although the

story has eight episodes, its over-all plot is constant, and wherever
it is found it remains a simple homiletic tale. The good girl is
made to jump into the well for her spindle. Pursuing various
objects, she finds herself on a road in the underworld. There
she obeys the requests of other objects, takes bread from an oven,
shakes apples from a loaded tree. For her kindness an old
woman, Mother Holle, gives her a shower of gold. The lazy girl
does not do the good deeds and receives a shower of pitch. The
story is known, but not widely known, in Europe and among
the French in America.

Among the Anglo-American folk the tale is found in the Scho-
harie hills, in Appalachia, and in the Ozarks. In Appalachia the
story takes on new vigor because of its cante fable form and its
tenser motivation. Mother Holle becomes an old witch from
whom the girls steal a bag of gold. The good deeds on the road
vary somewhat. For instance, in the story "Callymanders" in
Grandfather Tales the girl rubs a horse's sore back, milks a cow,
and breaks sprouts from a peach tree. The old witch in pursuit
calls out to these objects:

> Seen a little gal go by here
> With a jig and a jag
> And a long leather bag
> And all my gold and silver?

In one of my stories she chants these more singable verses:

> Cowl o' mine, cowl o' mine,
> Have you ever seen a maid o' mine
> With a wig and a wag and a long leather bag
> Who stold all the money I ever had?

Perhaps the best-known story in the world is described by Aarne
and Thompson as "Cinderella and Cap o' Rushes." It has been
aided in attaining this distinction by two printed versions by
Basile in Italy, two by Perrault in France, and three in the
Grimm collection. Besides the well-known "Cinderella" form,
it has two others: "The Dress of Gold, of Silver, and of Stars"
and "Love Like Salt." The story in its three forms is found in
most collections from China and Europe to America. In Anglo-
American collections, some forms are found in all volumes except

those of the Ozarks. The stories in the first two forms have the usual slipper test and the ring identification. The very few in the third form seem to be reworkings of the *King Lear* story.

My final story, which I will tell in full, is called "The Hunter" by Aarne and Thompson, and "The Skillful Huntsman" in the Grimm collection. It is not very well known in Europe and the only text in America besides mine is found among the Missouri French. This is exactly how it goes. I call it "Jack Outwits the Giants."

One time there was an old man and an old woman and they had two boys, Bill and Jack. They couldn't make a good living where they were and decided to leave the country. Loaded their house plunder in an old jolt wagon and started down the road. Went along till it begun to get dusty dark. They made camp and eat supper. Made 'em some pallets under the wagon to sleep on. They let Bill take the old rifle-gun and stand guard, afraid they were near the king's forest.

Bill walked around, walked around till way up in the night. About midnight he thought he saw a deer and shot at it. His pa and Bill come out from under that wagon and said, "What're you shooting at, Bill?"

When he said a deer they said, "You ortn't to shoot at the deer, liable to cause the king to come."

And Jack said, "It's about midnight. Let me stand guard the rest of the night."

They went back to bed and Jack walked around. Didn't see anything to shoot at. When it begun to get daylight he decided to climb a tree and see if he could see which way to go when they broke camp. Looked around over the wilderness, and over beyond a little dreen he saw a fire under a big kettle. And around it were three big old rusty giants. Looked like they were cooking cows. They had forks big as pitchforks and spoons like shovels. As they moved around the kettle, chunking up the fire, one of the giants run his fork in there and brought out a big haunch of meat. Jack up with his rifle and when the giant started to take a bite he went pow! Shot that meat off and the fork went into the giant's chin. Giant looked at the second one and said, "Was that you caused me to job my fork in my chin?"

Giant said, "Naw, wudn't me."

Jack grinned and loaded his rifle again right quick. Second one run his fork in the kettle and up with a big bite. Jack was ready for him. Up went the rifle and pow! knocked the meat off his fork and it hit his chin. He looked at the third giant, said, "Was that you made me job my fork in my chin?"

He said, "Now naw, wudn't me."

They fussed and looked around some. Third old giant run his fork in and come up with a big bite. Jack was ready and up with his rifle and cut the meat off his fork. He turned to the first giant, "That you made me job my fork in my chin?" and hit him.

First giant said, "Naw I never," and hit the second giant. Second hit the third and here they went around the kettle hitting and a-cussing. Jack was just dying a-laughing. Soon the first giant stopped, helt up his hand, "Hold up, you men." Said, "If we didn't make us job our forks in our chins, must be somebody around here."

They looked around and into the edge of the woods and saw this boy in a tree. First giant said, "Was that you a-causing us to stick those forks in our chins?"

Jack said, "I was trying out my rifle—must a-hit ye."

Giant said, "Why, Jack, we ort to kill ye for that."

Jack said, "No, no use to kill me. Maybe I can be of some help to you."

Giant thought a minute, said, "You're such a good shot with that rifle," said, "come down and you can help us get in the king's castle tonight." Said, "We want to get in there."

Jack come down and they helt him there that day. At dusty dark they took him along the woods and come to a wall about twenty feet high. Jack said, "Don't see how you can get over this wall."

One old giant said, "We know how to get in there." Said, "We're going to throw you up on the wall."

Jack said, "No, don't do that. Liable to hurt me."

Giant said, "Naw, won't hurt you. Grass up there. Just like a featherbed." He took Jack's arm and leg and throwed him about fifty feet high and he fell on the grass up there. Didn't hurt him much. Giant said, "Now Jack, look out for a little black-and-white-spotted dog. If it comes out and barks it'll wake the guards."

About that time Jack looked over in the yard and saw it come running out. He up with his rifle, shot, and the dog keeled over. Giants said, "That's good, Jack. Now you have to climb down and open the big gate."

Jack clim down inside and went down to the big gate, about twenty feet high. He jumped upon it, shook it. Called out, "Hey, giants. I can't open this gate. The bar is too heavy."

He looked around at the castle, walked up to the porch. There was a sword about ten feet long on the wall, and a horn below it. And there was a sign on the wall, said

> If you want to use me
> You have to drink what's
> In the horn.

Jack took down the horn and drunk, drunk. Couldn't empty it. He walked in the first room and saw the king sleeping in his bed. Saw the queen in another room, and soon come to the princess's room and there she was asleep. She was as purty as a speckled pup. He came back out there, took down the horn, held it up and gurgle, gurgle till he dreened it dry. Reached up and took down the sword and it was so light he could handle it like a cornstalk.

Went back out there where the giants were fussing. Called out, "Hey, giants, come down to this small gate. I can open it."

Jack opened the little gate and the first giant started through and bumped his head. Jack said, "You can't come through there standing up. You have to crawl through."

He got down and come crawling through and Jack up with that sword and cut his head off. Second giant said, "Hurry and let me in this king's castle."

Jack said, "He's hung. You'll have to shove him in."

Giant shoved him to one side, come on crawling through. Jack up with his sword and clipped his head off. The third giant was impatient, said, "Let me in this castle."

Jack said, "He's stuck. You'll have to shove *him* through too."

He shouldered him out of the way and came on in. Jack swung his sword and whacked his head off.

By that time it was getting light. The guards were up and stirring about. They found the dead giants down at the small gate and reported it to the king. King come out and asked how did it happen. Saw that strange boy standing there. Said, "Do you know who killed those giants?"

Jack said, "Yes, I killed about three out there this morning before breakfast."

King said, "Why, Jack, I've been trying to get shut of those giants for years. Been offering my daughter and half of my kingdom." Said, "Do you want the reward, Jack?"

He said, "Well, I left Pa and Ma and brother Bill down yonder. We're leaving this country, hunting jobs of work."

King said, "Go down and bring them. I'll give 'em jobs."

Jack went down and brought 'em all into the king's castle and they all done pretty well after that.

Other stories traditional in our land can only be mentioned. "The Little Red Ox" has come to us from northern Europe and from Ireland. "The Princess on the Glass Mountain" is often imbedded in the above story and in others. "The Table, the Ass, and the Stick" is our favorite folktale of revenge, along with its variations, such as "The Knapsack, the Hat, and the Horn."

"My Mother Slew Me, My Father Ate Me" ("The Juniper Tree") is well preserved here as a scare story to frighten children.

All these and many more magic tales have been told for hundreds of years in the islands of the Atlantic and in every region of the New World. These old stories ring true to the eternal essence of our nature. They appeal to our rational and irrational instincts, to our visions and dreams, and may in some cases connect us to our primitive origins. The race is richer in human and cultural values for its splendid heritage of old magic tales.

14

Legends and Tall Tales

RICHARD M. DORSON

In general usage the word "legend" implies an exaggerated and colorful account of an event. Legend in this sense differs from historical fact and is indeed disdained by historians. The folklorist attaches a more specific meaning to legend and regards legends with keen interest, for they form one of the staple categories of his subject. To him a legend is a traditional oral narrative regarded as true by its teller and by many members of the society in which it circulates, but containing remarkable or supernatural elements that follow a pattern. The folklorist recognizes these elements as part of the great floating stock of themes and motifs in constant circulation among the peoples of the world. Legends, or *Sagen*, stand in contrast to fairy tales or *Märchen*, the German terms brought into wide usage by the Grimm brothers. While the *Märchen* collected by Jacob and Wilhelm Grimm are well known in English translation as *Grimms' Fairy Tales*, the *Sagen* also collected by the Grimms have never been translated into English. The reason seems to be that *Sagen* are too local and episodic for the general reader, while the fictional *Märchen*, with magical adventures and well-constructed plots, have wider interest.

In the United States, folklorists have paid relatively little attention to collecting or defining the legend. In Japan, for instance, collectors have printed many books of local legends, but not a single book of orally collected American legends has been published. The older works of Charles M. Skinner, *Myths and Legends of Our Own Land* (1897) and *American Myths and Legends* (1903), represent the first attempt to report in any systematic way on the regional legends of the United States, but Skinner, a newspaper writer, provided no sources and presented the narratives in a literary style attractive to read but clearly far removed from the original words. Skinner seems to have discovered his most authentic legendary traditions along the Atlantic seaboard in various printed sources, but as he moved into the Midwest and the Far West he depended increasingly on collections of Indian tales, which he called myths. (A myth differs from a legend by being laid in ancient or prehistoric times and dealing with gods or other sacred beings.) More recently, Vance Randolph has published four volumes of Ozark folktales that seem much like legends. They customarily begin: "One time there was . . .," in contrast to: "Once upon a time . . .," which was used for the same plots by an earlier generation of storytellers in the southern Appalachians. There is a world of difference between these two introductions, for the first leads into a world of reality and the second into a world of fantasy. The most adroit rendering of local legendary traditions is *The Jonny-Cake Papers* of Shepherd Tom Hazard, set in Washington County, Rhode Island, and written in 1880.

Legends deal with persons, places, and events. Because they purport to be historical and factual, they must be associated in the mind of the community with some known individual, geographical landmark, or particular episode. Many or all of the members of a given social group will have heard of the tradition and can recall it in brief or elaborate form. This is indeed one of the main tests of a legend, that it be known to a number of people united by their area of residence or occupation or nationality or faith. These groups keep alive and pass along legends of heroes and badmen, of local visitations from demons and goblins, and of miraculous interpositions in battles and plagues. Printed sources such as town histories and newspaper feature articles often reinforce the spoken tradition. Let us look at these three main kinds of legends.

The personal legend may deal with a nationally famous statesman, an obscure eccentric, a celebrated outlaw, or a high-society wit. It can be divided into the heroic legend recounting the extraordinary feats of a superman, the saint's legend describing the miraculous cures of a holy man, and the anecdotal legend repeating the clever sayings and odd actions of a comical man.

In the formative years of the United States, pioneer and frontier conditions of living put a premium on the qualities of physical strength and stamina required for clearing the forests and erecting homesteads. Village tales reported remarkable feats of lifting and carrying that verged on the fabulous and incredible. In my *Jonathan Draws the Long Bow: New England Popular Tales and Legends,* I have brought together some of these strong-man anecdotes. They tell of titans lifting an 800-pound anchor, a 1,600-pound stone, a log thirty-five feet long and nearly a foot square, and barrels of molasses and cider. Once in a while a known incident can be recognized, as in the account of Joe Montferrat of Woonsocket, Rhode Island, credited with raising his plow from the furrow to point a direction to an inquiring passer-by. This feat is also ascribed to Old World folk heroes and to other figures in America, such as farm boys being recruited for college football teams.

Some of these locally renowned strong men achieve a reputation that extends to neighboring communities. As the stories about them accumulate, they take on the character of a whole cycle of legends, comprising a folk biography. This process is observable in the case of Barney Beal of Beal's Island on the Maine coast, who made his living lobstering and fishing. Barney died in 1899, but all the coast and island folk from Portland to Calais know the name and some of the exploits of Barney and, in 1956, I recorded a number of tales they continue to tell about him. Barney is certainly a real enough person, and I was shown an old tintype of him, standing like an oak alongside his little son, who stood on a chair beside him and reached only to Barney's waist. In the half century since Barney's death, caused by overstrain from pulling a fifteen-foot fishing dory over the sea wall, the tales have continued to grow, and some contain international folklore motifs, such as the following tape-recorded story of how Barney overawed the bully of Peak's Island:

Esten Beal:
Yes, I've heard that story told many a time, that he went into Peak's Island to get water for his fishing vessel. And the bully of

Peak's Island met him on the beach and challenged him to a fight. So he told him that as soon as he filled his water barrel why he would accommodate him. So he went and filled his water barrel. And they used to use these large molasses tierces for water barrels. So he brought the water barrel down on the beach, and he said, "Well," he said, "I guess before we start, I'll have a drink of water." So he picked up the water barrel and took a drink out of the bunghole, set it down on the beach, and the bully of Peak's Island walked up, slapped him on the shoulder, and he says, "Mr. Beal, I don't think I'll have anything to do with you whatever."

Whereas the legend of the strong hero emphasizes his physical prowess, the legend of a saint concentrates on his spiritual power. In the Middle Ages, the peasantry in Europe tended to locate the divine energies of the church in their local saint, to whom they prayed for assistance and to whom they ascribed their miraculous deliverances. Immigrants coming to the United States in the nineteenth and twentieth centuries brought with them their faith and loyalty to their village saint, and collectors have obtained saints' legends in profusion from Greek and Italian families now making their permanent home in America. The scene of these legends is the Old Country. They may describe how a Greek town was saved from attack by the Germans when St. Haralampos caused a fog to blanket the town, or how St. Anthony led an Italian girl to a sweetheart when she threw the saint's image out the window in despair and hit a young man who became enamored of her. But among the Mexicans of Spanish descent living in Texas and New Mexico, the saints' legends are laid in the New World. The healer of Los Olmos, as Pedro Jaramillo was popularly known throughout south Texas, where he first settled in 1881, effected so many wonderful cures that Mexican families placed pictures and statues of him in their homes beside those of canonized saints. Many stories are told of his cures, which customarily required some action to be performed nine times, such as drinking a bottle of beer for nine consecutive days while taking a bath.

On the frontier, Johnny Appleseed, who was born in Massachusetts in 1774 but spent his mature years planting apple orchards in the Midwest, has taken on the character of an American saint. Himself a Swedenborgian mystic, he is pictured in the guise of a primitive Christian tramping the back country barefoot, wearing a garment made from a coffee sack with a mush pot on his head, accepting the hospitality of frontier families to whom he read his religious tracts. Wild animals and Indians recognized his spiritual nature and allowed him to pass among them unharmed. Yet this conception of Johnny Appleseed seems to bear little relationship to the actual person, who was a rough, hearty fellow married to a Choctaw Indian woman.

The third type of personal legend, the comic anecdote, pervades American life. Anecdotes fasten on eccentric local characters in every country town, drawing their humor from traits of cunning, knavery, indolence, and ignorance exhibited by these odd individuals. The more or less true tales soon become mixed with apocryphal stories. New England is a special breeding ground for legends of eccentrics, due to the longer history of the region and to its settlement from the beginning in compact township units. Some examples may illustrate the main traits of local characters that furnish the humor of the anecdotes.

Stinginess, Meanness: Yankee characters, especially, display a miserly quality. The Yankee's grief at the death of a loved one is tempered by the fact he has one less mouth to feed. A Maine farmer expressed regret that his wife kicked down so many green apples when she hanged herself on the apple tree.

The family of Joe Swain, who had sent Joe on board a schooner bound for the West Indies with a load of their fowls to sell, crowded to shore when they saw the ship approach. The captain yelled out across the water, "Joe drowned." Joe's father called back, "Fowls drowned too?"

Then there was the hired man in Maine who stopped work at noon, saying he had to go to a funeral. "What a shame! Whose?" asked his employer. "My wife's," the down-Easter replied.

On his deathbed Hiram requested a piece of ham. His wife refused, saying she planned to serve the ham at his funeral.

A notoriously mean man offered his children a penny if they would go to bed supperless, then sold them nice hot biscuits at breakfast for a penny apiece.

Another miser put a piece of cheese into a glass bottle where his son could see it at dinner. One night he caught the boy rubbing the piece of bread that was his sole repast against the bottle and promptly whipped him, saying, "You can't eat bread and cheese every night!"

A similar character in Iowa, Mr. Mac, instructed his children to take long steps when wearing new shoes to save shoeleather. He pushed his car when starting it, to save gas, and told his son Willie to take off his glasses when he wasn't looking at anything, to save wear and tear. In this case the stingy man is verging on the fool.

Stubbornness: Some characters are known for their obdurate refusal to give in on an argument or concede a point, no matter what the cost. Or they may pursue a course of action in spite of all obstacles. Hazard tells in *The Jonny-Cake Papers* how brothers Sylvester and John Hazard fell out and would not speak to each other for ten years. A friend interceded, and Sylvester agreed to speak first. Seeing John on the other side of the street, he yelled out, "When are you going to bring home that iron bar you stole from me, you thief?"

Finally, as Sylvester lay dying, the brothers effected a reconciliation. Sylvester gasped out, "If I recover it's off." John concurred, "Yes, I only agreed because I didn't think you had a chance."

The Mississippi River overflowed its levees in one of its periodic floods. Two of the flood refugees perched on a housetop surveying the waters below them, on which various household articles floated by. One commented to the other, "Notice how that hat seems to float back and forth in a regular line." "Oh yes," replied his companion, "that's the hired man. He said he was going to mow the yard today come hell or high water." Here a comic anecdote has merged with a tall tale.

Sometimes two stubborn characters oppose each other. Meeting on a narrow road, two travelers belligerently faced each other, each refusing to move his carriage. One opened a newspaper and began to read. The other asked, "May I read your paper when you're through?"

In similar fashion, Dan and Dunk took to sea in a boat, quarreled, and divided up their craft. Dan took the wheel, Dunk dropped the anchor, and neither has been seen since.

Ugliness: On the early frontier, the ugly man was a constant figure of fun, since so many frontiersmen were marked and scarred by fever and ague, or eye-gouging, ear-biting brawls. Johnson Jones Hooper, one of the ante-bellum Southern humorists, wrote a sketch of a backwoodsman so ugly that flies would not light on his face; lightning glanced off him; and his wife practiced kissing the cow before she kissed him. Here again the tall-tale element enters into the character anecdote.

A current story tells of the ugly man walking home one night, when he is suddenly accosted by a stranger, who throws him to the ground, plants one knee on his chest, and presses a knife to his throat. The victim begs to know the reason for the assault. His assailant says, "I swore if ever I met a man homelier than myself, I would kill him." The prostrate man peers closely into the face of the other, then sighs, "If I'm homelier than you, kill me."

The trait of ugliness is a passive attribute of the local character, but it underscores his generally unkempt or grotesque appearance.

Knavery, Rascality: The village eccentric in one role is very much a rogue, given to petty deceptions and cunning tricks. An oft-repeated story relates how the town rascal turned up in the general store, ordered a doughnut, then changed his mind and requested a glass of cider. When the storekeeper asked him to pay for the cider, he said he had exchanged it for the doughnut. Asked to pay for the doughnut, he pointed out that he had not eaten it and walked away, leaving the storekeeper scratching his head.

One widely circulated legendary trick of similar nature is told on village characters around the country who seek to obtain liquor without cash or credit. The scalawag, having filled a gallon jug half full of water, asks the storekeeper to pour two quarts of whisky, rum, or gin into his jug. Then he requests credit, which is denied him, and he is obliged to pour back the two quarts. But he leaves the store with a mixture of water and liquor in his jug.

A vagrant enters a diner and asks if he can have a few potatoes to eat with his cold meat. After he is given them, he asks for a little cold meat to go with his potatoes.

Ignorance, Rusticity: On the other side of the coin, the local character exhibits a childlike naïveté and gullibility that make him the target of tricks and an object of laughter. Ben Hooper in Wisconsin took his first train trip to Chicago. He and his wife bought a bunch of bananas from a train vendor and started to eat them just as the train entered a tunnel. Mrs. Hooper asked Ben how he liked his banana. "I et mine and just went blind," he told her.

At a funeral Ben substituted for the big-horn player. Suddenly he let out a loud blast during the dirge. When asked why, he said he had played a fly that settled on his music sheet.

Another Wisconsin character, Bluenose Brainerd, was told by his wife to lose their meddlesome cat. He took the cat such a distance into the woods that he himself became lost and had to follow the cat home.

One time Bluenose went into town and had a number of drinks with the boys. Two wags reversed the large rear and small front wheels on his carriage while he was inside the tavern. On returning home he explained his tardiness to his wife by saying that he had had to drive uphill all the way.

A Massachusetts rustic bought a salmon priced at one dollar a pound and put it in his ice chest, waiting till the price went down to twenty-five cents a pound before eating it.

Pat Casey in Colorado was asked to contribute to the purchase of a chandelier for a new Catholic church. "Sure," he agreed. "But, begorry, I wonder who you can get up here that can play it after ye git it."

Pat was also confused by the suggestion that the town council buy half a dozen gondolas. "Why not buy one male and one female?" he asked.

Clever Retorts: The tart sayings and smart rejoinders of local characters deflating the pompous and self-righteous pass into oral legend. A summer visitor points knowingly to a tree in the orchard and tells the native, "You won't get a peck of apples from that tree." The Yankee replies drily, "Y'r right, it's ash."

A character in Maine known as "Uncle Daniel" Decker was asked by a self-important summer renter how he kept the squirrels from eating his corn. "I have no outside rows," he explained.

Then there is the classic story of the native in the back country accosted by a city visitor who has lost his way. The traveler is unable to elicit any information from the rustic as to where the road leads or how far it is to the next town. All the yokel says is, "I don't know." Finally the exasperated traveler asks, "What do you know?" "Well, I know I ain't lost," the answer comes back.

A thief in Rhode Island was heard to complain, "There is a great deal stole around here on my credit."

Dying Obadiah remained the skinflint Yankee to the end. Told his coffin was too short, he commented, "Oh, I can scrooch up a little."

Degeneracy: In fact as well as in folklore the village character frequently is unsound in mind and body, and so the object of sometimes cruel humor. One tale reported in Illinois, Maine, and Canada describes a misshapen and dull-witted fellow, four feet tall and nearly as wide, whose wife yoked him to the family steer to provide a second beast of burden to draw the plow. The steer broke and ran away with the wife chasing after him and whipping both ox and man. The husband called out, "God dammit, don't hit me. I'll stand."

A character in Ohio known as Temporary Thad lived alone in an unheated shack and used to beg for old newspapers, although he couldn't read. He explained that by burning the newspapers in his sheet-iron stove he could get enough "temporary heat" to change his clothes.

Laziness: A trait both regrettable and yet somehow endearing that leads to anecdotes is the shameless laziness and sloth of the local ne'er-do-well. Lazy Nathan, a Vermont character, hired a man to snore for him. A delegation called him as he was lying in his hammock to award him prize money as the laziest man in town. He asked them to roll him over and stuff the bills in his back pocket. Nathan said he was sorry he had missed seeing the sheriff's funeral that had passed by his house, but he had been facing the wrong way in his hammock.

One of the best-known American anecdotes concerns the starving man who was offered popcorn. "Is it shelled?" he asks.

Similarly, up in Maine Ab Yancey and his seven strapping sons borrow cordwood from a neighbor, then ask him to chop it for them.

Hazard recalled a Rhode Island lazy man who, told by his doctor that he must exercise, sat in his garden in his rocking chair pulling up weeds with fire tongs.

Then there was shiftless Ezra, who decided to raise hogs because they can mostly raise themselves and Cynthy could fetch the swill.

Absent-mindedness: The quality of absent-mindedness, like that of ugliness, seems to have received more attention from nineteenth-century humorists than from those of the present time. Long sequences of absent-minded actions appear in pre-Civil War newspapers and comic almanacs. We hear of Bill Jones, who placed the bucket alongside the well and lowered himself down and was drowned.

In our own day, the college professor rather than the village crank has become the symbol of absent-mindedness. Classic anecdotes, told of several professors at different universities, including the Harvard professor of transportation, has the preoccupied pedant drive away from the gas station leaving his wife in the rest room, or taking a train back from the city where he has attended a conference, forgetting that he has driven there.

General Eccentricity: The foregoing traits by no means cover every example of odd behavior, thus the broader term, "eccentricity," is needed to account for all cases. First and foremost the character is eccentric and his legend is built upon his deviations from normal and accepted conduct. He may be an inventor of useless contraptions, such as the Upper Michigan genius who invented a crooked shade, a door that would not open, and a bottle that could not be refilled. Or he can be a persuasive entrepreneur like the Wild Rice King of Grand Rapids, Minnesota, who sold carloads of wild-rice seeds to the state of New Jersey. When they did not grow, he sold the state half a carload of mud. According to legend, the Premier of Japan wrote him to come over and teach wild-rice culture to the Japanese. Or the character may be the victim of a lifelong obsession, such as the Old Darn Man of Connecticut, who wandered the roads searching for his bride in his tattered wedding suit, or Thunder River Frank of Wisconsin, who spent seven years digging for gold revealed to him by the Divinity in a vision, and another long stretch building an ark in anticipation of a second flood.

All kinds of anecdotal legends were inspired by Uncle Boney Ridley of Macon County, North. Carolina. Such stories were known as "Boneys" and they portrayed his comical mishaps and naïve mistakes. Going to the post office, he inquires for mail. "What is your name?" the postmaster asks him. "Why, you durned old fool, you, if I've got any mail, I reckon my name would be on it, wouldn't it?" sputtered Uncle Boney.

Another time a friend saw Boney at midnight leaning against a brick building writing a letter to himself, and asked him what he was writing. "How do you think I would know?" responded Boney. "I won't get it till the mail comes tomorrow."

Once Boney borrowed a quarter from his sister to get a drink in town. On his way he stumbled and dropped it, but he continued to Franklin and scratched around under the one street light there, looking for the coin. The hotel owner standing by asked Boney why he didn't look on the hill where he had lost the quarter. "It's dark up there," said Boney, "and my eyes are failing, so I better look where there is a light."

After a drinking party one night, Boney and his friend Dr. Snipe McCloud mounted the same horse. Boney fell off and remarked, "Shnipe, if I ain't the worsh mishtaken I ever wuz, I believe I heard something drap!" He remounted backward, bumped against Snipe, felt for the bridle, and said, "Shnipe, if I ain't the worsh mishtaken I ever wuz, it wuz this horse's head that I heard drap, for I shore can't find it on this end!"

On his deathbed Boney felt remorse and asked his wife Polly to pray for him. She knelt down and intoned, "O Lord, please have mercy on my poor old drunken husband." Boney remonstrated, "Oh, damn it, Polly, don't tell Him I'm drunk; tell Him I'm sick."

Place legends are connected with a locality rather than with a person. The story behind a haunted house or other haunted spot is such a legend, and when Cotton Mather wrote his *Magnalia Christi Americana* in 1702 he was able already to record well-established traditions of New England houses afflicted with spectral disturbances. Enticing accounts of buried treasure, sometimes left by Captain Kidd, along with the corpse of a murdered Negro slave whose spirit would guard the treasure, abound on the New England coast, while in the Southwest fabulous reports of lost mines keep alluring prospectors. These traditions, too, belong with place legends. Throughout many states one hears of a cliff or a mountainside known as Lovers' Leap from which two distraught Indian lovers, prevented from marrying by their tribal allegiances, jump to their doom. These Lovers' Leaps belong to a class of pseudo-legends, based on the white man's poetic misconception of the "noble savage" and promoted by Chamber of Commerce bureaus to titillate tourists.

Sometimes the name given a locality memorializes and also renews a tradition. Or a picturesque name may lead to apocryphal folk etymologies. One explanation for the naming of Gnawbone in Indiana is the poverty of the inhabitants, one of whom was seen by a passer-by to be gnawing a discarded bone for his supper. But a more prosaic version says simply that Gnawbone is a corruption of the French Narbonne, whence some of the settlers came. An example of a genuine folk tradition preserved in a place name can be seen in the legend of Yoho Cove, Maine. Here is the story of Yoho Cove as told by a retired lobsterman, Curt Morse, living on a country road near the coast:

> Cove about two mile below where I live called Yoho Cove and the old fellas years ago allus said there was some kind of wild man lived there, and all they could understand he holler, "Yoho, yoho" all the time, especially at night. So he kinda slacked off and there was some of the natives down around the shore, don'tcha know, and took kinda of a dugout canoe I call it, dug out of tree, went across there raspberryin'. Well they got about ready to come home and they heard this Yoho hollerin'—they call him a Yoho. So before they reached the boat this fella, this man, ran out and grabbed this girl and took her back in the woods with him and left the rest screechin'. So they went home, and a little while afterwards why it kinda died out, don'tcha know? They missed the girl a lot.
>
> Well they thought she was dead and about two years afterwards, or about a year and a half afterwards, they had kinda forgot about it and they was over there raspberryin' or blueberryin' again and they heard this screechin' and they look up and this girl there, their relation was runnin' and screechin' for help. So she had a baby with her chasin' along—a year old—some little year-old baby somethin' like that. And they got her in the canoe anyway, started off from the shore. And the Yoho come down on the shore and caught the baby, or took the baby, tore it apart, tore it to pieces, throwed one part at the canoe as it was leavin' and took the other part back in the woods. So it's been called Yoho Cove ever since. That's all of it that I know about. It's always been called Yoho Cove.

Folklorists know that this is a floating legend, because they have found closely similar traditions of a wild man mating with a local woman in Kentucky, Canada, and Persia.

Legends of events do of course involve persons and places, but their interest focuses on an action or a deed that excites the community. Such legends have not been well collected in the United States, because they fall between history and folklore, but the dramatic settlement and rise in power of the American people within a short three centuries has created a host of local historical legends.

The lynching of the McDonald boys in 1881 in Menominee,

a town in Michigan's Upper Peninsula on the Wisconsin border, is a historical event that rapidly grew into legend. Menominee was then a rough sawmill settlement where pioneer conditions still prevailed. A feud had flared between Billy Kittson and the McDonalds that ended, after a train of ugly incidents (described in my *Bloodstoppers and Bearwalkers*), in the fatal stabbing of Billy. Two McDonalds were jailed. A group of irate towns-people took the law into their own hands, entered the jail, and seized the accused pair whom they mauled and hanged. No trial was held, but the story spread that all the ringleaders would die with their boots on. In the Catholic version, a priest had uttered this prophecy as lynchers careened down the main street with their victims.

That a lynching took place is fact. The additions that pro-duced a legend lie in the curse of retribution—a universal motif in folklore; the ballad that commemorated the event; and the tales of the mysterious deaths that befell the lynchers. One was burned to death in his lumber yard, one tipped over in a boat and drowned, one was bitten by a rattlesnake, one was cut in two by a saw. Even those who lived longest and swore they would beat the curse, died with their boots on. But the crowning proof of the presence of legend appears in a parallel even re-ported as taking place in Gouger's Neck, in northern California, in 1901. Bizarre deaths overtook a group of men who broke into a jail and lynched a family of half-breed ruffians. According to the townspeople, "Hell overtook 'em, every one of 'em." The folk imagination has fitted episodes into a mythic pattern.

A number of legends of supposedly actual happenings circu-late in modern society—in fact, the coming of the automobile has given legend new wings. Ubiquitous urban legends deal with the ghostly hitchhiker, the maiden given a ride by a passing motorist who finds her gone when they reach her destination, and learns from a photograph that she had died some years before; the stolen grandmother, who died while traveling with her daughter and son-in-law, and whose corpse, strapped to the roof of their car, vanished while they were in a restaurant; and the death car, offered for sale at fifty dollars because the death smell of its former owner, who had committed suicide or had been accidentally killed inside it, could not be removed. In spite of the factual reports of these cases, no one has personally seen the hitchhiking damsel, or the deceased grandmother, or the ill-smelling car. The stories are told at second-hand.

A further word should be said about the categories of American legends. They need to be considered from two points of view: that of their themes and that of their sources. We can distinguish between folk legends, popular legends, and literary legends according to whether they are known chiefly through oral tradition, through a mixture of oral and printed sources, or chiefly through print and other mass media. Barney Beal can be called a hero of folk legend because the tales told about him are distributed chiefly by word of mouth. Mike Fink in the early nineteenth century was a hero of popular legend who benefited from campfire yarns and from stories in newspapers, almanacs, and giftbook annuals relating his feats as a brawling Mississippi keelboatman. Johnny Appleseed is today a hero of literary legend, known to the public through the poems of Carl Sandburg and Vachel Lindsay, the Walt Disney film, stories of his life written for children, countless newspaper feature articles, and a United States postage stamp. But no folk groups tell legends about Johnny Appleseed today.

It should be noted that the nature of the folk hero, whether historical or mythical, has no bearing on his legend, so long as the folk believe he exists.

Already in our glance at anecdotal legends we have seen tall-tale elements appearing. Barney Beal is well on his way to becoming a hero of humorous exaggeration, and some local characters are credited with impossible performances. Still the legend and the tall tale belong to different realms, for the legend, however remarkable and fantastic, is meant to be believed, and the tall tale, however specific and solemn in presentation, is intended as a deception.

The tall tale grew naturally out of the travelers' tales that flourished in the seventeenth century when curious explorers visited the Americas and the Far East. In their writings for the home market, the travelers intended to convey the truth, but they also wished to satisfy the thirst of their readers for marvels, in the vein introduced by Marco Polo three centuries earlier. Then, too, the travelers had truly beheld strange savages and beasts and plants and landscapes. Early chroniclers of the American colonies described a horn snake which struck a locust tree with its venomous tail and caused it to wither within eight hours; bears who slept during the whole winter, sucking their paws for nourishment; a tulip or poplar tree so large that a settler lived inside one with his house and furniture; an oyster as big as a ship's cabin; a whirlpool at the mouth of the Mississippi that swallowed up every craft on the river and even the river itself.

These and similar wonders were written down as true travelers' tales in colonial times, but by the nineteenth century these marvels are being told as tongue-in-cheek tall tales. A jestbook of 1808 contains a piece called "The Diverting Club" which describes a liars' contest, the institution that has stimulated the competitive telling of unlikely stories. One raconteur related the wondrous incident of the Split Dog, which ran into a sapling and cut himself in two, whereupon the owner patched him together again, but in his haste placed two legs up and two down. Thereafter the dog proved a tireless hunter, for when weary on the first set of legs he flipped over onto the other two. This has proved one of the most popular American windies.

The most celebrated of all made its first appearance in print in the United States in *The Farmer's Almanack* for 1809. It was titled a "Wonderful Story related by George Howell, a mighty Hunter, and known in that part of the country where he lived by the name of the Vermont Nimrod." Howell reported how he had with one lucky shot brought down a deer, a sturgeon, a rabbit, three partridges, and a woodcock, while honey was oozing out of the hole in the tree where the bullet had lodged. This feat would be duplicated many times throughout the nineteenth and twentieth centuries, and we can trace the tale through printed sources up to the field collections of recent times. It is an international folktale, identified by the number 1890, *The Wonderful Hunt* in Antti Aarne and Stith Thompson's *The Types of the Folktale*, but particularly cherished by American sportsmen and backwoodsmen.

The free-and-easy masculine society of the frontier and the back country relished tall tales of hunting, fishing, changeable weather, fast-growing crops, mythical animals, and the reversal of natural laws. Before the Civil War the daily and weekly press often printed tall tales and humorous anecdotes, and a type of journalistic fiction, customarily referred to as the humor of the

Old Southwest, drew themes and characters from this folk humor. In the figure of Davy Crockett, born on the Tennessee frontier in 1786, elected to Congress in 1827, and killed at the Alamo in 1836 defending the mission fort against the Mexicans, the currents of tall-tale humor and anecdotal legend mingled and produced a comic legendary hero. Davy was both a storyteller and a subject of stories; he was both an eccentric character and a superman. In these respects he differed from other personalities in American folklore, who tend to be either the teller of tall tales or the subject of local anecdotes. On a field trip in Maine in 1942 I collected a number of tall tales, including "The Wonderful Hunt," from Slick MacQuoid, who at one point took me to see the town character, Old John Soule, a wisp of a man. Slick told windies about Old John, saying he was so light he always carried a rake on his shoulder to keep from floating off the earth, and that once when Old John was shingling his roof, he sailed twenty feet into the air and Slick had to lasso him to bring him down. But Old John himself told no stories.

The comic legend of Crockett is known to us through a series of humorous almanacs that entertained readers from 1835 to 1856. There is good evidence that these almanac tall tales did derive from oral stories told in barrooms, general stores, hotel lobbies, and other meeting places. In the case of such twentieth-century tall-tale heroes as Paul Bunyan, the giant lumberjack of the north woods, and Pecos Bill, the giant cowboy of the Southwest, the evidence points to only a slender thread of oral folk legend underneath the literary and mass-culture adornments. Lumberjacks tell very few yarns about Paul Bunyan and cowboys very few about Pecos Bill. The incentive to write about these whimsical titans has come from authors sensing a market —mainly a children's market—for fiction about made-up American gods and heroes. From the folklore viewpoint, these accounts are neither genuine legends nor genuine tall tales.

15

Trickster, the Outrageous Hero

ROGER D. ABRAHAMS

One of the most remarkable features of folklore is its adaptability and endurance. Man does not give up the results of his creative acts easily. Instead, he is inclined to change either their form or substance, adapting them to new needs and stresses. Nowhere is this stubborn fondness for his own artistic creations more apparent than in the persistence and proliferation of stories about that outrageous hero called "Trickster." In the form of small creatures such as Spider or Rabbit, in the guise of the jesters and fools Stupid Jack and Punchinello, or as Moron and Hophead, he has performed his antics in the traditional entertainments of most groups throughout the world: aboriginal, peasant, and urban. In North America, among the Indian tribes, he may appear as a mythic hero like Raven or Coyote. In communities of Negroes, he may crop up as a fictional prankster like Br'er Rabbit or Aunt Nancy (the Spider). Or, most recently, he may be found playing the main role in joke cycles. Whether he populates myth, general folktale, or jest, his undertakings are audacious, rebellious, egotistical, and always performed with the idea of giving freedom to personal action in the face of group restrictions.

Trickster is also the most paradoxical of all characters in traditional narratives—at least as far as the Western mind is concerned—for he combines the attributes of many other types that we tend to distinguish clearly. At various times he is clown, fool, jokester, initiate, culture hero, even ogre. This contradiction is brought out by the anthropologist Paul Radin in his book on Trickster: he is "at one and the same time, creator and destroyer, giver and negator, he who dupes and who is always duped himself." He is the central character for what we usually consider many different types of folk narratives. When he appears as culture hero, he brings fire or food to his people and teaches them how to use such resources; his role of trickster is directed in these cases against the constraints of the gods. But just as often he will direct his actions against the others in his group, stealing food, seducing women, satisfying all of his voracious hungers.

His outstanding characteristic is his lack of morals. As Radin says, "He wills nothing consciously. At all times he is constrained to behave as he does from impulses over which he has no control. . . . He possesses no values, moral or social, [and] is at the mercy of his passions and appetites." Yet the stories about him exist in communities with ethical values; though he represents amorality, he does so in a moral context. His actions must be condemned at the same time that they are laughed at and admired. As the enemy of constraint, he seems to function as a representative of the lawless, indeed anarchistic, aspect of ourselves which exists in even the most social creatures.

As the classicist, Karl Kerenyi, says of Trickster, he is the very "spirit of disorder, the enemy of boundaries." Essentially, we seem to be fascinated by him because he represents the principle of pure unbridled energy, directed into human shape and impelled by primal human needs. But this only explains about half of the stories about Trickster, those in which he actively dupes others. But as often as not, he tricks himself. And when he does so, his exploits are nothing less than clownish and his mask is that of the noodle, the simpleton.

The duality of Trickster's acts is most dramatically seen in the stories about him which were told as a cycle of tales among such American Indian groups as the Chippewa and the Winnebago. For instance, in the celebrated cycle collected by Radin from Sam Blowsnake, a full-blooded Winnebago, Trickster begins as an unnamed chieftain who unwittingly commits all kinds of taboo acts leading him to retreat from his group and his role as leader. He then goes through a series of close to fifty incidents, equally divided between those in which he tricks others and those in which the duper is duped, generally by himself.

Characteristic of the tricking type of story is the one in which Trickster persuades Skunk to dig a hole in the hill which he then uses to trap mother raccoons and thus provide himself with a sumptuous meal. In another, he dupes Coyote into being tied to a horse's tail.

On the other hand, there are a number of stories in which Trickster appears to be an absolute fool. In one case he finds himself in the sea, and though he is just off shore, he must ask all of the creatures of the ocean how to get to land; and in another, he jumps into a lake thinking that there are plums at the bottom, only to find that he was misled by the water's reflection. This latter story is one which is often found as a moron or simpleton tale in more sophisticated traditions.

There is one type of story that is associated with Trickster that virtually defies understanding. In these tales, Trickster's conscious mind becomes dissociated from his body and its excrescences, and consequently he commits acts that soil or maim him severely. In different episodes, he finds himself awash in his own feces, or burning his anus as punishment, or eating his own intestines. Such stories betray the fascination of Trickster with his own body and its products—an attraction which must paradoxically be interpreted as both humorous and self-destructive.

It is clear that Trickster's actions are not to be considered models for behavior. He cannot be seen as a norm of sanity; he does not clear our vision, but rather clouds it with hints of potential chaos. In social terms, his actions are extremely aggressive, destructive, and forbidden. Therefore, his acts must be countenanced because of some aspect of our dream world; his actions must represent a way of getting around taboos and other restrictions without actually upsetting the order of society. In other words, Trickster functions primarily as a release value for all of the anti-social desires repressed by the men who tell and listen to his stories. He behaves as the members of the society would behave if they were not constrained by fear from acting. Vicariously, sympathetically, through the acts of this egocentric sensualist, man expunges the pressures that might otherwise destroy both his ordered world and himself.

To evoke this sympathetic response, the stories of Trickster must be removed from the everyday world and put in a ridiculous context so that we may laugh the laugh of superiority. In the Indian tales this removal is effected in a number of ways. First, Trickster is represented as existing in the mythical world, the world as it was in the beginning or before man came to his present state. Second, he is given powers such as the ability to change shapes, or sexes, and so is somewhat removed from the sphere of man. He is generally portrayed as an animal. Third, and perhaps most important, he is always presented as a creature with many human characteristics, but one who lacks exactly those features which would qualify him as a member of the tribe. Specifically, he often is shown to be a lawbreaker; the fact is, however, that he is too minatory, too childlike, too insane to be conscious of the law.

In this regard, it is interesting to look at the beginning of Sam Blowsnake's cycle of mythical events. Here Trickster appears first as a chief who calls for a war dance only to frustrate the expectations of the assembled group by cohabiting with his wife, in direct violation of ritual war procedure. As the incident proceeds, it becomes clear that the chief has in a very real sense lost his mind, his sense of order, and has taken on the characteristics of an insane man. He has regressed from his adult role to one of essential innocence or childishness, and it is in this guise that he is able to get away with his acts.

This regressive infantilism is underlined in a number of ways. Most obvious to the Westerner is his fascination with and attachment to his own body parts and to the products of his body, which he often mistakes for detached objects. Furthermore, he does not seem to coordinate well, especially when his role is that of a clown, and he is almost always presented as a *small* creature usually in contention with those larger than he is. He does, however, enjoy a certain self-sufficiency. He is interested in play, but needs no one else to play with; and surrounded by the bounties of nature, his deprivations are most often temporary.

Given these primal, childlike elements in all representations of Trickster, it is interesting to notice how the figure recurs in different cultures in response to different focuses and artistic conventions. Among the American Indian groups he seems to fulfill a need not only to explore prohibited subjects and acts but also to serve as a representation of what might be termed original or mythic energy. However, few collectors of Indian lore have explored the way in which Trickster functions in specific tribes, and those who have attempted to do so have not been conspicuously successful.

On the other hand, some extremely suggestive remarks have been made by Melville Herskovits, Richard M. Dorson, and others, on the way in which American Negroes have channeled Trickster's energies to serve specific psychic needs. As Herskovits pointed out, "Psychologically, the role of the trickster seems to be that of projecting the insufficiencies of man in his universe onto a smaller creature who, in besting his larger adversaries, permits the satisfactions of an obvious identification to those who recount or listen to these tales." The gains in increased self-confidence to be achieved through such a process was especially important to the slaves, inasmuch as they had to contend not only with a hostile universe but also with a social system in which they were stereotypically cast as animalistic, primal, and forever trying to trick the white "Marster." By embellishing upon the African trickster tradition of Rabbit and Spider, these Negro storytellers were able to convert these stereotypically condemned traits into characteristics which were to be admired (if not by the whites, at least by other Negroes). Consequently, a large group of stories concerned with the clever doing of Br'er Rabbit achieved wide currency in the Southern United States, stories we know best through the collections of Joel Chandler Harris.

Perhaps the best known of these is the one in which Br'er Rabbit confronts the tar-baby:

Once, after Br'er Rabbit had fooled Br'er Fox, Br'er Fox decided to catch him. He set up a tar-baby in the middle of the road, and then he hid in the bushes to see what would happen. He didn't wait very long, for by and by there came Br'er Rabbit pacing down the road. When he came upon the tar-baby he stood up on his hind legs very much astonished. "Good morning!" said Br'er Rabbit. "Nice weather this morning!" Tar-baby made no reply. "Are you deaf?" said Br'er Rabbit. "If you are I can holler louder." Tar-baby kept still and Br'er Rabbit said, "You are stuck up, that is what you are. And I am going to cure you. I am going to teach you to talk to respectable people if it is the last thing I do. If you don't take off your hat and tell me 'How do you do' I am going to kill you."

Br'er Rabbit kept on asking and the tar-baby made no reply. Finally he raised his fist and struck tar-baby on the side of the head.

It stuck. "If you don't let me loose I'll knock you again," said Br'er Rabbit, and saying this he struck with his other hand, and that stuck also. "Turn me loose or I'll knock the stuffings out of you," said Br'er Rabbit, and he kicked with his feet and they also stuck. Then he cried to the tar-baby to let him go or he would butt him. And he butted him and his head stuck.

Br'er Fox came out of the bushes and laughed and laughed until he could laugh no more. He then went to prepare a fire to roast Br'er Rabbit. "I don't care what you do with me, Br'er Fox," said Br'er Rabbit. "You can roast me and eat me if you want to, but don't fling me in that briar patch." Br'er Fox in turn threatened to hang, skin, and drown Br'er Rabbit, and Br'er Rabbit went on saying he didn't care as long as he wasn't thrown in the briar patch. So Br'er Fox caught him by the hind legs and twirled him around and threw him in the briar patch. "Born and bred in the briar patch, Br'er Fox, born and bred in the briar patch," laughed Br'er Rabbit as he ran off.

This is just one of many tales, often of international currency, which assert the pattern of the small animal outwitting the larger animal or human. This sequence of events in which he functions to trick others is almost the only mask worn by Trickster in American Negro tales. Though in some accounts the sneaky beast does get paid back for his knavery, rarely do we find the trickster playing the clown or the self-devourer, as we do in Indian tales. Clearly the Negro storyteller focuses on Rabbit or Spider because of the gains implied in the victories of the small animal.

The implications of this strategy are a great deal clearer in another series of narratives told by American Negro storytellers, the "Marster John" stories. In these the trickster role is carried out not by a small animal casually associated with the Negro, but by a slave himself. And John, the slave, generally is able to dupe his master, even though the latter often starts out to pull a trick on John.

Old Marster killed a lot of hogs every year. He had John helping him. When it was time to pay off he said, "John, here's a hog's head, hog's feet, and hog's ears." John killed hogs for a long time that way. That was his pay. Then John got an idea and bought himself some hogs. Old Marster never knew. When Old Marster came around and wanted John to kill hogs for him, John said, "What are you paying?" "I'll pay you what I always have, a head, four feet, and two ears." "Well," said John, "I can't. I'm eating higher on the hog now!"

Clearly such stories emphasize, as do the Br'er Rabbit tales, that the stereotyped characteristics of Negroes can be used by the Negroes themselves to good aggressive purpose. By accepting the childlike, lazy, and animalistic image into which they are cast, they are able to gain an upper hand, at least psychologically, through such tales. This strongly aggressive and amoral content is still to be observed in more urban Negro lore, but here the trickster figure has been replaced by the vicious badman who carries out his aggressions quite overtly. Drinkers, sadists, wenchers like The Great MacDaddy, Devil Winston, Railroad Bill, and Aaron Harris break the law of the whites and are energetically described as "the baddest man in this 'hole world" or as "mean enough and bad to whip his mammy and shoot his dad."

Among the American Indians, Trickster appears in full-blown myths and is assumed to have lived at the beginning of time. Among the American Negroes, though not necessarily among the the West African tribes, his doings are regarded as totally fictitious, although his exploits are still recounted in elaborate tales. However, his amazing versatility and adaptability is testified to by his recent appearance in joke cycles in the white urban culture of the United States, where in the form of Moron, Hophead, Drunkard, Moby Pickle, or Kilroy he has reared his outrageous head. In such a milieu he is, of course, no longer part of a formal narrative tradition, but has found his place in quips which rely on conciseness for effect. Though there are narrative jokes about trickster figures in today's culture—for instance, the traveling-salesman series—his most vital existence has been in the short riddle or conundrum. Why does Kilroy keep cutting his knee? To see if there is any beer in the joint.

Most commonly in these short jests, Trickster is characterized not so much by his ability to trick as by his clowning tendencies. The clown is, of course, the figure who seems to be a man, but who cannot control his words or acts and so reduces himself to childishness. As in the Winnebago narratives, this aspect of Trickster arises out of his resignation from society in favor of directing his energies along egotistical, primal, amoral lines. This is the role assumed by the drunkard and the hophead in our society, and because of this resignation we can make fun of their inability to act correctly. Thus we tell of the drunkard mistaking telephone poles for speeding projectiles and the hophead mistaking an auto accident for a baseball game. Furthermore, this type of trickster often causes harm to be directed at himself, waiting at the corner with a slice of bread for the traffic jam, only to be hit by a truck which gives him a jar; throwing his cigar butt down a manhole and breaking his leg trying to stamp it out.

Similarly clown-like are the doings of the Moron, on whom a persistently popular joke cycle centers, or of the Polack, the Moron's recent first cousin. In these jests the focal character is so childishly unknowing that he commits absurd acts such as jumping off the Empire State Building to make a hit on Broadway or using four men to screw in a light bulb, one man holding, three turning him around.

The recent joke cycle concerned with Elephant resuscitates Trickster in his guise of minatory creature, capable of transformations and of finding himself involved in the strangest of actions because that is his nature, no matter how immoral these acts may seem. Elephant is a being of indeterminate proportions; though he appears to be huge, he nevertheless can be found in the bathtub or a Volkswagen or next to your wife in bed. He is capable of changing sex, appearing in one form as a marauding male figure jumping down on natives from trees, and then as an effeminate ballet dancer, distraught at the tightness of his slippers. He is capable of impregnating women (for twenty-eight months) and yet of being subdued and made to float down a river flat on his back, with his feet in the air. Clearly, with Elephant, we have a figure very close to that of Indian Trickster but in modern dress, for he conforms almost completely to Radin's description: "a figure of undetermined proportions . . . foreshadowing the shape of man. . . . Laughter, humor and irony permeate every act [he] does. The reaction of the audience . . . to both him and his exploits is prevailingly one of laughter tempered by awe." The presence of such a primal and amoral character in the midst of contemporary oral traditions shows that the vitality and usefulness of Trickster has remained ever present, and that he is as capable of changing shapes from one era and society to another as he is of assuming different forms within an individual story. He is a masquerader and a marauder that we will obviously encounter as much in future traditions in the United States as we have in the past.

16

The Folk Games of the Children

BRIAN SUTTON-SMITH

Although this chapter is about the folk games of American children—that is, about games like marbles, jump rope, hide-and-seek, and hopscotch—it is important first to mention some of the recent developments in the academic investigation of games. These bring a new sense of significance to the study of children's play itself.

1. Deserving prior mention are the remarkable effects that the analysis of the two traditional adult games of strategy and chance have had on the whole of the social sciences in the past thirty years. Thus, games of strategy such as checkers and chess, under the name of "game theory," have provided models for analyzing decision-making as it is found in business, war, and even marriage. And games of chance such as dice and roulette, under the name of "probability theory," have provided models for analyzing statistical outcomes in a wide range of social problems. Such realistic applications of the processes modeled by the games themselves would certainly seem to imply that though games may be fun to the players, they are also doing some serious work for the cultures of which they are a part. These games of strategy and chance, after all, have emerged from thousands of years of folk activity and presumably have been teaching their lessons in some implicit way throughout that long period of time.

2. Evidence that this is indeed the case has been provided by recent cross-cultural studies of games in which from 100 to 200 of the known tribal cultures of the world have been examined, with the aid of a computer, in order to find systematic interrelationships between the presence of games and other aspects of culture. The results from the study of games of chance show that these games first occur in cultures where there is great uncertainty about basic food supplies or about the conditions of survival. The games are a part of the general view of these people that the help and occasionally the benevolent assistance of the gods can be solicited both through prayer and through games. Children in such cultures are made anxious about acting upon their own resources alone. They are taught to rely on such outside decision-making. On the other hand, games of strategy arise in post-neolithic times with the emergence of complex military cultures where young children are trained in the arts of leadership and obedience, so that they can fit into the hierarchical social arrangements of these cultures and be masters of the arts of deception and strategy so necessary in the diplomacy and wars that characterize these cultures. In each case the games of chance or strategy seem to provide the group members with a way of practicing necessary skills without real-life consequences.

3. These cross-cultural studies have led further to psychological studies of individual game-playing American children. To give one example: studies have been made of the most elementary game of strategy played universally by American children which is called tick-tack-toe (or noughts and crosses in the British Isles). In this game, which is played with pencil and paper, each player marks with crosses or circles on a diagram trying to get three crosses or circles in a row. The diagram is like a street intersection with two parallel lines intersecting two other parallel lines at right angles. It has been shown that boys who are winners in such tick-tack-toe tournaments are perceived by the other children as leaders because of their ideas (but not because of their physical strength); they are boys who are also good at problem-solving processes. It is not difficult to argue from such data that the child is exercising and learning a strategic approach to life partly through the game.

4. Or we can take yet another development in theorizing about games which adds up to a similar interpretation. This is the view long expressed by psychoanalysts that play is a child's emotional

language and that what a child does in play has to be read as a picture of his underlying feeling and motives. This view has gained particular urgency as a result of recent programs for under-privileged children where it has sometimes been discovered that children of the same ages but from different economic levels do not know how to play together. They do not have a common play and game language. The importance of having detailed structural analyses of children's play and games in order to know what to do in such circumstances is obvious.

5. Finally, the extensive psychological study of the nature of creative talent in this country following the advent of Sputnik has created a new appreciation for the role of purely expressive behavior such as play, humor, etc., in the life of the very creative person. It has been discovered that the more creative person tends to have more humorous ideas and to be more playful. It is thought that in so doing he builds up a wider repertory of potential responses for future use. Similarly, the culture with the greater number of games may well train children in a wider repertory of potential future responses. Play and games widen repertories of potential response. From this discovery as well as the others mentioned above, children's folk games have once again gained an importance as subjects of investigation which they have not had since the end of the nineteenth century when they were investigated for the remnants of historical customs that were to be found in them.

With such ideas in mind, then, let us look at the current picture of children's games in America. The first and most strik-ing impression one gets is that there has been a considerable amount of change going on, with some games disappearing while others have been getting stronger. But at the same time as these changes have been occurring, there has also been a constant and, as it were, sideways, infusion of novel elements from new immi-grant groups. The most notable example is that provided by the Negroes who brought with them their own dances and rhythms, many elements of which persist today in children's lore. Of the many examples in singing, jumping, and ring plays, the hand-clapping games seem particularly distinctive. Although the words usually have a contemporary reference, the movements and rhythms are non-European. Negro children usually clap on the offbeat while white children playing the same game clap on the downbeat; in addition, the Negro children clap various parts of their body as well as their hands, perhaps simulating the different sounds once produced on drums of different timbre. Again, the Negro children's ring games are more of a cooperative enterprise than those of white children. The center player is supported by the others as she satirizes the life she lives—there is not the contest between the center player and the rest of the group which is more characteristic of European circle games. The words of one hand-clapping game suggest a proud assertion of ethnic distinctiveness:

> I ain't been to Frisco
> And I ain't been to school
> I ain't been to college
> But I ain't no fool.

More characteristically, however, as new immigrant groups are assimilated into the general stream of American life and come into increasing contact with other children, they begin to play the Anglo-European variants of the traditional games which they first brought with them as well as the new games being played by other children. This occurs necessarily because folk games are generally acquired from other children in the districts and schools to which the immigrants move, not from their parents. Immigrant adult folk materials are, of course, somewhat more resistant to such assimilation.

But to return to the major stream of American children's folk games. One of the most interesting examples of the way in which children's games have both changed and yet in a sense continued to serve the same function is provided by the fate of the *singing games* and dialogue games of young girls. At first sight it would look to the visitor to an American playground as if these games had almost disappeared. Where, he would ask, are all the singing games first recorded by the American folklorist William Wells Newall in 1883? To answer this question, however, requires different answers for different types of singing games. Thus, some of the very simplest have been retained and are still widespread. These are games in which players take turns at being in the center of the circle of players as in "Farmer in the Dell," or where the players make simple movements going around together in a circle as in "Ring-around-a-Rosy," "Looby Loo," the

"Mulberry Bush," and "In and Out the Window." Most children of four to seven years of age still get some experience of these simple games. The games that one does not find very frequently, however, are the games of courtship once played by older children and adolescents where the players are arranged in two groups or lines and which had names such as: "The Knight of Spain," "Here Comes a Duke," "Here Sits the Queen of England," "King Arthur Was King William's Son," etc. The names reflect by and large the European and predominantly British origins of most of these games. In the nineteenth century these games were a part of the larger group of couple games that were played by adolescents at church socials, evening parties (the play-party as it was called), husking bees, and country fairs. They were played without musical accompaniment with everyone singing and dancing. They were often thought to be less sinful than ballroom dancing. Some of them contained the opportunity or the penalty, whichever way you took it, of kissing your partner or the lady in the middle of the circle. While a few of such games have persisted into recent times, they are generally to be found only where the children are isolated from the rest of the society, as in Harlem or in the Appalachian mountain communities.

It is interesting to note what has happened to the various elements of these games: the dancing, the kissing, the rhymes, and the altercations between mother and daughter. Dancing has in general taken more individualistic forms. In the past, the child proceeded from "Farmer in the Dell" to the "Three Knights" to "Skip to My Lou." Today, after "Farmer in the Dell," the child is likely to proceed directly at the age of seven or eight to such dances as the monkey, the jerk, the pony, the Watusi, and the swim, which are dances where the child makes rhythmic movements in time with the music, dancing alongside rather than with her partner. When the children begin to go to parties and dances as couples, they simply carry on the same dances, or new forms of them. But even a girl of seven or eight can do these dances while listening to her toy recorder. There is, therefore, dancing today at the various stages of growth, just as there used to be, but it is of an individualistic rather than a group-patterned character.

Kissing is no longer proscribed in the way it once was, and instead of being given a furtive excuse by the game, kissing is now the sole purpose of some games. Most thirteen- and fifteen-year-old children still get some experience of these games, although there is usually little to prevent them from kissing even without games. With thirteen-year-old children the most popular kissing game is "Spin the Bottle," in which the central player spins a bottle around in the center of the circle and kisses the player to whom it finally points. That player then takes her place and the game proceeds. With fifteen-year-olds, by contrast, the most popular game is "Flashlight," where the central player is the only one without a partner. All the other couples are supposed to be kissing. If the central player turns on his flashlight (the game is played in a dark room) and finds a boy *not* kissing, he then gets that boy's partner and proceeds to kiss her in order to stay out of the center, or not to kiss her if he wants to get back in the center. And there are many others of a similar sort of which we shall mention only "Endurance Kissing," which is a contest to see which couple can maintain a kiss for the longest period of time, usually for the length of a phonograph record. While older persons might wonder at the necessity for such games, it appears that young teen-agers are both embarrassed about and yet interested in kissing, and the games partly solve their problem by allowing them some experience without commitment or responsibility.

The parts of the old singing games that have continued most abundantly in other game forms, however, are the rhythm and rhymes. Grade-school children still have as many rhyming and rhythmic games as did children in the nineteenth century, but the major vehicles of expression are now the jump-rope, ball-bouncing, and counting-out rhymes, rather than the singing games, as used to be the case. The girls in most schools can still provide the collector with some twenty to thirty jump-rope rhymes, and about the same number of other rhymes of various sorts. While there is individual jump-roping, and sometimes two children swing two ropes between them, most characteristically two children swing one rope while the other players skip in and out.

Here are several of the jump-rope rhymes which have been most widely recorded throughout different parts of the country with only minor variations from state to state. Notice in this first one that the child jumps until she trips and that the count when she trips, in a sense, determines her fate. Thus:

Johnnie over the ocean,
Johnnie over the sea,
Johnnie broke a bean pot
And blamed it on me.
I told Ma
Ma told Pa.
Johnnie got a licken,
Ha. Ha. Ha.
How many lickens did
Johnnie get?
One, two three, etc.

When she trips, that is the number of smackings, or "lickens,"
that Johnnie gets. More often the count when she trips decides
how many kisses the girl is supposed to get from her lover. Thus:

Down in the meadow,
Where the green grass grows,
There stands Mary
As pretty as a rose.
Along comes Johnnie
And kisses her on the nose.
How many times did he kiss her?
One, two, three, etc.

The rhymes themselves have many origins, most often in the
singing games or songs of earlier days. In general their contents
are much more topical and mocking of adult life than were the
contents of the earlier singing games, although the latter did
contain a certain amount of disputation among mothers, daughters, suitors, and witches. Children today are apparently freer
to laugh at the adult world than were their forebears. Thus:

Here comes Susie,
The American beauty
She can do the rhumba
She can do the splits.
She can wear her skirts
Up over her hips.

or

Polly drinks lemonade
Polly drinks beer

Polly drinks everything
That makes you feel so queer.
Oops goes the lemonade
Oops goes the beer
Oops goes everything
That makes you feel so queer.

or

Minnie, Minnie, Ha Ha
Went to see her Pa Pa.
Papa died, Minnie cried,
Minnie had a baby
And named him Tim.
She put him in the bathtub
To see if he could swim.
He drank a gallon of water
And ate a bar of soap.
Minnie called the doctor
To see if he would croak.
How many minutes did he live?
One, two, three, etc.

The thing to notice about these jump-rope games is that, like the modern children's dancing, they are more individualistic than the older games and dances, and they are also more competitive. Each girl takes the center spot in turn and competes against the others. It is perhaps not surprising that in a world where a girl's achievement counts sometimes for as much as her charm, the games she plays should thus emphasize success by achievement rather than success by arbitrary choice—that is, by being chosen by one of the three kings, as in the more patterned singing games of yesterday. The tendency for girls of today to be more interested in games involving competitive achievement is reflected in their much greater interest in and play at games which used to be pretty much restricted to boys: games like marbles, baseball, basketball, chasing, leapfrog, etc., and activities like skating, swimming, and kite flying. Although we have suggested that the young girls of today are more like boys in their play than they used to be, we would emphasize that in certain respects the sexes remain very much unalike. Boys still have wrestling, football, boxing, and cowboys and Indians pretty much to themselves, and girls still dominate the play world of house, jackstones, hop-scotch, and ball-bouncing. One characteristic type of girls' game which boys don't play, for example, is the "Leader Game," which seems to reflect so nicely the mother-hen role that girls will have to play as they get older. An example is "Mother, May I," in which one girl stands out in front of the others. They try to move forward toward her and the first one to reach her takes her place. But the other girls can only move when she says so, and only if they display the proper manners. They must say "please" and they must say "thank you." "Mother, may I take three granny steps, please?" "Yes, you may." "Thank you." . . . "Mother, may I take two lamp posts?" "No, you didn't say 'please.'" And so on, with an elaborate vocabulary for the types of steps to be taken, and much cheating by the players in an attempt to creep up and take Mother's place when she isn't watching.

So to sum up this account of girls' singing games, it is clear that many of their major elements persist but in other forms and with new emphases. The dancing and the rhyming are now more individualistic. The jump-rope rhymes are less formal. There is still a concern with marriage, but it is somewhat less a matter of arbitrary choice and somewhat more determined by the skill of the girl who jumps the rope. She may recite the alphabet instead of counting. If she trips on the right letter, she can thus determine the first letter of the name of the one she will marry. Kissing now also has its own games, or no games at all. And again, there is much more open commentary on the world of adults.

Another group of games that show a similar transformation— that is, the forms of the game played by young children persist, while those once played by older children are replaced—are those known as *chasing and tagging games*. The younger children's chasing games are as popular as they ever were under such names as tag, hide-and-seek, stoop tag, red rover, and pom pom pullaway.

What has happened in the modern world is that these simple chasing games no longer lead gradually into more complex ones, as they used to when games like "Fox and Hounds" and "Prisoner's Base" were the school favorites of twelve- and thirteen-year-old boys. Their place has been taken by the formal sports of baseball, football, and the others. The new national sports, however, have had a broader effect than this. They have tended to displace many other types of skill games once played with knives, sticks, stones, buttons, tops, hoops, peashooters, and whips. Of course, the displacement of some of these has come about because their dangerous character is unacceptable in the modern playground.

Still, as has already been apparent, continuity is more obvious than loss. If the modern sports appear to be somewhat more physically confining to children, children have freer access to a wider variety of informal physical activities than ever before. More children today participate in roller-skating, cycling, camping, fishing, hunting, boating, and swimming than was formerly the case. And again, while variety may have been lost in physical sports, it has not been lost in intellectual board and card games, which have multiplied enormously, although usually along fairly traditional lines. It is on this intellectual or verbal level, in fact, that the modern child's play has shown its most remarkable developments, and we turn now to these.

It is clear that if the modern American playground is less turbulent than its forerunners with respect to physical skills, it does seem to be a much freer place with respect to its *verbal games*—or to the verbal aspects of older games as we have already seen in the case of jump-rope. If one were to point out a single feature that distinguishes today's children from their forebears, it would have to be their verbal facility. Encouraged by a more permissive form of education, by a greater freedom in their homes, and by the stimulation of movies, comics, radio, and television, today's children are both socially more mature and verbally more sophisticated. Which means that the collector of child lore often gets many more riddles, rhymes, and jokes than he does games. One is tempted to say that children today do not, to the same extent, need to have games to structure their social relationships. They are socially so much more mature that many of their relationships can be carried on in conversational terms. For example, young children love riddles. They compete in terms of moron riddles (and many other types):

Q. Why did the moron throw the clock out the window?
A. To see time fly.

Older children compete in terms of absurd riddles:

Q. What has six legs and barks at the moon?
A. A dog. I put in two extra legs to make it harder.

Q. Why do elephants wear red tennis shoes?
A. Their blue ones are in the wash.

Adolescents compete in terms of logic riddles:

Q. A lawyer and a doctor were having lunch together when the doctor suddenly looked up and exclaimed: "My God, there's my wife." The lawyer pulled out a gun and shot the doctor. Why?
A. The lawyer was a woman in love with the doctor and she didn't know he was married.

And children of all ages today seem to relish humor that an older generation has labeled sick or sad:

Q. Mummy, can I play the piano?
A. No, your hooks will spoil the ivories.

Q. Mummy, I don't want to go to Europe.
A. Shut up, kid, and get into the Care package.

Q. Mummy, I don't want to go to China.
A. Shut up, kid, and keep digging.

Something of the same smartness is to be found in the ball-bouncing games of young girls where they chant rhymes while bouncing balls under their legs, against a wall, with a one-two, one-two beat to match the rhythm of bouncing and catching:

> Bouncie, bouncie, ballie,
> I lost the leg of my dollie.
> My mother came out
> And gave me a clout
> That turned my petticoat
> Inside out.

The counting-out rhymes which were always used by players about to begin a chasing game in order to decide who would be "it"—that is, who would have to chase the others—appear to continue strongly though not with the same increase in numbers

that characterizes both jump-rope and ball-bouncing games. A
brief one is:

> Ink, mink, pepper, stink
> Alley, cally poo
> O.U.T. spells out
> And out goes you.

But as well as these more game-related rhymes, there are scores
of miscellaneous rhymes; some for teasing, some for nonsense.
Many verses have a contemporary American ring to them:

> I should worry, I should care,
> I should marry a millionaire.
> He should die, I should cry,
> I should marry another guy.

or

> Cinderella dressed in red,
> Went to town to buy some thread.
> Along came a fellow whose name was Red.
> And shot her with a bullet that was made of lead.

Nonsense, of course, covers anything and everything:

> The sausage is a cunning bird
> With feathers long and wavy
> It swims about the frying pan
> And makes its nest in gravy.

or

> Thirty days has September
> April, June, and November
> All the rest eat peanut butter
> Excepting grandma
> And she drives a Buick.

There are thousands of such verses, rhymes, and jokes in the
play of children today: a vast repertory for thinking differently
about ordinary events and a model, we would argue, of the
divergent, unconventional thinking of the modern American

child growing up in a less traditional society than ever before, but paradoxically creating his own play traditions to bring some order out of the changing situation.

In conclusion, it is the intention of this chapter to indicate what seems to be the beginning of a radical change in folk-game analysis. Instead of viewing games within the traditional Puritan Western cultural perspective as trivial phenomena or as phenomena merely reflecting earlier cultural practices, modern scientific analysis suggests rather that games are always essentially representative of the life and times of their players. Within this perspective, the more detailed analysis of the folk games of American children has much to offer in understanding the psychology of the children, the creativity of the modern generation, the character of the times, and the continuity of these games with earlier historical periods and earlier methods of folk representation.

17

"The Wisdom of Many": Proverbs and Proverbial Expressions

RAY B. BROWNE

Proverbs and proverbial expressions are now and apparently always have been an integral part of people's lives. They are an element of the culture of people on all levels of society, from the most ignorant to the most sophisticated. The various levels, to be sure, possess and employ proverbs in different ways. To the most credulous members of society, proverbs and proverbial expressions are the accumulated knowledge of the ages, the voice of history; they are tried and true, and as such are pragmatic, unassailable wisdom. Proverbs to these people are so true that to a certain extent they are a folk exemplification of the words of George Santayana that if one does not remember history he will be doomed to relive it. Except that, essentially conservative as these people are, reliving history would be pleasure, not doom.

At the other intellectual extreme, among the most sophisticated people, proverbs are considerably less important. They are to be viewed with great detachment, perhaps with condescension, often with derision and humor. With such people, proverbs must be avoided at all costs. In the intermediate strata of society, attitudes toward proverbs are modifications of these extremes. But regardless of the society in which they are used, proverbs and proverbial expressions are always recognizable coin of the realm, a part of the currency of all members, both high and low.

Despite the fact that proverbs have existed for a long time and among many peoples, not much critical and analytical attention has been paid them by serious scholars. This lack of critical attention is perhaps understandable, for proverbs are in many ways so elusive as to frustrate scholarly analysis, especially in the matter of definition. Like the weather, which Mark Twain said everybody talks of but nobody does anything about, proverbs simply exist; they are. Even the matter of definition scarcely satisfies everybody. The narrow ones are too exclusive to admit all aspects; the broader ones are so inclusive as to be without sharp boundaries and therefore are virtually meaningless.

Perhaps definition, as Archer Taylor said in his thorough study *The Proverb,* is "too difficult to repay the undertaking." Professor Taylor, of the University of California at Berkeley, is undoubtedly the greatest living authority on this subject. After a lifetime of working on the genre, he still approaches definition in cautious and general terms. The old description of proverbs as "short, plain, common, figurative, ancient and true," as Taylor and B. J. Whiting, another authority, say, is "as good as any formal definition." In probing for more preciseness, these authorities characterize the proverb as a saying which "summarizes a situation and in its own inimitable way passes some sort of judgment on it or characterizes its essence." It must be in tradition: that is, it must have or must have had currency among the people. The old definition—"the wisdom of many and the wit of one"—is perhaps as sharp and effective as any.

Such definitions, however, fail to distinguish precisely between proverbs and other similar categories, such as clichés, aphorisms, sententious remarks, and familiar quotations. Especially is the demarcation inexact when the category is expanded to include proverbial expressions, as it generally is. But the actual line of demarcation between these similar types and proverb, if it in fact does exist, is often so indistinct as to be indistinguishable.

Some caution of course must be used when one is insisting on the currency of proverbs as a criterion for their legitimacy, especially if the only examples are to be frozen in the printed word. A single inclusion in print, though the example may seem to have the trappings necessary for wide currency, is proof of only a single use. But even if the particular item may in fact have been severely limited in circulation, it is not necessarily invalidated as a legitimate proverb. Though one swallow may not constitute a summer, sometimes one printed example of usage may in fact attest to a sufficient amount of currency to constitute legitimacy.

In classification, proverbs fall into two categories: the literary and the non-literary or traditional. Despite the fact that Professor Taylor and others insist that there is only a negligible difference between the two, there is a very important distinction. These terms do not refer to point of origin—which we shall turn to in a moment—but rather to means of transmission, and consequently to differences in sophistication, to level of language, and to attitude.

The literary proverb is obviously wittier, more polished, usually less terse, less idiomatic, less earthy than its "popular" counterpart. A good example is the Biblical proverb, "To every thing there is a season, and a time to every purpose under the heaven." In Shakespeare's *Comedy of Errors*, these words became, "There's a time for all things." The traditional, or non-literary, proverb is rougher, less polished, more homely in its references to daily life, more idiomatic and slangy. Thus the proverb just quoted attains in tradition a greater brevity still, and consequently a greater thrust: "There's a time for everything."

Another example will cast further light. Thales of Miletus (636–546 B.C.) is supposed to have advised, "Take time by the forelock." Edmund Spenser, the English poet, rhapsodized, "Tell her the joyous time wil not be staid / Unlesse she doe him by the forelock take." In American usage the proverb has received varied treatment. Nathaniel Hawthorne kept it dignified: "Father Time, together with the old gentleman's gray forelock." James Fenimore Cooper made it more idiomatic: "To have l'arnt to take time by the forelock." The humorist Benjamin Shillaber made it even more idiomatic: " 'I'll take Time by the foretop,' as Solomon says." Louisa May Alcott and others have wrenched that proverb even further from its original, by saying, "I will try to take time by the fetlock." Another proverb, "He who hesitates is lost," has been tainted in American idiom with a great amount of anti-feminism: Oliver Wendell Holmes, in *The Autocrat of the Breakfast Table*, changed it to read, "The woman who 'calc'lates' is lost," and other authors have altered "hesitates" to "deliberates."

The origins of proverbs, although in many instances demonstrable, often are shrouded in mystery and ambiguity, and thus baffle the most assiduous speculation and scholarly spadework. Sometimes *a* point of origin, if not *the* point, can be found. Frequently, however, all the student can say about this aspect of proverbs is a paraphrase of what Topsy in *Uncle Tom's Cabin* said about herself: they just growed. Sometimes the growing is circuitous, obscure, even hidden. For example, the proverb usually attributed to Abraham Lincoln—"Don't swap horses in the middle of the stream"—quite possibly was only a re-use or a retooling by Lincoln, the politician, of an older and widespread bit of folk wisdom. Petrarch voiced the apothegm, "A good death does honor to a whole life." But nobody knows much about the origins of the burlesque version of the same philosophy: "A good flight saves life again." Franklin D. Roosevelt's call for a "New Deal" was a re-use of a plea that has been ascribed to numerous persons, among them Mark Twain, all of whom may in fact have "invented" it; the thought probably is as old as cards. Parenthetically, President Harry Truman's call for a "Fair Deal" consciously paralleled Roosevelt's "original" so closely as to be merely a variant.

"When in Rome, do as the Romans do" has only the most distant and questionable paternity in the words of St. Ambrose, as quoted by St. Augustine. On a trip, so the story goes, Augustine observed that the Romans did not observe the same fast day he had been used to. To learn which day he should fast on, Augustine asked Ambrose. Ambrose, according to Augustine, replied: "When I am here, I do not fast on the Sabbath; when I am at Rome, I fast on the Sabbath. To whatever church you come, observe its practice, if you do not wish to suffer or to create a scandal." In the earlier, longer, and much less quotable statement lies only the seed for the growth of the much more effective mutant.

Proverbs are developed in any of several ways. Professor Taylor believes that: "Some [proverbs] are simple apothegms and platitudes elevated to proverbial dignity, others arise from the symbolic or metaphoric use of an incident, still others imitate already existing proverbs, and some owe their existence to the condensing of a story or fable." Others spring from variations of existing proverbs, some are based on narratives, some are apparently verse, some are created by individuals, some are translated from other languages, and many are taken from the Bible. Other proverbial or proverb-like expressions clearly spring from verbal slips, conscious coinages, humorous perversions or alterations of existing serious proverbs. Though the life of some or most of these may not continue long enough to justify their being called proverbs, they are obviously short-lived variants which possess many characteristics of more "legitimate" proverbs.

Those proverbs which originate as apothegms carry the burden of instruction and sententious precept or maxim contained in such platitudes as: "A man can die but once"; "Seeing is believing"; "Truth crushed to earth will rise again"; "Truth wears many faces"; "All's well that ends well"; "The proof of the pudding is in the eating." Much more picturesque and effective are those proverbs growing from metaphorical observations of life. Since they spring from event or act, some are as old as time, while some are as young as today's happening: "New brooms sweep clean"; "Barking dogs don't bite"; "It pays to advertise"; "Half a loaf is better than none"; "Look before you leap"; "A miss is as good as a mile"; "Mistakes will happen"; "Nobody's perfect"; "Politics makes strange bedfellows"; "Put up or shut up!"

The inventive power of the human mind and the great love for variation have led to numerous proverbs: "Politics makes strange bedfellows," probably, though not necessarily, derived from, "Misery acquaints a man with strange bedfellows" and "Poverty makes strange bedfellows." But because of the inviting nature of the statement about politics, its derivation from the older ones might indeed have been totally unconscious. "The nearer the church, the farther from God," dates from 1300. Chaucer said, "The ner the fire, the hatter is." Variations of one form or another are numerous and are found in German, Dutch, French, Italian, Latin, and many others. Some examples are: "The nearer to church, the later in"; "The nearer the Pope, the worse Christian"; "The nearer the bone, the sweeter the meat."

Numerous variants occur through transmission, possibly more in oral transmission than through the printed word. Probably one of the most widely varied proverbs is our familiar "A bird in the hand is worth two in the bush." John Heywood said in 1562, "A birde in the hand is worth ten in the wood." An even older form has it "three in the wode." Rumanians say that the captured bird is better than *a thousand* on the house. Other variants include the following: "Better one bird in the cage than four in the arbor" (Italian); "A bird in the pan is better than many in the air" (Frisian); "A bird in the snare is worth more than eight flying" (Latin); "One sparrow in the right hand is worth more than four out of it" (Latin); "Better a sparrow in the hand than two flying" (Portuguese); "Better one bird in the pot than ten in the wood" (Swedes in Finland); "Better a sparrow in the hand than a crane on the roof" (German); "A sparrow in the hand is worth a vulture flying" (Spanish); "A finch in the hand is better than a thrush afar off" (North Italian); "Better a feather in the hand than a bird in the air" (North Italian); "Better a sparrow in the pan than a hundred chickens in the pastor's yard" (North Italian); "Better a wood-grouse in the fist than nine or ten on the branch" (Finnish).

Numerous proverbs are thumbnail sketches of fables; in fact in many nations there is little distinction between fable and proverb. Many examples spring from Aesop: "Sour grapes"; "A dog in the manger"; "Don't kill the goose that lays the golden eggs." Ballads and folk lyrics generally originate in the creative mind of a single individual, thereafter to undergo numerous variations, perhaps even improvement. So, too, do many proverbs originate, if the sources could only be found. If a stroke of wit, an observation, is sufficiently valid, witty, appropriate, and quotable, it will catch on and be paid the supreme compliment of imitation and variation. Shakespeare was undoubtedly the greatest single creator of quotable and proverbial expressions. An old lady once taken to her first production of a Shakespearean play was asked afterward how she liked it and what she thought of the author. She replied that he would have been a fair writer if he had not used so many clichés. Shakespeare's expressions are indeed well worn and familiar, but hosts of other writers have enriched the genre. Francis Bacon supposedly gave us, "Knowledge is power." Benjamin Franklin floated hundreds of proverbs in the American language. Even so undistinguished a person as Calvin Coolidge gave us "The business of America is business."

Many proverbs are translated from other languages: "The die

is cast" (Caesar's words on crossing the Rubicon) and "A rolling stone gathers no moss" (Greek, recorded by Lucian); Latin contained two translations of the Greek version of "There's many a slip 'twixt the cup and the lip." Several other items that were probably translations are: "All that glitters is not gold"; "Rome was not built in a day"; "Strike while the iron is hot"; "Love is blind"; "Two heads are better than one"; "Beauty is in the eye of the beholder"; "Better late than never."

The Bible supplied many: "Money is the root of all evil"; "Pride goeth before a fall"; "Man proposes, but God disposes"; "The more he has, the more he wants."

Existing and serious proverbs are frequently altered or perverted. The serious proverb, "Don't throw pearls before swine," has its comical, academic variant in, "Don't throw fake pearls before real swine." Just as proverbs often are epitomes of longer stories, sometimes longer versions—anecdotes—are built humorously and jokingly from proverbs, as this example, which seems to have been popular the last few years, demonstrates. Based on the proverb, "Don't count your chickens before they hatch," it elaborates as follows. During the French Revolution, Robespierre was having unusual trouble with a particular nobleman, whom he was determined to capture and subdue. One day there was a pitched battle in Paris. The Count and his men were holed up in the houses on top of a hill, and were causing the Revolutionists considerable trouble. Finally, however, the Count's position was overrun and the Count captured, though his men escaped. The nobleman was brought to trial. He would not name his fellow troublemakers and was therefore condemned to be guillotined. He was taken out to the guillotine and his neck properly positioned, though Robespierre kept hoping that the Count would relent and reveal the names of his fellows. Finally Robespierre started counting to three. After the count of two, the nobleman realized that the execution was indeed going to be carried out and, blanching with terror, called out, "I'll tell." Robespierre raised his hand to stop the blade, but the executioner mistook the gesture for the sign to release it, and he allowed it to fall. Robespierre, frustrated and angered, chastised the executioner in these words: "You were too hasty. Didn't you see my sign? Haven't I told you, Don't hatchet your Counts before they chicken?"

No matter how obscure the origins of proverbs, their vitality and longevity are undeniable. These sayings, often with variants, surface on the wide stream of literature frequently enough to demonstrate how important the "wisdom of many and the wit of one" has been through the ages. The ancient injunction, "Know thyself," was attributed to the oracles and was inscribed on the walls of the temple of the Delphic Apollo. But it probably had been proverbial long before that time. Juvenal may have been searching for too much age and weight of authority when he said that this saying came from heaven, but it is a comment on the undoubted age of the proverb. The history of this particular proverb is paralleled by that of numerous others.

Anglo-Saxon writings contain numerous proverb-like expressions. For example: "The frost shall freeze, fire consume wood, the earth sprout, ice shall form a bridge. . . . The sea shall be restless. The solemn way of the dead is longest secret. Holly shall go to the fire. The property of a dead man shall be divided. Fame is best."

In the Middle Ages great stress was placed on generalized wisdom, and thus on the importance of proverbs. This stress continued up through the Renaissance. In 1562, for instance, John Heywood published his *Dialogue Containing the Number of the Effectual Proverbs in the English Tongue.* This collection, purporting to be "all the proverbs" then in English, is a treasure trove of sixteenth-century English proverbial wisdom. Like many people before and after him, Heywood felt that his proverbs "much may profit both old and young." Three examples from his many will have to suffice as windows into his world of proverbs:

Look ere thou leap; nay, thou canst in no wise brook
To look ere thou leap, for thou leapst ere thou look.

Thou canst hold my nose to the grindstone.
So cannot I thine, for thou hast none.

One nail driveth out another with strokes so stout
That the hammer-head which driveth them wear'th quite out.

There were also during these centuries numerous collections of a particular kind of proverb, the *brocard,* or short traditional legal principles used as textbooks. This tradition lasted on through the Renaissance, the Elizabethan Age, and into the Neo-Classic period. Francis Bacon collected these *brocards*, as did William Noy, who in 1641 published his *Treatise of the Principal Grounds and Maximes of the Lawes of this Kingdom.*

In America the most famous single compiler and user of general proverbs was undoubtedly Benjamin Franklin, who in his *Poor Richard's Almanac* not only capitalized on them—utilizing the most practical in his collection called *The Way to Wealth*—but also strengthened the sense of their authority simply by endorsing them with his imprimatur. Franklin's sources were various publications and the people. In the preface to *The Way to Wealth*, Franklin commented that though few learned authors quoted his proverbs, the people, "the best judges of [his] Merit," often quoted him. Examination of Franklin's proverbs reveals the strength of the traditional proverb, for Franklin rewrote most of the ones he used, turning them into more earthy, sententious, idiomatic statements. Comparison of Franklin's sayings with the originals indicates the marked difference between the literary and the traditional types. Unfortunately we have space to quote only a few of Franklin's adages: "A fat kitchen makes a lean will"; "A small leak will sink a great ship"; "A word to the wise is sufficient"; "The sleeping fox catches no poultry"; "Early to bed, early to rise, makes a man healthy, wealthy and wise."

The importance of proverbs in American everyday life remained steady up until the Civil War. After that holocaust, however, new forces began to work at more sophisticated levels. In urban literature in particular there was an increased demand for realism in attitude and expression, with a consequent and necessary use of everyday idiom and exploitation of customs and humor, and with great emphasis on proverbs. Especial interest centered on the particular kind of proverb called a "Wellerism," that is the type that ends with the tail "as . . . says." This type is very old and extremely widespread. It is known now as Wellerism because of its particularly effective use by Sam Weller in Dickens' *Pickwick Papers*. It was widely used in America during the nineteenth century because of the comical qualities it supposedly possesses. For example: "Every man to his own taste, as the man said when he kissed the cow"; "What next, as the woman said to the man who kissed her in the tunnel"; "Didn't

I tell ye so, as the old woman said when the hog et the grind-stone."

In content—an aspect that has excited considerable specula-tion—proverbs range as widely and deeply as life, being formed from practically all elements of existence, though some areas quite naturally feed more readily than others into proverbial lore. Customs and superstitions provide fewer proverbs than might be expected. The Devil is far and away the most wide-spread supernatural figure in them: "Give the Devil his due"; "The Devil drives a hard bargain"; "The Devil is beating his wife around a stump." Superstitions and customs deriving from racial, ethnic, national attitudes and characteristics supply a good number, as do differences in sex: "Redheads have bad tempers"; "Rats desert a sinking ship"; "A whistling girl and a crowing hen / Will surely come to no good end."

Proverbs that grow out of historical events are often short-lived unless they are generalized and thus made more useful. "One if by land and two if by sea," referring to the hanging of the signal lamps in the belfry of the Old North Church in Boston at the beginning of the American Revolution might be classified as proverbial, and it has endured because of the significance of the event. Also the current use of "Minute Men" among the extreme rightist groups in America today is proverbial, and persists because of the importance of the historical reference. But proverbs usually have to do with matters of common knowledge, rather than with teaching dates and events.

One of the richest sources of proverbs is man's fear and hatred of his fellow man, his xenophobia. Man is always willing, even eager, to characterize, deride, spoof his fellow man, especially if in so doing he thinks he is raising himself in the eyes of the world or in his own. In such proverbs there are of course numer-ous examples of man's earliest objects of derision, women—anti-feminism, fear and hatred of women, especially wives. Two or three American examples will suffice: "No Irish need apply"; "The only good Indian is a dead Indian"; "Kentucky for fast horses and pretty women"; or its comical variant, "Kentucky for pretty horses and fast women."

The weather provides many proverbs, often in the form of rhymes: "If the geese go out to sea, / 'Tis good weather there will be"; "Evening red and morning gray / Speeds the traveler on his way"; "If loudly sounds the distant bell, / A coming rain it does foretell."

Somewhat less numerous are medical proverbs which suggest ways of achieving and maintaining good health: "Never drink milk with fish"; "After dinner rest a while / After supper walk a mile"; "A hair of the dog that bit you." Also less numerous are such conventional phrases as "Ask me no questions and I'll tell you no lies" and "A little bird told me"; and such political lore, as, in America, "As Maine goes, so goes the nation."

The study of proverbs, though a fascinating subject, has generally proved a fruitless area for study. Proverbs vary too much and in too many ways to be schematized. One characteristic of some proverbs is alliteration: "Many men, many minds." Some contain figures of speech, but many do not: "People who live in glass houses should not throw stones." Some contain metaphors: "Hunger is the best cook." Some exhibit parallelism and contrast: "Like father, like son," "Nothing ventured, nothing gained." Many proverbs rhyme: "A friend in need is a friend indeed." Some are dialogues, and some are epigrammatic: "Time and tide wait for no man." There are undoubtedly other, relatively minor, types.

Proverbial phrases differ from proverbs only in lacking the rigidity of the latter. They are looser and more subject to change. Consequently they are harder to identify and classify, more difficult to distinguish from other, allied forms. Proverbs and proverbial phrases blend one into the other, and to try to separate them, except in a detailed study, is perhaps without real point.

Both, however, are important in the life of a people, perhaps more important than many persons recognize. In his essay "The Function of Proverbs in the Intellectual Development of Primitive Peoples," published in *Scientific Monthly*, in February, 1952, Edwin Loeb, of the University of California at Berkeley, insists that proverbs "were man's first great attempt at abstract thinking." In phasing man's growth in thought, Loeb says: "First comes play or magical thinking, the let's-pretend kind, then proverbs, next deductive reasoning . . . and finally the objective reality of inductive science."

In less primitive societies the importance of the "folk mind" has long been recognized. In early eighteenth-century England, for example, Andrew Fletcher said, "Give me the making of the songs of a nation, and I care not who makes its laws," a popular aphorism that emphasizes the importance of the sinew of songs in the body of a nation. No less important are a country's proverbs, for, as Francis Bacon long ago observed: "The genius, wit, and spirit of a nation are discovered in its proverbs."

18

Riddles: "Do-It-Yourself Oracles"

WILLIAM HUGH JANSEN

What more fitting way to open a discussion of riddles than to pose a question, particularly a question to which everyone knows the answer and yet no answer for which agrees with any other? What is a riddle?

A riddle is a question, direct or indirect, complete or incomplete, in traditional form whereby the questioner challenges a listener to recognize and identify the accuracy, the unity, the truth, in a statement that usually seems implausible, or self-contradictory, but that is in its own peculiar light always true. The riddle is universal, as every folklore collector who has ever tried to collect riddles has discovered—once he has also discovered the proper local term by which his informants identify the riddle concept.

Probably no single factor explains the universality and the popularity of the riddle, but certainly of major influence is the fact that the riddle affords man the opportunity to exercise his reason or, more accurately, to witness reason being exercised. And man has always proudly considered the power to reason a most precious talent, if not a distinction and a justification for a sense of his own superiority. Man has long been concerned with reason, and perhaps more particularly with deception and with the ability to unravel deceptions. Indeed many cultures or mythologies have considered divine both the power to deceive and, naturally, the power to recognize and frustrate deceit. For most of us today, it is to be supposed, such a concept of wisdom seems rather limited if not shoddy. Yet to man's awe for this limited wisdom must be attributed the trickster gods in many of the world's mythologies. And, more to our point, to that same awe can be attributed the popularity of many traditional patterns that are kin to the riddle.

Such is the oracle of classical antiquity with its frequent ambiguity. Thus the ancient Greek must have been delighted when he himself was not misled, as Psyche's parents had been, by the oracle which predicted that their daughter would never marry a man (she didn't—she married a god). And the same ancient Greek must have felt a kind of intellectual pride when he recognized or solved a Homeric epithet and equated the "city of the broad roads" with Troy and the "goddess of the white arms" with Hera or when he recognized the artfulness in that ambiguity which today is termed dramatic irony. So, too, the Saxon of long ago must have felt satisfied with himself when he recognized that the kenning "whale's road," with its ambiguity (how can there be a road at sea?), meant the ocean. And I venture nothing is so old—or so modern—as man's self-congratulatory pleasure in his ability to resolve the ambiguity in such oxymorons as "wise fool," "cruel mercy," and "cold comfort."

The oracular prediction, the Homeric epithet, dramatic irony, the kenning, and the oxymoron are, of course, neither riddles nor the ancestors of the riddle. Indeed it is not impossible that riddling antedates some or all of these devices. But all of these devices have one element in common: they flatter the audience by allowing it to feel that it shares with narrator or performer a superior mental ability that enables one to see through an ambiguity or a kind of anonymity. The riddle very often, perhaps even more often than is always realized, creates exactly the same flattering effect in the auditor.

Allow me one other point of pontification about that dangerous generalization, man. In addition to being intrigued by ambiguity and uncertainty, man has been fascinated by analogy for a long time. How old is allegory, symbol, or metaphor?

Aristotle recognized a relationship between riddle and metaphor —a relationship which I would guess is a prerequisite to the concept of riddling, although admittedly not all riddles are explicitly or implicitly metaphorical. Living as we do in a world where athletic organizations rejoice in such names as Tigers, Wildcats, Lions, Eagles, Bears, Giants, and now Jets, we should have some sympathetic understanding of totemistic myths or of the enthusiasm evoked by a Homeric simile. Again man feels superior by the very act of recognizing likeness, particularly of understanding the comparison of incomparables.

Let us see how two famous riddles illustrate these two rather broad and abstract concepts: (1) satisfying man's desire to be assured that he can understand ambiguity, and (2) allowing him to see analogies. The first is the Sphinx riddle widely circulated by both folk and literary means: "What is it that walks on four legs at sunrise, on two legs at high noon, and on three legs at sunset?"

The ambiguity is easily isolated. What walks on four legs but a quadruped? What walks on two legs but a biped? And is there anything in nature that walks on three legs? Further, there is a kind of deceit in the initial phrasing whereby crawling on hands and knees is trickily called walking on four legs. Remember that, in the folk mind, successful trickery equals admirable wisdom. So ambiguity boils down to the inference desired by the riddler that there is one being who is somehow quadruped, biped, and "triped."

The analogies are a little more complex, and of course from the recognition of them comes the solution of the riddle. The first has already been spelled out: the similarity between an infant crawling about and an animal walking on its four feet. The second analogy is between an old man's cane and a supplementary leg necessary to hold up that old man in his infirmity. And the third (not always present in the folk forms of the riddle, incidentally) is the appealing cliché comparing one man's life to the course of a day. If one could not answer the riddle of the Sphinx, or if he were merely the witness of someone else's inability to answer that riddle, I contend that once he heard the answer given he would still be pleased and flattered by his consequent ability to comprehend both the ambiguity and the metaphorical aspect of the riddle.

My second example is a riddle whose very wide distribution

seems to owe nothing to literature. At the risk of seeming
facetious, I am going to repeat the form in which I have collected
it several times. Its crashing innocence of conventional grammar
gives to this form for me a whimsical charm:

> White as snow, but snow it ain't;
> Green as grass, but grass it ain't;
> Red as blood, but blood it ain't;
> Black as ink, but ink it ain't;
> What is it?

Part of the ambiguity is, of course, spelled out *seriatim* in the
very riddle itself. However, there is more than the separate
ambiguities. How can one item be simultaneously like snow, like
a plant, and like two different liquids? And how can one item
be four colors at the same time? Here again is the deceit. The
riddle doesn't say that the object is all four colors at once, but
the riddler's victim is likely to make this inference. Certainly
these is nothing to prevent such an inference. Or is there—in
the progression of snow, grass, blood, and ink?

Again the analogy becomes obvious once the answer is known
—and I doubt that many contestants ever solve this riddle the
first time they hear it. In urban English the answer is a blackberry, a name which gives a key to the answer, a key that is not
present in the only names for the same fruit that my mountain-
residing informants know: brambleberry or briarberry. Whatever its name, the fruit starts in the early spring as a snowy-white
blossom, then forms a tiny green fruit which turns red before it
finally ripens into a purplish-black, smallish berry about the
size of a thimble. Again, the auditor upon hearing the answer
sees the ambiguity resolved and the unreasonable analogies made
reasonable. That auditor therefore feels that he has performed
a mental act—he has understood.

In a broadly and abstractly psychological sense, two functions
of the riddle have just been illustrated. In even more general
terms, those two might be grouped into a single function: the
riddle develops or strengthens the ego of the riddler, of his opponent, and of the audience present at any riddle contest. And
this, I believe, is a true function of riddles wherever and whenever they are told. Certainly, the folk themselves do not so
understand or define the function of riddles. From their point
of view, riddling is usually entertainment, a pastime, "something

to do." In certain cultures, however, riddling has now or has had in the past various religious connotations as an appropriate activity during the harvest, or funerals, or other rituals. For the members of such a culture, riddling at inappropriate times might invite fears of attracting undesirable supernatural spirits or of offending desirable spirits—fears that would hardly be defined as entertainment.

Various scholars have identified other more specific or more limited functions for riddling. Riddles are, it is claimed, instructive and therefore elders encourage the young to perform them. I doubt that this is a major function, particularly in a literate society; and unlike some other folk genres, riddles thrive in literate cultures. And I doubt that any great rational powers are developed by the practice of riddling. Further, I venture that riddling contests are usually not tests of skill and wit but rather tests of performance and memory. When a contestant hears a familiar riddle, he does not halt his opponent with "I have heard that one before"; instead, he hears the riddle to the end and then gives the answer to the discomfort of the riddler and the delight of any onlookers. Field experience with American riddlers yields an interesting bit of evidence to support the contention that, at least in America, riddling is more nearly a performance than a contest: American riddlers do not *ask* riddles or *set* riddles; they *tell* riddles—the same idiom that is used for tales and jokes.

Other functions cited are the relief of anxiety and the socially acceptable venting of aggressive tendencies. Probably both of these are valid functions, but certainly they must be subconscious and not recognizable by the riddlers themselves. A minor function fully recognized by American riddlers (and I feel sure by other riddlers as well) is the provision of social communication between elders and children, particularly—in rural America, at least—between visiting elders and the children of the family being visited.

Next to function in importance, and receiving far more attention from scholars, is the problem of structure. Here there is a vast area of disagreement; such disagreement is compounded by confusion about the demarcations separating *structure* and *style* and *content*. Modern conceptions of the riddle structure seem to stem, either negatively or positively, from the German Robert Petsch's dissertation published in 1899. While Dr. Petsch implied that an ideal true riddle contained five elements (an opening formula, a naming of the subject to be described, a descriptive statement about that subject, a misleading statement about the same subject, and a closing formula), he also realized that a true riddle may exist without the first, the fourth, and the fifth elements. Indeed, in English there are even a few riddles which contain only the third element: the descriptive statement. Necessarily, from the nature of the English language, in which a statement must have a subject, such riddles are grammatically incomplete. And in the nature of communication, it can be said that the subject is implied or "understood," and thus by a liberal interpretation such riddles contain both the second and third of Petsch's elements. Indeed, if one is sufficiently generous in his interpretation of what is implied or understood and of what is formula, he could make a challenging defense of a statement that the vast majority of true riddles, in English, at any rate, contain explicitly or implicitly at least four of Petsch's five elements. And let me add that there are in American English a number of riddles that contain quite explicitly all five of the Petsch elements and that to me these seem the most aesthetically satisfactory of all American riddles. What we know about the processes of degeneration and regeneration experienced by other folk genres, such as the folktale, during oral transmission could well give rise to some interesting but probably footless speculation about the disappearance and reappearance of various of the Petsch elements in the case of a given riddle.

Be that as it may, however, scholars—including Petsch—have realized that a true riddle is a true riddle whether it does or does not contain all five of the Petsch elements. Certainly opening and closing formulas are matters of form or style rather than structure. The greatest riddle scholar of modern times, Archer Taylor of Berkeley, has struggled valiantly over the years to define analytically the structure of the riddle in terms of the ambiguity which seems most commonly characteristic of true riddles: a paradox, a self-contradiction, a conflict within the riddle itself in terms of what it seems to be describing rather than in terms of the answer it is seeking. Taylor's masterpiece, *English Riddles from Oral Tradition*, (1951) will long dominate folklore research, not only in the English riddle but in the riddle in general. It classifies 1,749 riddles and hundreds of variants into eleven categories, basically in accordance with Taylor's emphasis upon what the desired answer is being compared to.

Not finding ambiguity or contradiction so common in the riddle as does Taylor, more recently Robert Georges and Alan Dundes have proposed a structural definition of the riddle which differs from Taylor's. Georges and Dundes allow for one or more descriptive elements (i.e., statements complete or fragmentary) about the riddle's subject instead of Taylor's two descriptive elements. Moreover, they point out only the possibility of "opposition" between two such elements, whereas Taylor makes the ambiguity very nearly a *sine qua non*. With their structural definition, Georges and Dundes then suggest a categorization into two great classes: "oppositional," riddles that fit the Taylor definition, and "non-oppositional" riddles. Further, they propose three subdivisions of the oppositional category according to the type of ambiguity involved. This is a very useful suggestion certainly and it is tightly and logically bound to structure, whereas the Taylor classification is basically tied to content. The two classification systems are really complementary rather than alternate possibilities.

Less essential to an understanding of the concept riddling than either function or structure—but significant in the appreciation of the aesthetic impact of the riddle—is the factor of style. Stylistically the riddle is frequently related to folk poetry. In English it may be heavily rhythmical or rhymed or both. And the meter or rhyme may rather artfully stress the oppositional elements in the riddle.

Consider, for example, the simple and very common riddle which goes:

> Riddle-dee, riddle-dee, I suppose:
> How many eyes and not a nose.

In addition to the rhyme, note that the four stresses established in the near-nonsense, near-baby talk of the opening line are used in the second line to stress the seeming contradiction and to make it a statement rather than a question. The answer, of course, is a potato, whose sprouts are called "eyes."

But even a riddle that has neither rhythm nor rhyme is likely to be in the form best suited to emphasize its seeming ambiguity and usually reserves the emphasis of the final position for that purpose. For instance:

What is black and white and read all over?

would place less emphasis upon its misleading pun if it were phrased: What is read all over and is also black and white? Or even if it were phrased: What is black, white, and read all over? Need I say that the answer is a newspaper?

The prose riddle also often demonstrates a keen understanding of the values of parallelism. The second "and" in the newspaper riddle just cited illustrates this point, but even better is:

What has four eyes and cannot see?

How less effective is: What cannot see although it has four eyes? Or: What has four eyes although it cannot see? The greater effect of the original depends at least in part upon the misleading impression, created by the parallel structure, that both descriptive elements are of equal significance. The answer to this riddle, which of course can be told only to and by literate people, is "Mississippi," depending upon the ambiguity created by the fact that the word "eye" and the letter "i" are homophones.

Obviously one of the stylistic devices of the riddle is the pun, utilizing both homophones and homonyms. The humor of the pun clearly is cherished by literate and illiterate alike, except of course where the ability to spell, as in the last citation, is a prerequisite to understanding the riddle. However, it should be admitted that it is fashionable among literate riddlers to greet answers that depend upon puns for their understanding with groans or howls of pretended disgust at the alleged unfairness of employing such a device. This, of course, shows that there is style even in the social context of riddling. All orally transmitted folklore implies, of course, a teller and a listener. A few folk genres, including the riddle, imply through their form a teller and a respondent, a kind of two-way communication. Even fewer, but still including the riddle by virtue of the rather complicated formality of its performance as a contest, imply two-way communication before an audience.

Thus the folk riddle, at least the English-language riddle in America, has style to a perhaps surprising degree. It employs such poetic or near-poetic devices as rhyme, rhythm, alliteration, personification, symbol, and metaphor—not all of which I have had the space to illustrate. It shows a realization, probably empirical, of the impact of such rhetorical devices as the climactic series and parallel structure. It reveals a rather sophisticated skill in wordplay and implies an even more sophisticated or pseudo-sophisticated reaction to such wordplay.

Let me digress for a moment to point out that such stylistic potentialities in the folk riddle probably explain the enormous popularity of the complex and often charming literary riddle, as this form was developed from the sixth century of our era in medieval Latin, Byzantine Greek, and Anglo-Saxon down into the seventeenth and eighteenth century, when it was still being practiced by such famous German, British, and French poets as Schiller, Swift, and Voltaire.

Such stylistic formality also explains why the riddle belongs to what Dundes aptly terms the fixed-phrase form rather than the free-phrase form of oral folk material. That is, a specific riddler is likely to use the same wording every time he recites a given riddle, although the form of that same riddle may vary from riddler to riddler or from one geographic area to another.

The stylistic formality, the wordplay, and the fixed-phrase aspect of the riddle all lead to the conclusion that any given riddle must be inextricably bound into the linguistic peculiarities of the language in which it is recited. Obviously, the riddle is a folk genre most difficult to collect through the medium of an interpreter. Yet it would be a rare foreigner indeed who could so completely master a language that he could perceive the delicate overtones of meaning and aesthetic experience that may be present in that language's riddles. However, this emphatically does not mean that all of the riddles in any one language are peculiar to that language and culture. While it may be true that the anomalies giving rise to some riddles are so striking that each of these riddles has been invented dozens of times, I think it safer to assume that the popularity of the riddling concept and its functions is so great that any good riddle could pass successfully through any language or cultural barrier and soon be adapted to the physical facts and cultural peculiarities of its new home. Thus the blackberry riddle cited earlier exists in dozens of languages, some as dissimilar as Russian, English, Armenian, and Spanish. That it might have been invented more than once is conceivable; that it was invented dozens of times is unthinkable.

It should be pointed out, too, that the popularity of the riddling concept has attracted to the pseudo-riddle form many other types of traditional folk questions and puzzles that are not true riddles: numerical puzzles, shrewd questions, questions that cannot be answered without special knowledge, practical jokes, and so on. It should also be pointed out, however, that in general the folk do not distinguish between these false riddles and true riddles; such distinctions concern and disturb scholars alone.

There are a number of aberrant subforms of what are really, I think, still true riddles. There is the riddle with a double ambiguity that leads to two answers, one obscene; it serves as a kind of comic relief in the pretended contests that riddling performances actually are. There are pantomimic riddles, in which the riddler asks, "What is this?" as he gestures through an action that suggests fanciful analogies and sometimes ambiguity, the answer to which frequently even involves wordplay. There are visual riddles, in which the riddler asks, "What's this?" as he quickly draws a few lines on paper that again create analogy and ambiguity. And again the answer may involve wordplay.

Finally there is a subform which I term the story riddle and for which I have a kind of personal affection. This type of riddle, not a true riddle in Taylor's sense, is also called in English the neck riddle and in German the *Halslösungratsel* (the neck-liberating riddle), since most of the stories relate how a condemned prisoner escaped his sentence by posing a riddle that the judge or the king or the jailer or the executioner, as the case might be, could not solve. In America the story riddle is rarely encountered, and it seems no less rare in other folk cultures.

Although I have heard of other methods of performance, in my own experience the riddler first tells the riddle and then, when his opponent "gives up," tells the story which incorporates the riddle. Incidentally, in various locations quite different stories are told featuring the same riddle. So in southern Appalachia the riddler begins:

> Riddle me, riddle me right:
> Where was I last Friday night?
> I sat high and looked low.
> Oh, how the wind did blow;
> Oh, how the leaves did shake;
> Oh, how it makes my poor heart ache
> To see what a hole that sly fox did make.

After being assured that his competitor does not know the answer, the riddler then tells the tale—with considerable documentation, as though it were true—of a young woman who had agreed to marry a handsome Mr. Fox, a newcomer in her village, and who had become suspicious of his intentions. One cold evening, seeing him slip furtively into the forest, she follows him until she hears him engaged in some laborious activities. In order to observe his actions, she climbs a tree from which she discovers to her horror that he is digging a grave. A few days later at a prenuptial party she recites her riddle:

> Riddle me, riddle me right:
> Where was I last Friday night? and so on.

No one can answer her riddle, but Mr. Fox disappears from the party and is never again seen in that village.

19

"*The Fear of the Gods*": *Superstition and Popular Belief*

WAYLAND D. HAND

The relentless climb of man from the primitive state to a life of increasing knowledge and culture has been marked by the retention of age-old folk beliefs—irrational ideas and superstitions that he has been unwilling or unable to discard. Whether these beliefs are idle bits of whimsy that have lingered on from a bygone day, or whether they are superstitious practices actively fraught with harm, they spring from the same seedbed of misinformation, ignorance, and darkness. Superstition has always flourished best where the mental horizon of man is low and his reasoning powers limited. If the connections between cause and effect are not properly understood, the untutored person of any time or circumstance may be prone to seize upon the first explanation of a phenomenon offered, and may, in the same precipitate way, even favor a striking or intriguing solution over one more sane and reasoned.

As we search back in history for explanations of the proclivity to interpret phenomena and events in subjective terms, we are confronted with the fact that not all so-called superstitious pronouncements were made as a result of purely personal inference. There seems always to have been a body of thought inherited from an earlier time, a residual element, a *superstes*, or a *superstites*. This residuum often carried the connotation of a suspect or rejected element. The exact etymology of "superstition" has never been agreed upon, but the Germanic equivalents would seem to support the notion of a faith or a false faith that has either lived on or has grown up outside the bounds of an accepted faith or belief. The German *Aberglaube*, the Dutch *overgeloof*, and the Danish *overtro* are terms that bear out both aspects, going somewhat beyond the Latin term in the matter of a non-canonical body of thought or a fabric of questionable ideas. Another Dutch term, *bijgeloof*, clearly establishes the fact that such questionable notions lie outside accepted norms of thought and faith.

Still another facet is seen in the closest Greek equivalent to superstition, namely, *deisidaimonia*, "fear of the gods." More clearly than any other definition, this Greek word expresses man's concern for the imponderable forces that lie behind the visible universe, awakening in him not only feelings of awe, but those of fear as well. It is this basic confrontation with the forces that surround him, whether they be animate or inanimate, that compel man to order his own world of thought and action. This compulsion appears to be universal, involving man, to a greater or less degree, in all stages of civilization, and prevailing upon him to profit from favorable conjunctures where he can, or to try at any cost to, counteract the supposed untoward or evil forces that beset him.

As noted, it is the belief in the internal and hidden forces that affect his life, as well as the outward events which he experiences, that drives man to seek out underlying causes and an inner logic. Since those motivating circumstances can never be objectively determined and proven once and for all, man speculates about them endlessly. He does not speculate alone, however, for his fellows have also been subjected to the same or similar experiences, are gripped with the same wonder about things, and suffer the same bafflement. They, too, contribute their own notions toward an analysis and a solution of the problems at hand; and together, in a constant give and take, they evolve what to them are plausible lines of cause and effect. Once causes have been determined, then necessary courses of action may be prescribed.

Since these measures accord with the best knowledge on the subject available within the group, they soon become an approved method of treatment in much the same way that factual and scientific data are handed down within the various trades and professions in modern life. Moreover, because the efficacy of the treatment or procedure has been "proved" to everyone's satisfaction, it can safely be recommended to others, and is thus passed on and finally handed down to posterity.

While it is commonly supposed that these old beliefs and superstitious practices are the legacy of people still in a primitive or benighted state, on the one hand, or that, on the other, these quaint and erroneous ideas are kept alive in the civilized community only by the unlettered folk, experience has taught otherwise. Superstition exists in all strata of society and is encountered among people of all degrees of formal education.

Leaving primitive man out of account, since much of his mental and spiritual life is based on but the most rudimentary knowledge of the physical world that surrounds him, let us look rather to representative people of our own time and condition for examples that will suggest the range of irrational beliefs and practices that help to make up the total body of modern-day mental baggage known as superstition: A New York financier feeling compelled to wear only a certain "lucky" necktie to the stock market; a merchant in Hamburg making the first sale of the day, at any cost, so that, analogically speaking, good sales may be guaranteed through the whole day; thrifty Dutch burghers believing that the clergyman celebrating the mass is able to detect witches in the congregation by lighted beehives dimly visible on their heads; North Carolina mountaineers pulling youngsters through split tree trunks to rid them of asthma and other ailments; English fishermen throwing part of the first catch back into the water so that the take from the sea will be bountiful; French fraternity boys "interring" an effigy of one of their number who has taken unto himself a wife; a former President of the United States campaigning with a rabbit's foot in his pocket; a sports announcer's not mentioning the fact that a no-hitter is in progress, lest the mere mention of the fact jinx the pitcher and nullify the effort; the belief in the eastern Mediterranean countries that vampires must be interred on islands separated by salt water so that these evil creatures cannot return; the strange notion, reported from several countries, that the mates of husbands or wives with so-called white livers die soon after marriage; the almost universal belief that blood innocently shed cannot be expunged; the strange faith in many parts of Europe that by making a pact with the devil a person may gain wealth and superhuman wisdom, and learn such diverse skills as playing the fiddle, shooting a magic bullet (*die Freikugel*) with unerring accuracy, sewing the seamless seam, or becoming an irresistible lover; the widespread belief that only innocent youths and maidens should pluck herbs intended for healing; the widespread dislike of a visit by a red-headed or light-complexioned person on the first day of the year, and the consequent securing of dark-complexioned "first-footers" or "early birds"; the universal taboo against three persons lighting a cigarette on one match; the numerous hunches reported from many countries that evil would befall the *Titanic*; the widespread faith in the magical efficacy of the numbers 3, 7, 9, and the universal dread of 13 in most parts of the Western world.

So the enumeration could go on through literally hundreds of thousands of items constituting the stock-in-trade of popular beliefs and superstitions in the civilized world. No one knows even approximately how many such outmoded beliefs may exist in any given country, since variations are easily devised and new items readily formed on old models by the processes of associate thinking. It is precisely this creative quality of mind that accounts for the wide ramification of simple ideas, and makes folk belief and superstition easily the most prolific genre of folklore surviving from an earlier time. One example of associative thinking will suffice to illustrate the easy movement of material from country to country, and the simple adaptability of individual items from situation to situation. It has to do with the taboo against whistling. This taboo seems to have been most prominently connected with ships at the time of sailing, when a sailor, merely by whistling, might inadvertently bring on a gale. On the other hand, when a vessel was becalmed, some canny salt could "whistle up the wind," as the saying went, but this act constituted a magical invocation and was not lightly resorted to. The taboo against whistling soon was discovered to exist also in the mines, but here the obvious connection with the wind was lost. The evil consequences of whistling later were thought to apply also to the theater, and particularly to actors' dressing rooms. How the taboo finally reached the city rooms of newspapers and other kinds of establishments has not been traced, but the fear that it might cause bad luck apparently was reason enough for the credulous to accept it without question on the basis of a seemingly logical association. Whether the original interdict rested on some thought that one would "whistle up the devil," as many scholars think, or whether it went back to the time when women were said to have stood by and whistled indifferently as gypsy tinkers forged the nails for Christ's cross, will never be known. The present-day aversion, in the folk mind, to a whistling girl, as contained in an old verse:

> A whistling girl and a crowing hen
> Will surely come to some bad end

is said to date from the alleged circumstance at the time of the Crucifixion. In Germany to this day, however, a whistling girl is thought to be of easy virtue, and some go so far as to say that she will surely end up in the world's oldest profession.

Superstitions are usually differentiated from folk beliefs by the fact that they are at once more intimate and demanding; generally they are of such importance that they may not be viewed simply as bits of passing fancy, but, on the contrary, must be espoused and followed. Moreover, compliance with the dictates of superstition invariably leads to error and eventual harm. The failure, for example, to render assistance to those struck by lightning, as in classical antiquity, or, in more modern times, the refusal to save a drowning man—both on the grounds that the gods or other forces were claiming their due—is superstition at its worst. Similar examples from our own time may be found regularly in the daily newspaper. Two examples from the field of medicine alone will suffice to illustrate the harm that can come from superstition, ignorance, and religious fanaticism: Negro mothers eating cornstarch to lighten the color of their unborn children, and thus made chronically ill; children dying because of the refusal of their parents to have them vaccinated or given other kinds of necessary medical attention.

For harmless ideas that rest on mistaken judgment or error many writers now use the term "folk belief" or "popular belief." These are the age-old ideas that arouse awe and wonder, on the one hand, or simply evoke idle amusement and delight, on the other. The ideas need not necessarily be false or misplaced; they may, as a matter of fact, rest in whole or in part on fact. Let us consider as an example the reported fact that prairie dogs, snakes, and owls live together in peace and amity in the selfsame burros on the Western prairies. This has been reported as a fact by trappers, naturalists, and other observers from the circumstance that skeletal remains of all three creatures have been found in the warrens. Little or no thought, apparently, has ever been given to the notion that these creatures might have lived in the burros at different times. Because of the outward circumstances, attention seems to have been focused wholly on the paradox that two well-known predators could possibly live together, let alone share quarters with the harmless prairie dog. Here one is so engaged and so enthralled by the mere suggestion of the paradox, that, far from investigating the underlying facts, he is ready to accept the report as true, and thus to take delight in the thought that sworn enemies can somehow coexist. Folk belief, then, is often a matter of attitude and a matter of faith. As in the folktale, one may speak here of "thé willing suspension of disbelief." Add to this the active will to fantasy, and one can account for how folk beliefs get started, and how they are propagated. All this, as I have said more elaborately elsewhere, is another way of saying that folklore and folk beliefs of all kinds are products, ultimately, of the imagination of man. From some points of view, one can apply Zola's famous dictum about literature to folklore, and paraphrase it somewhat as follows: folklore is fact refracted through human temperament, and enlarged upon by the wondrous and inexhaustible powers of the imagination.

Now that we have seen a random sampling of folk beliefs and superstitions which are encountered in Europe and America today, it will be instructive to look more closely at the whole field of such beliefs. First of all, let us return to the basic phenomenology of folk belief and superstition, as discussed above in a consideration of the thought processes of primitive man and, with modifications, of the untutored folk in our own society. In his simple view of the universe and in his daily nearness to nature as the source of his existence, man has always felt a close kinship to animal and plant life, has pondered the cosmic forces that surround him, and as a sentient being has also been keenly aware of the inanimate world. Even though he has often felt sovereign in his limited world, quite as often, perhaps, he has felt a loneliness and at the same time a great sense of dependence upon all things that his mind could compass. His lack of certainty about many of the things that surrounded him and the things he experienced tended to sharpen his senses and to alert him to every change, however slight. Lacking a body of dependable knowledge about the weather and the seasons, his simple animal and plant husbandry, and other pursuits which he followed as part of the daily regimen, he was forced to develop his own rudimentary science.

Since much of this body of knowledge or lore is based on associative thinking, false premises, or faulty logic, scholars, notably Sir James George Frazer, have assigned the term magic to the whole process. The dividing line between science and magic, as Frazer has pointed out, is often very slight, and the unprejudiced student will often have cause to wonder at the ingenuity with which certain propositions and practices are arrived at. Let us start with ominal magic. Ominal magic, or predictive magic, as it is called, rests on the premise that events or states of being can be foretold by observing things which are not immediately related yet which may possess some inner connection perceived only by the person who is able, or claims he is able, to read these signs. Thus rain might be predicted by the way birds fly, the shape of the clouds, the movement of insects, one's aching joints, or moisture forming on the pump, to mention just a few of countless such passive indicators. (Whether there is scientific merit to any of the signs cannot enter into our discussion here.)

Causal magic, on the other hand, must at least involve the observer in an attempt to see why the person wishing rain, for example, does certain things, for he acts specifically with a purpose in view and applies definite means to attain his ends. Stepping on ants, for example, reduces the poor creatures to a liquid mass resembling the water sought, but this is never stated, and may not be the real reason for doing it after all. Certainly the killing of frogs, the hanging of dead snakes belly-up over fences or the limbs of trees, or the hanging up of a daddy-long-legs does not in and of itself suggest the intended symbolism and magical effect. In a twentieth-century setting among literate country folk dare one even think of the carry-over of ancient animal sacrifice in this simple connection? While causal magic usually depends on something the performer does or perhaps says, as in the case of verbal magic, there are instances of magical results by failure to act, whether by design or inadvertence. A person who fails to inform bees of the master's death may lose the swarm as a consequence. Similarly, if in planting a field of corn, the sower inadvertently skips a row, there will be a death in the family that year. This last example serves to show the fine line often separating ominal and causal magic. As in the case of homoeopathic and contagious magic, which we shall discuss next, elements of one form may often be operative in the other.

In his classic discussion of sympathetic magic, Frazer differentiates two classes of magic that rest on associative thinking and the symbolic association of things not immediately related. For the first of these kinds of magic Frazer suggested the terms homoeopathic magic, which is a system of magic based on the law of similarity of things, and the general premise that like begets like. Mimetic magic and imitative magic are other terms for homoeopathic magic, and the latter term is still often used. Illustrations are best adduced from the field of folk medicine, where there is a belief that cures are effected by agents possessing similar characteristics or properties. The ancient dictum, *similia similibus curantur*, "similar things are cured by similar means," raised to a classic doctrine by Paracelsus, and elaborated further in the so-called doctrine of "signatures," decrees that jaundice, for example, should be treated only with plants of the same yellowish color, or that kidney ailments, to take another example, should be doctored with plants having kidney-shaped leaves, and so on. In other realms of folk belief one can also see homoeopathic principles at work: "If the first person who comes to your house on New Year's Day is a woman, nearly all your young chickens will be hens, but if the first visitor is a man, they will be largely roosters." Another example from the realm of husbandry decrees that "if you want to raise lots of strong pepper, make a person with a strong temper mad and get him to sow the seed." It will be noted that the first example is ominal in cast, since the host has no way of telling who will pay the visit. The second example, on the other hand, is definitely causal. Both are symbolic and imitative, of course.

Contagious magic, also subsumed under the rubric of sympathetic magic, rests on the law of contact, and envisions the

magical association of things even after separation. The notorious "hand of glory," or dead man's hand, known in the British
Isles and elsewhere in Europe, as well as in America, is an excellent case in point. The hand of glory is usually the hand of a
thief severed at the gallows, or exhumed, which other thieves are
eager to possess since it is thought to confer upon the owner the
skill and dexterity of the dead criminal in the matter of working
with locks and executing other skills of the burglar's art. Specifically, it may render the housebreaker invisible, or deaden the
sound which he might make. Contagious magic underlies much
of sorcery and witchcraft, particularly in magical operations where
parts of the victim's body such as nail parings, hair combings,
etc., are used in dolls (spite dolls) or other representations of
the victim. These dolls are then pierced, scourged, and even
burned. By the magical principal of *pars pro toto,* "the part for
the whole," the torments are not only symbolically visited upon
the victim, but actually so—at least in the folk mind—in terms
of the magical extension of the person resident in his severed
parts.

Our Victorian forebears apparently never gave thought to the
connection between the innocent gift of a lock of a sweetheart's
hair to the powerful magical and aphrodisiac uses to which
workers of magic put human hair. A superstitious practice—nay,
a serious folk ritual—reported from North Carolina, involves
contagious magic on two counts and a sort of symbolic magic as
well: "To keep a woman true, take some dirt from her right foot
track, and a wisp of her hair on the back of the neck, and stob
it into the hole with a hickory stob." The girl herself is presumably liable to control by virtue of her lover's having obtained
some of her hair, and a foot track which she has left. Addition-
ally, she is symbolically arrested from straying by his possession
of her foot track. Finally, she is vicariously held safe in a tree
by a magical process known as plugging. This single item will
suggest the intricate underlying ideas in a single magical pre-
scription, and I am sure Freudians might suggest additional
twists.

Additional kinds of magical practice may be seen in folk medicine, a field sadly neglected with regard to studies in medical
magic. Scholars in the British Isles, and even more so in America, have been mainly concerned with folk botanicals and regular

folk therapeutic procedures. As a first example of medical magic, diseases are transferred from the patient to other humans, including the dead, to animals, to trees, and occasionally to inanimate objects. This is often done by contagious magic, whereby a rag, a string, a kernel of corn, or something of the sort is brought into contact with the diseased part and then communicated to trees, bushes, or even fed to animals. Sometimes effluvia or excoria of the victim are plugged into trees in holes made with a gimlet, or nailed or wedged into bark, crevices, and the like. Magical riddance is further achieved by measuring the affected part with a string or a straw and then disposing of the agent in a damp or sequestered place, where it may easily rot and thus take the disease with it. The notching of sticks is done in much the same way, but these are disposed of either by being thrown over the left shoulder or cast into a flowing stream. Passing young children suffering from rickets, asthma, and other ailments through split tree trunks, through horse collars, under the rungs of chairs, or under rerooted vines is still encountered in America as a means of stripping off the disease. Likewise, crawling through the holes in stones caused by the action of water is still reported from the British Isles and France. These forms of magical divestment are very old.

Verbal charms and incantations are not only encountered in folk medicine, but throughout the whole range of folk belief and custom. They range from simple, childlike implorings for the rain to stop:

> Rain, rain, go away;
> Come again some other day!

to highly ritualized verbal adjurations involving either Christian or pagan elements, or, often, combinations of both. A charm for a burn will illustrate this more arcane kind of charm. People in the Pennsylvania German country who "blow out burns" repeat the following verse:

> The blessed Virgin went over the land.
> What does she carry in her hand?
> A firebrand.
> Eat not in thee.
> Eat not farther around.

In the name of the Father, and of the Son,
And of the Holy Ghost.

Saying these words, the healer then strokes the burn slowly three times with the right hand, bending down each time to blow on the wound.

In the various examples given, the reader will have noted a connection between mere folk beliefs and superstitions, on the one hand, and, on the other, the working out of these ideas in customs, practices, and rituals. There are all degrees of involvement; many of these practices are magical, others are not. Believing, for example, that it is bad luck to walk under a ladder, a person may make a habit of going around a ladder placed against a house or building. This is hardly a custom, for it involves but a single person. If villagers congregate in the fields at the end of the harvest, however, and dowse the last reapers with water or beer, they are carrying out an old custom which is based on the belief that this act will ensure the fertility of the fields for the coming year. An even more elaborate custom, also based on folk belief, is illustrated by the involved love divination ritual known as the "dumb supper," whereby girls meeting in a house silently set a table and serve a meal, often walking backward and working with their hands behind them, in hopes of luring the would-be lover to the home at midnight, where his face could be seen in a mirror.

As in the case of customs, there is also a close connection between folk beliefs and legends. Just as customs often represent the acting out of a belief, so legends illustrate belief and superstitions in actual examples. The great ten-volume dictionary of German superstitions, *Handwörterbuch des deutschen Aberglaubens*, rests more on collections of legends and customs than it does on compilations of superstitions *per se*. This circumstance can be explained, of course, by the extent to which folk beliefs and superstitions are actually believed. No mere listing of superstitions in books and articles can convey the intimate part these old notions play in the life of the people. It is for this very simple reason that folk beliefs and superstitions usually come up in actual life situations. They are rarely, if ever, discussed in a detached way; they are lived and experienced.

In one chapter it is impossible to treat all the genres of folk belief and superstition. Historically, and particularly in classical antiquity, great interest was attached to beliefs concerning the universe, and especially astral bodies. So great and lasting was this interest that astrology later became a more or less independent field of study. Likewise, early magic and divination subsequently gave way to a preoccupation with sorcery and witchcraft. Today witchcraft and black magic are fields of study apart from superstition proper, although the general principles of magic that apply throughout the whole field of superstition are operative in these special fields as well. Alchemy is a field of pseudo-science that never did figure importantly in superstition itself.

For purposes of classification, popular beliefs and superstitions may be grouped in categories that involve, first of all, the human body and folk medicine; then the life cycle, e.g., birth, marriage, and death; then economic and social relationships, including travel and communication, legal matters, the domestic scene, the school, the church, etc.; then witchcraft and magic, including divination; then ghostlore and the realm of the dead; then numbers and cosmic phenomena; and, finally, a group of subject fields that revolve around farm life—namely, the weather, animal and plant husbandry, and hunting and fishing.

The inquiring student of superstition must certainly speculate as to the eventual fate of a body of outmoded beliefs and ideas. No final answer to this question, of course, can be given, other than to reiterate what was said earlier about the astonishing tenacity of these old beliefs. Even though some of the more outlandish items are now barely believed, or only half believed, they somehow linger on as heirlooms of the hoary past, finding harbor with succeeding generations of people in all walks of life. It is safe to say, however, that the uncertainties and hazards of life, and the myriad unexplored and unexplained facts that man constantly faces, will always serve to inspire approaches and modes of thought that inevitably lead to the speculations and irrationalities that underlie superstition. To believe in the persistence of superstition, one need only witness the flourishing quackery in medicine, the inveterate preoccupation with gambling and assorted bunco schemes, the rising interest in astrology, and all the rest. In the light of this, it seems safe to say that although many age-old superstitions are no longer really believed, people somehow take delight in repeating them, and in musing about them. Perhaps this is only an idle soliloquy on how man has tried to rid himself of a cargo of superannuated beliefs and customs that, in the long run, have only brought harm, even though many of them have brought comfort as well as amusement to countless generations of people.

20

Folk Speech

RAVEN I. McDAVID, JR.

Although no one talked about folklore in my boyhood in South Carolina, it was a part of our everyday living in a way that the middle-class commuter of the 1960's can hardly imagine. True, my home was near the wealthiest block in the city, in perhaps the best residential neighborhood; but in a small industrial city in a region where distinctions of caste and class have always been important, it was impossible to be unaware of the presence of other groups. In fact, only half a block away was one of the Negro enclaves that characterized small Southern cities—originally the homes of the servants in our part of town—and between the Negro section and our street was a small buffer zone of local poor whites and some of the few recent European immigrants. To the north we could see the Blue Ridge on a clear day—an outpost mountain was almost at the city limits—from which, on Saturdays, the mountaineers came down in their covered wagons, bringing their produce, some of them having jugs of moonshine for local patrons hidden underneath the watermelons and string beans.

Summer camps in the mountains were just beginning to develop, and many of us hiked casually over the scenes of bloody feuds, and learned the history from the survivors. All of us had country relatives, and there was visiting back and forth. We felt that there were some differences between country Negroes and city ones, as between country whites and city ones. We knew that there were some educated Negroes, and some who were successful in business, but we never met any in our normal routine.

With the Negroes we did know, however, whether servants in the home or tenants on the farm, our relationships were characterized by a code of respect for each other's dignity, perhaps as outmoded in an industrial society as the traditions of the English rural gentry—and like that gentry, many of us showed a lack of wealth distressing by the standards of that same industrial society. Industry, in our experience, was represented by the fiercely paternalistic cotton-mill village, with houses and store, schools and churches, all owned and controlled by the mill management; we were more uneasy in proximity to the cotton-mill operatives than we were in similar proximity to the Negroes, and if we were incredulous at the idea of Negroes voting, our elders were often indignant to think that the mill workers could and did vote.

Our region was one of relatively small farms, worked by the family and—for the largest—a few tenants. Although cotton was the principal crop, and the rural school year was governed by the growing season (a two-month "lay-by" school in July and August, with vacation in September and October so that children could help with cotton picking), cotton had never dominated the rural economy in the way it did elsewhere in the South, and there had never been a true plantation in the county. But as one drove toward the coast, cotton and the plantation became ever more in evidence, though the surviving plantations retained little of the elegance they were supposed to have once possessed. In the coastal plain we found Negroes far outnumbering the whites, and living in mysterious, half-isolated communities where a white man seldom appeared except as the merest transient. In the coastal cities we found the remnants of older traditions of aristocracy and commerce, which we inlanders might publicly mock but secretly envy. And halfway to the coast we passed the Dutch Fork, a tenaciously maintained religious-centered community descended from eighteenth-century German settlers, with few Negroes, a farm economy based on fruit and vegetables and dairy products, strange-sounding names, and an architectural tradition as peculiar as the Charleston side galleries with a door denying visibility from the street—the custom of not centering the chimneys on the ridgepole of the house but putting them a few feet forward, so that the back rooms had no fireplace.

The society was, in essence, a folk society—that is, one in which the important rules of conduct were not enacted formally by legislation or learned from books, but handed down from one generation to another. This was as true of the Episcopal merchant and the Baptist banker-deacon in the city as it was of the mountain moonshiner that both of them patronized. The assumption was that each group had its own customs, which other groups were morally bound to respect. In language, as in other kinds of behavior, this assumption worked implicitly; we knew that it was normal for cotton-mill workers to speak differently from store clerks, Negro farm hands differently from house servants, mountaineers differently from college professors. It was expected that a man's talk should reflect his upbringing and his personality; the notion that an outsider should sit in judgment on the speech ways of anyone in the community was as incomprehensible as the idea that, say, a Fijian should pass judgment on American mores. This attitude extended—and properly, we thought—even to the programs for teaching English in the schools. We may have had teachers who disapproved of particular words or pronunciations or, especially, grammatical constructions we used from time to time; but the disapproval was always based upon an appeal to the appropriate usage of educated men, not upon any fancied notions of correctness. No one would ever have thought of appealing to a dictionary to justify /grizī/ or /grisi/; dictionaries were for more advanced problems, such as whether "negotiations" was properly stressed on the first or the second or the fourth syllable. In short, it was assumed that the surest guide to good usage was the observation of what one's neighbors and friends said. Later, of course, I was to learn that there was a serious branch of linguistics, called "dialectology," concerned with the ways in which people use their language; still later, I was to shift my career to the study of these variations in the field, and to the analysis of the forces behind these variations. But the experiences I had faced as a child in a small town in the South Carolina up-country always stuck with me: languages are used by living human beings for communication in concrete situations; within a language, these differences can be explained in terms of the different experiences brought to the particular situation, or of the different purposes behind the intercommunication.

Unfortunately, the technical terms that scholars use for talking about these variations in language are not too well understood by the general public. Take, for example, the term "dialect." To some people, the term simply means the old-fashioned usage of old-fashioned people in out-of-the-way communities; it is to be applied to words or pronunciations or grammatical constructions that have survived from the past, but not to things that have been brought into existence and which may even be spreading. To some European scholars it seems incredible that Americans should be studying regional and local names for *kerosene* or *the baby carriage*, or pronunciations of such a word as *library*; these are characteristic of industrial civilizations, recent in their intro- duction into general usage, or the concern of educated people rather than the unsophisticated. And yet it is clear that *baby coach, baby cab,* and *baby buggy,* that *coal oil, carbon oil,* and *lamp oil* appear in clearly defined regional patterns, regardless of the education of the speaker; whether or not such words are characteristic of the dialect vocabulary in the traditional sense, they clearly set off regions of the eastern United States, and they are to be studied in the same way that one studies regional dif- ferences in names for pancakes or for the side meat of a hog; they are terms which one learns from his common experience rather than from books.

It is for this reason that students of American speech have adopted a method that is slightly different from the methods used by their predecessors in Europe to investigate regional and local differences. In investigating the local varieties of German, the scholars of the University of Marburg asked local school- masters for samples of what they considered local dialect. In organizing the *Atlas Linguistique* of France, Jules Gilliéron in- structed his field investigator, Edmond Edmont, simply to seek a good natural speaker of the local dialect in each community he visited; the same kinds of instructions were given the interviewers for the atlases of Italy and southern Switzerland, though—includ- ing larger places for the first time—they were advised to talk to more than one speaker in each city. But even in this investigation the persons interviewed were basically drawn from the oldest, least-educated, and least-sophisticated segments of the population.

These procedures did have something to say for themselves in the European situation—in France, in Italy, and in Germany. In each of these nations there is a sharp distinction between the standard language, a particular form learned by all educated people as a part of their education, and the more local forms of speech which are usually spoken by the least educated; in each of these countries there has been a long tradition behind making the upper-class speech of an important city or region the national model of excellence. But in English-speaking North America a different situation has prevailed: Bostonians, New Yorkers, Philadelphians, Richmonders, Charlestonians, Pittsburghers, Torontonians, and the rest base their standards of linguistic excellence on the usage of local people with good education and social standing. To ignore these variations in educated speech would be to ignore one of the principal characteristics of North American English; so it has been the practice to interview the highly educated as well as the uneducated, in all important centers and perhaps a fifth of the other communities. And because American society is traditionally fluid, with those of modest status in one generation frequently becoming the parents of the next generation's elite, an intermediate group of speakers has been investigated. In the *Linguistic Atlas of the United States and Canada*, the major survey of regional and social differences in American English, the three types of language represented by these three groups are often described as Cultivated Speech, Common Speech, and Folk Speech—the last being applied to the speech of the oldest, least educated, and least sophisticated.

Yet this classification, perhaps better than some of the others, is still not completely satisfactory. It uses too mechanically the index of formal education and formal exposure to the present-day dominant culture, and tends to overlook the ways in which each speaker group accepts and participates in and hands down the traditional language and lore of those with whom he grew up. John Voelker of Ishpeming, Michigan, a former justice of the Michigan Supreme Court and the author of several widely known books, is essentially a folk speaker, thoroughly identified with the traditional mores of his community, but many relatively uneducated Americans—principally, but not exclusively, in urban and suburban areas—have rejected the speech and the customs of their elders.

Thus, despite the well-known tendency to dichotomize between folk speech and the speech of the educated, there seems no justification for it in the American situation. Many of us are multidialectal in our speech, switching from one code to another as the situation demands, talking in one way to cotton-mill hands and in another to our fellow professors, without mixing the styles. In fact, it may be that some of the aspects of folk speech—the terms of hunting and fishing, of gardening, of home cooking—are best preserved among the highly educated, who are so sure of their position that they need not worry about conformity to other patterns.

Nor, though one traditionally associates folk speech with remote and isolated rural areas, is there any reason for it not being discovered in cities. In Chicago, for instance, my colleague Lee Pederson, in the course of his study of local pronunciation, uncovered a host of words not known elsewhere: *prairie* for vacant walk, *gangway* for a passage (usually but not necessarily covered) between two apartment buildings, *clout* for political influence, *chinaman* for one who supposedly can wield political influence (as in altering one's rank in civil-service lists), and *tax-eaters*, as a self-deprecating term used among city employees. Recently *juice* has become a well-known term for usury, usually for the kind extorted by strong-arm tactics with the help of the underworld (it is almost literally squeezed out of the victim); the *juice racket* has been under constant investigation, and several *juice-workers* have been sentenced to prison. For things characteristic of urban life, local innovations may arise spontaneously in several parts of the nation: in South Carolina I had no name for the strip of grass between the sidewalk (British *pavement*) and the street, but from my Minneapolis-born wife I learned that the term in her city was *boulevard*. In the past fifteen years I have encountered a variety of other terms for this strip: *parkway*, *parking strip*, and simply *parking* in various parts of the Middle West, *tree lawn* in Cleveland, *devil strip* in Akron (less than twenty miles south of Cleveland), and *tree belt* in Springfield, Massachusetts.

Nor is it accurate to assume that folk speech—the speech arising more or less spontaneously from day-to-day contacts—is limited to the phenomena of old-fashioned life. Things associated with modern technology and mass merchandizing can also have their own peculiar patterns of occurrence. In most of the United States, one takes woolen clothes to the *cleaners* (or, perhaps more formally, the *dry-cleaners*); in metropolitan Boston they are taken to the *cleansers*; similarly, in the Boston whole-saling area one uses *tonic* to describe the carbonated non-alcoholic bottled beverages that elsewhere in the United States are marketed as *soda*, *soda pop*, *pop*, or simply *soft drinks* or *cold drinks*. Some generations ago New Orleans gave to the world the *poor boy*, a sandwich of many ingredients served in a small loaf of bread sliced lengthwise; in the past two decades the same kind of sandwich has appeared in many other communities, under other names—*hero* in New York City, *submarine* in metropolitan Boston, *grinder* in upstate New York, *hoagy* in Philadelphia. Refrigeration has taken to the remotest crossroads the concoctions made from ice cream; but in eastern New England —unlike most of the United States—a *milkshake* contains only milk and flavoring and a little ice. Here, if one wishes a drink with ice cream, he orders a *frappe* /fræp/ or a *cabinet*. And I still recall my disappointment the first time I ordered a *chocolate soda* in Washington and received no ice cream; in South Carolina, to omit ice cream would have been unthinkable. With such variation in products of the soda-fountain age, it is no wonder that the older generation still hotly argues as to whether the essential propellant in a *mint julep* should be bourbon, rye, scotch, rum, or brandy, or that the inlander is aggrieved when he discovers that in New York City bars the label *rye* is applied to blends of neutral spirits and that the traditional Maryland and Pennsylvania rye whisky is unknown.

It is clear, then, that the study of folk speech involves more than the tracking down of Middle English or Celtic survivals in remote areas; it also involves the discovery of innovations, and the ways in which they are disseminated. It is inextricably related to the general study of the regional and social distribution of linguistic forms, and to their relationships to the historical and social and cultural forces to which we are all heirs. It concerns the distribution of old-fashioned words like the common names for curdled milk—*loppered milk, bonny-clapper*, or *thick-milk*—and the names for varieties of fancy doughnuts (*long John, Bismarck*) or breakfast pastries: Chicagoans have an array of terms such as *sweet roll* and *crescent*, whereas New Yorkers seem content with *Danish*. It involves older grammatical constructions like *ain't* and the multiple negative, and innovations like the eastern Kentucky *used to* as a sentence-beginning adverb: "*Used to*, everybody around these parts baked their own bread." It involves older pronunciations like /dif/ for *deaf* and newer ones like the introduction of the /l/ *palm, calm*, words that have had no /l/ since they were brought into English during the Middle Ages, but where it has been recently introduced under the influence of ignorant schoolteachers and because of the spelling. It involves patterns of stress, like the rural Southern initial stress in *po*-lice and *De*-troit, or elegant urbanisms of stress like that of Clevelanders in the noun per*mit*, meaning a license to operate a saloon or carry a pistol. It even involves gestures, whether the retention of peculiar ones limited (like some of mine) to the northwestern corner of South Carolina or the spread of new ones, like the expansive hand gestures associated with the eastern Mediterranean or the Russian ghetto. It involves all the ways people habitually interact in a communicative situation.

In studying folk speech, as in studying other aspects of folk culture, we have long since passed the stage when a professor would simply record the quaint and curious language he observed during a summer on Cape Cod or in the Great Smokies. Such simple recording, valuable as it was in the earlier days, has long passed the point of diminishing returns; besides, we need to know what is the significance of what we have recorded. However interesting it is to note in a certain county in Kentucky a number of words and meanings once used by Chaucer, it is more important to find out how common these words are in adjacent territory and, should they be more common in one area than another, to suggest the reasons for their greater frequency. And in settling such matter, however tentatively, it is not only important to investigate other communities than the Kentucky hills but to find out about other kinds of words than those which seem to be derived from Chaucer's time. For this reason, it is customary to have a network of communities in the area under investigation—large and growing cities, most of the earliest settlements, stopover points on old routes of transportation, isolated communities with declining population, communities with homogeneous settlement from the eastern United States, the British Isles, or other countries, all the while maintaining a fair distribution according to both the area and the population of the region. In a community under investigation it is usual to interview at least the most old-fashioned and the moderately sophisticated, and often the cultivated; in more intensive studies, or in larger and more complicated communities, it is common to have many more speakers, with finer gradations of age and social standing. And the persons interviewed are chosen not because they happen to be available but because they belong to certain types the investigator is interested in.

The evidence is gathered by various means, but always with particular features of language in mind. A good deal of evidence on the vocabulary can be gathered by questionnaires mailed out to people in the community, but for pronunciation and grammar it is necessary to have a face-to-face interview. In either situation, however, it is economical and profitable to proceed from a prepared questionnaire of items that promise to be useful because they are familiar, are easy to talk about, and are known or suspected to have regional or social variants. Some of the items that have proved to be interesting and profitable are the pronunciation of *greasy* (which has an intervocalic /-s-/ north of Philadelphia, the negative of *ought* (*hadn't ought*) in the area of Yankee settlement), and the various names for the seesaw, cottage cheese, the dragonfly, and the earthworm. The last one illustrates the advantage of having a questionnaire to work from: Wright's *English Dialect Dictionary*, published in the first decade of this century without the benefit of systematic questionnaires, listed relatively few of the synonyms that have been found in North America—only the Rhode Island *eaceworm* and the Hartford-Windsor *angledog*, besides *angletwitch*, so far unrecorded in the New World. But the American patterns of distribution of such terms as *fish worm, fishing worm, mudworm, rainworm, eelworm, ground worm, redworm,* and the Canadian *dew worm* suggest that a variety of terms came to the United States with the earliest settlers; one speculates that the rural clergymen who collected so much of Wright's evidence simply would not recognize as dialectal the ordinary terms for the worm which they used themselves when fishing.

The gathering of the data is simply the first stage. Next comes the charting to see what are the patterns of distribution, and finally the explanations. Although in an absolute sense no two words or pronunciations pattern in exactly the same way, enough of them pattern alike for us to draw up dialect boundaries and to offer some characterization of the dialect areas which these boundaries enclose. Where words or pronunciations or grammatical constructions seem to radiate out from a well-defined cultural center—such as Boston, Philadelphia, Richmond, or Charleston —and where the marginal communities show that the younger and better-educated speakers are adopting the words and pronunciations favored in the center, we have a "focal area." Where there is no well-defined center, and where the typical words of the area seem to be surviving only in the oldest and least-educated speakers—especially in the marginal communities—we have a "relic area." Where the area is caught in the cultural influence of two or three cultural foci outside, and has no established cultural focus of its own, we have a "transition area." The Maine and North Carolina coasts are typical relic areas; the Shenandoah Valley and the South Carolina Piedmont are transition areas.

In the relationships between the study of folk speech and that of other aspects of folk culture we see the most significant differences between the attitudes of the older collectors and the younger scholars. An older generation of investigators would have concentrated on the relic areas, feeling that in such communities one would find the only true folklore—Border ballads, Scottish proverbs, East Anglian and Devonshire words. And in one sense they were eminently correct: in such areas one is most likely to see the survival of rapidly disappearing ways of life. But it is also true that in the focal areas a new kind of folk speech and folklore is developing, out of the interaction of different traditions. Metropolitan New York shows the mingling of southern British, Irish, Yiddish, Negro, and Puerto Rican traditions, each of which is rubbing off on the others; the same is true of Chicago, Detroit, Minneapolis, New Orleans, and San Francisco. The study of any of these communities in depth is likely to be more than anyone can handle in a single lifetime; but one job well done—like the survey of Chicago speech by Pederson— points out ways in which other jobs can be done to fill in some of the gaps in our knowledge. What all studies of folk speech accomplish is to point out the richness and diversity of our heritage and to develop on American soil a fuller understanding of each group's cultural traditions—an understanding that may result in a more intelligent appreciation of the common traditions of all mankind and a deeper respect for the particular traditions of other nations.

21

American Literature and American Folklore

HENNIG COHEN

The relationship between the folklore and the literature of any country is subtle and complex, for folklore and literature both attract and repel each other. Literature nourishes folklore, and folklore nourishes literature. But literature is fundamentally associated with literacy, a fixed text and a printed page, and folklore is associated with illiteracy, a fluid text and word of mouth. Where literacy thrives the folk decay, while a flourishing folk culture is evidence of a relatively low level of literacy.

The relationship becomes even more complicated in a country like the United States which, contrary to the experience of most nations, became self-governing before it had developed a distinctive national literature or folklore. The political independence of the United States was proclaimed on July 4, 1776. Art moves at a slower pace than politics, and although literary independence was often called for in the decades that followed the American Revolution, its attainment was less dramatic and required a longer period of time. The literary tradition and the folk tradition of the United States were largely borrowed, for time was needed to establish the distinctive cultural identity that is the seedbed of both. It is not simply coincidence that the Romantic Movement in Europe in the late eighteenth and early nineteenth century was characterized by a concern for the past, by nationalism that ranged from the sentimental to the political, and by a scholarly and literary interest in folklore. Herder's studies of myth and primitive poetry, Sir Walter Scott's ballad collecting, and Paulin Paris' editions of Old French epics imply a search for national identity.

Lacking a usable past and not yet having evolved a usable lore, the United States sought its national identity in the present. It looked to the common landscape and shared experiences, particularly the experience of immigration—the movement toward the Western frontier—to modify and replace the European traditions that the early immigrants brought with them to the New World.

Almost imperceptibly American literature came into being. The beginnings were the chronicles of settlement and factual descriptions of the American landscape and its inhabitants, human and otherwise, some of which bordered on the fabulous. For example, John Josselyn, an English naturalist, visited the Massachusetts Bay Colony in 1663 and reported on his travels in a little book called *New-England Rarities Discovered: in Birds, Beast, Fishes, Serpents, and Plants* . . . (1672). Like many a subsequent traveler to the backwoods of America, he let himself be hoodwinked by the natives who couldn't resist telling him tall tales that he accepted as gospel. Josselyn solemnly records: "The Pond *frog*, which chirp in the Spring like *Sparrows*, and croke like Toads in Autumn: Some of these when set upon their breech are a Foot high; the *Indians* will tell you, that up in the Country there are Pond *Frogs* as big as a child a year old." After describing the venomous rattlesnake, Josselyn reports: "The *Indians*, when weary of travelling, will take them up with their bare hands, laying hold with one hand behind their Head, with the other taking their Tail, and with the teeth tear off the Skin of their Backs, and feed upon them alive; which they say refresheth them." Clearly there was a humorous side to Indian-white relations which is not so well known as it should be, and an indebtedness to the Indian for establishing the frontier folk tradition of telling whoppers to gullible strangers who presumed to be superior to the unlettered natives.

The modest beginnings of American literature are also evident in the intrusion of American matter into the European literary forms, the only forms they knew, used by early American writers. Thus, when Ebenezer Cooke wrote a satire on life in colonial

Maryland called *The Sotweed Factor* (1708)—the title means tobacco merchant—he followed the form and style of Samuel Butler's *Hudibras*. But he packed his poem with local references to manners, customs, food, drink, and folkways. He, too, was plagued with prodigious frogs and rattlesnakes. He tried to sleep one night in an orchard but

> Hoarse croaking Frogs did round me ring,
> Such Peals the Dead to Life wou'd bring.
> A Noise might move their Wooden King:
> I stuff'd my Ears with Cotton white,
> And curs'd the melancholly Night,
> For fear of being deaf outright:
> But soon my Vows I did recant,
> And *Hearing* as a Blessing grant,
> When a confounded *Rattle-Snake*
> With Hissing made my Heart to ach, . . .

Meanwhile, as the chronicles of early observers and the imitative verse of early poetasters recorded and incorporated the American scene, the European folklore the early settlers had brought with them was also being altered; and gradually, as it acquired a history and heroes, the new nation was building up a body of indigenous legend and lore.

At this point, before we deal further in specifics, some definition is necessary. The term "folklore" is defined as the songs and stories, proverbs and riddles, beliefs and superstitions, the traditional ways of doing and saying things, that are passed along by imitation among a relatively stable, homogeneous people and created anew with each repetition. This is a narrow definition. It fails to take into account mythic patterns, ritual, archetypal figures, or even American stereotypes such as the Yankee peddler, the Uncle Tom, the frontiersman. Though these are provocative approaches to the comprehension of any literature, they are either too imprecise or too dogmatic for the purpose at hand, which is to describe in a general way how folklore appears in American literature.

Folklore appears in American literature in two ways: passively or actively, transcriptively or functionally. The most elementary way is passively. A writer presents a more or less authentic transcription of genuine folk material possessing considerable literary appeal in its original state. Joel Chandler Harris' *Uncle Remus*,

His Songs and His Sayings (1880), is a notable example of this kind. Harris, a native of Georgia, was sufficiently emancipated to recognize the charm as well as the less attractive slavish streak in the animal tales he heard from plantation Negroes. His first and most famous, "The Wonderful Tar-Baby Story," he once stated, "was written out almost by accident." It was begun as an exercise in the accurate transcription of Negro dialect. Closely related to the West African folktales of Anansi, the spider, it tells how Br'er Rabbit, the helpless weakling, outwits his more powerful foe, Br'er Fox—and beneath the surface how the slave outwits his master. A journalist and a modest man, Harris had no literary pretensions for his Uncle Remus stories but saw himself as recording faithfully folk material that he knew at firsthand. The setting of the tar-baby story is Uncle Remus' cabin. The story is held together by questions from a "little boy" addressed to the elderly Negro. Thus the literary framework is close to the situation of the anthropologist in the field, tape recorder at his side, interviewing an informant.

A Northern counterpart to Harris and a writer whose work he admired was Harriet Beecher Stowe, author of the anti-slavery novel, *Uncle Tom's Cabin* (1852). Mrs. Stowe wrote local color sketches of New England in the 1830's, long before this term gained currency. She is at her best, however, in *Old Town Fireside Stories* (1871) of a generation later in which she transcribes folklore and in other respects uses a pattern that Harris followed. She states her transcriptive intent in the preface to this book: "I have tried to make my mind as still and passive as a looking-glass, or a mountain lake, and then give you merely the images reflected there. I desire that you should see the characteristic persons of those times and hear them talk. . . ." She uses dialect and has a folk informant, the Yankee storyteller Sam Lawson. The setting is the hayloft of an old barn, and Sam is encouraged in his performance by an audience of country boys who ask leading questions, the procedure that Harris followed with Uncle Remus and the little boy in the cabin. Sam is assisted by a Negro hired hand who plays the fiddle and sings a ballad on the hanging of Captain Kidd. Kidd's gold—along with lost gold mines in the West and the Seven Cities of Cibola sought by the Spanish conquistadors—is the American equivalent of the Nibelungen hoard. Washington Irving in "The Money Diggers" part of *Tales of a Traveller* (1824) has stolid New York Dutch burghers search in vain for Kidd's treasure on Long Island Sound, and he gives us a few stanzas of the ballad on the hanging of Captain Kidd by way of background; and in "The Gold Bug" by Edgar Allan Poe an impoverished Southern aristocrat recovers Kidd's treasure on the Carolina coast.

Akin to the transcriptive occurrence of folklore in American literature is what might be called the pseudo-transcriptive, the attempt to produce something that passes for the real article. The imitation ballads of such Romantic poets as Thomas Chatterton or Gotfried Bürger are within a recognized convention, the literary ballad, but England and Germany were aware of their genuine native ballads, and for this reason the fabrications of the American poets, Whittier and Longfellow, are not precisely the same. Longfellow wrote "The Wreck of the Hesperus" within two weeks and fifty miles of the shipwreck that inspired it, yet he did his best to make it sound as much like the medieval ballad, "Sir Patrick Spens," as possible:

> "Last night, the moon had a golden ring,
>   And tonight no moon we see!"
> The skipper, he blew a whiff from his pipe,
>   And a scornful laugh laughed he.

"The Wreck of the Hesperus" is good of its kind, but one cannot help wondering to what extent Longfellow was writing within the European convention of the literary ballad and to what extent he was trying to supply his country with a made-to-order folk tradition. The work is transcriptive, in any case. Like Uncle Remus' animal stories and Sam Lawson's yarns about buried treasure, "The Wreck of the Hesperus" is an attempt to provide a sense of place, of tradition, of identity.

But literature is creative. It is not simply transcriptive. And this brings us to the second of the two ways in which folklore appears in American literature. Writers who are concerned with creating works of art rather than providing transcriptions from life (or when they cannot find what they would like to record, producing a synthetic substitute) use folklore functionally. Folklore is recognizably present, with all of the appeal and power that it has in its own right, but it is put to work. Folklore in American literature has been put to work in a number of ways —among them, to advance the plot, to characterize, to provide structure, and to defend, explain, and raise questions about the nature of the society. It is the last use on which we will focus our attention.

In 1765 Benjamin Franklin was in London as agent for the Province of Pennsylvania. One of the problems that beset him was defending the commercial position of the American colonies from neglect and from disadvantageous British regulations made on the basis of misinformation or misrepresentation. The British seldom bothered to get at the facts. A device that Franklin used was the hoax, in its Americanized version, the tall tale. With mock sobriety, he wrote a letter to the newspapers arguing on behalf of the credibility of foreign travelers who brought back with them seemingly incredible information. To prove that the apparently preposterous was perfectly true, he served up a couple of illustrations that he claimed he could vouch for, illustrations that happened to be pertinent to the wool trade and the fishing industry. "The very Tails of the American Sheep are so laden with Wooll," he wrote, "that each has a little Car or Waggon on four little Wheels, to support & keep it from trailing on the Ground." The second illustration is one that John Josselyn's Indian informants would have appreciated. Franklin soberly stated:

> . . . the account said to be from Quebec, in all the Papers last Week, that the Inhabitants of Canada are making Preparation for a Cod and Whale Fishery this "Summer in the upper Lakes" [is true]. Ignorant People may object that the upper Lakes are fresh, and that Cod and Whale are Salt Water Fish: But let them know, Sir, that Cod, like other Fish when attacked by their Enemies, fly into any Water where they can be safest; that Whales, when they have a mind to eat Cod, pursue them wherever they fly; and that the grand Leap of the Whale in that Chase up the Fall of Niagara is esteemed, by all who have seen it, one of the finest Spectacles in Nature.

Franklin was not indulging in the kind of private joke that the Indian played on the gullible John Josselyn. His success depended on his hoax being recognized as a hoax. Herodotus tells of Arabian sheep that hauled their tails after them in wagons, and so does Rabelais, who credits the story to Jean Ternaud. The point is that the story was well known. The leaping whale is of less ancient lineage. In fact, it has an American smell about it. But it is equally fabulous. Should Franklin's readers have swallowed his tall tales, he still stood to gain. Taken seriously, they were evidence against the popular theory that animal and plant life degenerated in the wilderness of America. What should be noted here is that Franklin used folklore for his own special purpose, that of defending an American cause.

Joel Barlow, an American diplomat and ardent supporter of Thomas Jefferson, Tom Paine, and the French Revolution, was in Savoy in 1793. One morning he was served a bowl of porridge that reminded him of the mush or hasty pudding made of Indian corn meal boiled in salt water that he had eaten as a boy in Connecticut. He is said to have retired forthwith to his room and written a mock heroic, mock pastoral poem, "The Hasty-Pudding." This poem is in the tradition of Alexander Pope, and is of a type then in vogue extolling such staples of diet as potatoes and apple pie. Barlow uses neo-classic literary conventions, but he introduces American folk customs and folk speech, particularly words of Indian origin for food items like "suppawn" and "succa-tash." He describes the process of cooking hasty pudding and of growing Indian corn, and he concludes with an idyllic account of an American folk festival, the husking bee:

> For now, the corn-house fill'd, the harvest home,
> Th' invited neighbors to the *Husking* come;
> A frolic scene, where work, and mirth, and play,
> Unite their charms, to chace the hours away.
>   Where the huge heap lies center'd in the hall,
> The lamp suspended from the cheerful wall.
> Brown corn-fed nymphs, and strong hard-handed beaux,
> Alternate rang'd, extend in circling rows,
> Assume their seats, the solid mass attack;
> The dry husks rustle, and the corn-cobs crack;
> The songs, the laugh, alternate notes resound,
> And the sweet cider trips in silence round.

Here, indeed, is a pastoral golden age, but not mythic Arcadia or even Goldsmith's elegiac *The Deserted Village* from which Barlow borrowed for his husking-bee passage. Against these materials from the dead past as his backdrop, Barlow depicts a pastoral golden age that is manifest in a healthy, viable folk life, a golden age that has been realized in the agrarian society of the young republic. Barlow's conventional neo-classic poem on a simple American dish becomes an explicit call to his countrymen for a life of simple habits, personal dignity, and democracy—in short, for the Jefferson ideal.

If Barlow, who belonged to the generation that took part in the American Revolution, was a radical and an optimist about the future, Washington Irving of the post-revolutionary generation was inclined to cherish that past and to have misgivings about the place and the direction his country was taking along what was generally believed to be the path of progress. Opposed to both Jefferson's egalitarianism and Hamilton's commercialism because they disrupted the social order, Irving tried to foster a sense of tradition through his writing that would make for stability and continuity. Folklore, legend, and local custom were capable, in Irving's words, of "binding the heart of the new inhabitant to his home," and these commodities being in short supply "in our new country," he imported them. His typical method was to borrow a German folktale and Americanize it. In his most celebrated story, "Rip Van Winkle," the engaging but irresponsible Rip takes to the hills to avoid domestic tyranny, encounters hospitable strangers who ply him with strong drink, miraculously sleeps for twenty years, and awakens after the Revolution to find the world changed and not entirely for the better.

Irving's immediate source was the German tale of Peter Klaus, the goatherd, from Otmar's *Volkssagen*. The motif is widespread. For example, the Seven Sleepers of Ephesus were Christian martyrs walled up in a cave by heathens and miraculously preserved through a sleep of two hundred years. Irving was writing a complex fable. In terms of character, his subject was the eternal American adolescent, and the existential absurdity of growing up, and Rip is the literary ancestor of Mark Twain's Huck Finn "lit out for the territory" and Faulkner's Ike McCaslin, who fled the wilderness and never quite grew up. But in terms of theme, Irving transformed the miraculous folktale of Peter Klaus into a miracle that does not quite take place. For a miracle requires of the person who has experienced it an understanding that the experience was miraculous and regenerative, and Rip's transformation is merely physical. It must also be accompanied by the recognition of the experience as miraculous by those who witness it, and their consequent redemption. The villagers make room for Rip but continue to pursue their petty affairs, and social change apparently continues at an accelerated pace. Finally, a miracle must be taken seriously by those who recount it and those to whom it is told. Rip, a dotty old man, repeating his legend until every villager "knew it by heart" and telling it "to every stranger that arrived" is not Lazarus raised from the dead, and Irving's tone is such that readers find Rip's experience touching but hardly sacramental.

Yet the folk motif served Irving well. As he intended, it has helped to bind the hearts of Americans to their homeland, permeating the culture at all levels through the means of literature and the mass media, and even finding its way back into oral tradition; and Irving uses the motif to carry a warning that revolutions have a way of upsetting the cycle of growth and decay and progress that he saw as the historical process.

The generation of writers that succeeded Irving continued to use folklore to explain and question the society (and, of course, for other purposes). These writers were more distinguished than he, more ambitious, and more fortunate in that they had a much richer store of native materials to draw upon. A few examples must suffice. The bulk of Nathaniel Hawthorne's work derives from New England tradition and legend which he put to use as a way of exploring social and spiritual questions. In "Young Goodman Brown" a witches' sabbath attended by the most respectable as well as the most disreputable villagers of Salem becomes a device for examining the effects of evil that lurk in the institutions of the community and the hearts of men. Herman Melville frequently makes functional use of folklore in his sea stories. In *White-Jacket* (1850), a novel about the United States Navy, two old sailmakers, while sewing the body of a shipmate into his hammock for burial at sea, debate the need to conform to the demands of a nautical superstition—taking the last stitch through the nose of the corpse to make certain that it sinks when cast over the side. One sailmaker favors the tradition, but the other, troubled by the indignity of the mutilation, wishes to disregard it. This debate helps to carry the theme of the novel, an attack on rigid naval laws, customs, and traditions that debase and dehumanize the individual. In "The Man That Was Used Up," Edgar Allan Poe transforms the old joke about the beautiful girl who is discovered to have false teeth, a glass eye, a wig, and to otherwise depend upon cosmetic and prosthetic appliances, into a sardonic comment on a society so devoted to mechanical ingenuity that human beings become mechanical men. Mark

Twain in "The Celebrated Jumping Frog of Calaveras County" uses a jumping contest between two bullfrogs as a way of stating the values of civilization as opposed to the values of the frontier. William Faulkner, the most distinguished American author of recent times, uses a hunting tale in "The Bear" to present, among other things, the same conflict.

In American writing today one rarely encounters examples of transcriptive folklore. The need for transcription has passed, and most writers have come to realize that from a creative standpoint mere recordings or imitations of folklore are essentially lifeless, for such transcriptions become fixed and frozen when they are removed from the folk, whose creation they are, and put into print. In a special sense, however, when folklore is made to function in a literary work it retains its vitality. In this sense folklore in American literature has had a long life and remains very much alive today.

III

FOLKLORE AND MODERN TIMES

22

The Workers in the Dawn: Labor Lore

ARCHIE GREEN

As the United States grew from a colonial outpost to a powerful nation, the traditions of craftsmen, industrial workers, and trade unionists drew together into a complex which I will call "labor lore." Artisans carried to the New World folklore, already ancient, as well as their hand skills and guild secrets. Old ways were localized in new homes. However, there is no precise marker to separate the transported from the native. On both sides of the Atlantic songs, stories, and proverbial speech were used to soften the blow of hard times. But hard-times pieces also made wry comments on the failings of mechanics and, indirectly, provided fine documents of workers' perceptions of their customs.

Was this early craft song flavored with English ale or Yankee rum?

> The Carpenter will tell you he'll build you a house
> So tight and so snug, that it won't harbor a mouse,
> For two dollars a day—but he won't take a job—
> Though himself and apprentice won't half earn their grog,
> In these hard times.

Besides carpentry, half-a-hundred callings were satirized on Boston and Philadelphia broadsides printed before and after the Revolution. Some of this occupational humor is of remarkable longevity. Newfoundlanders still sing:

> Then next comes the carpenter to build you a house,
> He'll build it so snug you will scarce find a mouse,
> With holes in the roof and the rain it will pour,
> The chimney will smoke and 'tis open the door,
> And it's hard, hard times.

When factories emerged dominant over cottage crafts, workers responded to strange and difficult conditions with time-tested expressive forms. Children were toiling in Samuel Slater's cotton mill at Pawtucket, Rhode Island, in 1793. Neither their talk nor their yarn is available today, but their heritage is not entirely lost. Textiles led America's industrial revolution and our earliest true factory folksongs came, appropriately, from New England. "A Factory Girl" was the most popular; it commented on new routines by projecting wishful dreams of the young operatives and by verbalizing their desires for escape. A Massachusetts broadside declaimed:

> I do not like my overseer
> I do not mean to stay
> I mean to hire a depot boy
> To carry me away.

During 1962 I had the good fortune to hear Nancy Dixon, a retired North Carolina textile worker, sing her "Factory Girl," a direct descendant of America's oldest traditional industrial song:

> I'll bid you factory girls farewell,
> Come see me if you can.
> For I'm gonna quit this factory work
> And marry a nice young man.

But of course Pawtucket boys and Lowell girls, as well as their sisters and brothers for decades ahead, did not quit factory work. Instead, they went into forges, foundries, roundhouses, garment shops, shipyards, mold lofts, and countless other work sites. High steel, the bowels of the earth, assembly lines, cotton gins, sky-scraper offices—any place where hands were needed—there work-ers gathered. And many joined unions.

Long before labor gained formal organization, free journey-men or bound workmen took collective action to strike, to slow down, or to desert. In 1636 fishermen on Richmond Island, Maine, "fell into a mutiny" (struck) after their year's wages were withheld. In 1643 obstreperous shipwrights were locked out (a strike in reverse) of the Gloucester, Massachusetts, yards. In 1741 the radical Boston caulkers refused to accept paper-money notes from employers. They were strong enough to win their demand for hard money without striking. In pre-Revolutionary times, unions (under various names such as friendly societies) were impermanent, but after the war they achieved some continuity and cohesion—prerequisites for conveying institutional lore.

Labor history in the United States is not usually told in folk-loric terms. Yet parallel to unionism's economic practices and development is found a network of tale, balladry, ritual, and belief which embodies its tradition. This material can be labeled "folk wisdom," "verbal art," "debris of history," or "old fogey stuff," but, regardless of name, it is the same substance as the folklore of ethnic, religious, and geographic societies. One cam-paign alone—the eight-hour-day drive—generated widespread traditions from torchlight processions and fervent prayers to maudlin ditties and bloody demonstrations. "Eight hours for work, eight hours for rest, eight hours for what we will," was a slogan and a song's chorus well before the American Federation of Labor was founded in 1886. Yet after the A.F.L. achieved the "short" workday, the song was forgotten. No one knows how much labor lore was verbalized, codified, transmitted, and lost before antiquarians began a conscious search for such material. We can examine here but a few items which were retained by workers or gathered by collectors.

Words were extended from old contexts to serve fresh purposes by the builders of our earliest unions. Such terminology (*dialect*, *slang*, *argot*) became traditional when set off from formal lan-guage by special usage and association. Where unionists were harassed and fighting for a place in the sun, they had an especial need for negative terms to scorn enemies. Such words (*scab*, *rat*, *blackleg*, *yellowdog*, *fink*) also, by inference, denominated the good laborite: militant, loyal, generous, disciplined.

Perhaps the most traditional labor usage is *scab*. We do not know when or where it was first applied to a non-unionist, but we can fix it in Philadelphia speech as early as 1794. The shoemaker's calling, at that time, was in a transitional period, since it was separating into distinct functions: merchant, master, journeyman. A single person could no longer combine these diverse economic specialties. Consequently, the Federal Society of Journeymen Cordwainers was organized; it managed to survive for more than a decade, but in 1806 it was broken in the first major criminal conspiracy prosecution against American organized workers. *Commonwealth of Pennsylvania versus Pullis* is a legal case of great significance; it also tells us in ordinary words how *scabbing* (and its countermeasures) began.

During the prosecution testimony, taken down by stenographic report and privately printed, Job Harrison, a plaintiff's witness, told of entering the trade at Germantown (1794). When his fellow cordwainers solicited his membership, they suggested that he "was liable to be scabb'd" if he did not join. But Harrison was a newcomer (from England) and did not know the term's meaning. The men explained both the word and practice: "No man would set upon the seat where I worked; that they would neither board nor work where I was unless I joined." Harrison joined the Society, but later, in the "turn-out" (strike) of 1799, he pulled away. "I concluded at that time I would turn a scab unknown to them." He was discovered by the union "tramping committee" and fined. His subsequent troubles were carefully entered into the record and helped convince the jury of the union's criminality (the long bill of indictment reads in part "did combine, conspire, confederate, and agree together"). We learn from Harrison how it felt to be a "notorious scab," and also gain insight into the probable circumstance of the word's extension into labor lore. After paying fines and veering from membership to non-membership, Harrison, alienated from his fellows, stated, "I felt myself after all but a scabbed sheep and visit the body [union] as seldom as possible . . . for I know they are not pleased with me to this hour."

Unionists have manifested their displeasure at *scabs*, which Harrison articulated, through a century and a half of song, story, and slang. For example, Joe Hill's song parody (now traditional) of "Casey Jones" alters the brave railroad engineer's role into that of a strikebreaker, rewarded by the despicable job of *scabbing* on the angels. This development need not detain us. However, a footnote to the scabbed-sheep analogy may point up the frequent use of fish-flesh-fowl figures in a pejorative sense. While a young shipwright, I was curious about a fellow unionist's attack on hated *salmonbellies*—men who worked in Alaska canneries during the summer and at California drydocks in the winter. It was charged that these men would bring casks of choice pickled or smoked salmon fillets to curry favor with their bosses, and would slither around like salmonbellies while undercutting the standards of good (year-around) unionists. To my knowledge the term was not traditional, nor was it used beyond our locale, but it illustrates the force of hostility and the imaginative use of labor lingo which welds *scabs* and *salmonbellies* into a composite profile to be scorned.

The characteristic frontier tall tale (put to literary use by Mark Twain and other writers) is heard in modified form wherever laborers gather for a bite to eat: the lumber pile, the loading platform, the water bucket. Some workmen "just naturally talk funny" about heroic exploits, dangerous events, or luck. An anecdote may be told because a pretty girl walks past the crew, or simply because it is not yet time to resume the job. A tale may be highly stylized (and part of an ancient cluster) or it may be a casual elaboration on a fragment of memory. It may be bawdy and salty or light enough to be repeated to the family at the day's end. More often than not it is presented as a true event and against the backdrop of a troublesome job problem.

Traditional narratives were frequently used as actual stories or to establish atmosphere in proletarian fiction of the 1930's. Novelists who identified with labor were "folklorists without credentials." *Red Neck*, by McAlister Coleman and Stephen Raushenbush, portrays a work scene lightened by a remembrance:

[A group of miners descend to work.] At the bottom they stepped out of the man-cage and got into the empties waiting for the man-trip. The motorman looked over his shoulder, saw that everyone was aboard, crouched down in the cars, and then he started off down the main entry. . . . [At the first parting] the men got off and started down the sub-entries to the working places. They were in a great blackness now, slashed only by the lights from their caps, a blackness that the darkest night on top could never equal, all-enveloping, as though you could reach out and touch it, and yet you could not see the reaching hand three inches before your face. They went in single file steadily, swiftly through it. It was the element in which they moved for eight hours of the day, as familiar to them as the sunlit airways to the pilot of a plane. But more often than not the bravest visitors from above ground balked at the head of the sub-entries and begged to be taken up again. There was the widely-advertised "Demon Driver, the Bravest Man Alive," who with great thundering and aplomb had driven a weirdly balanced motorcycle around a mere shell of a track at a breakneck speed. When he had asked the Black Queen men [who had stood at the county fair watching him with their mouths hanging open] to take him below, they had been proud to escort such a hell-for-leather bully boy. But he had not gone ten feet from the parting when the blackness got him and he ran down the track yelling like a baby and had to be taken back and up again. They thought this was pretty comical and talked about it for days.

Did a motorcyclist's courage really fail him on a mine visit? Was there an actual happening which embedded itself in the minds of the Black Queen men so they talked about it for days? Was this a traditional fragment borrowed by miners from tunnel stiffs, marine divers, or bridge erectors, who also face darkness in their familiar scenes? Whether or not a tale is "true," it serves to bypass gloom and to dissolve danger.

At times stories are put to specific union use. Labor missionaries, walking delegates, and pioneer organizers were masters at talk. They carried a stock of clichés and commonplaces, not unlike Balkan epic singers. The soapbox at a plant entrance, or perhaps on skid row, where itinerant workers gathered, was an ideal spot from which to disseminate philosophy.

One soapbox tale told to me by John Newhaus, a San Francisco machinist, is typical.

The iron ore miners were on strike up in Minnesota. It was a long, hard strike but the men held out pretty good. A lot of them were Finns—Finns believe in solidarity. One day a striker's wife was about out of money. She went to the butcher shop to try to buy some cheap cut of meat that might last the family for a week. She saw a calf's head in the case and figured it would make lots of soup. So she asked the butcher, "Is this a union shop; is your meat union?" He was surprised but replied, "Sure, I'm a member of the Amalgamated—I cut my meat by union rule—there's my shop card in the window."

The lady said, "Well I don't want any union meat. Don't you have a scab calf's head?" The butcher was stumped but he was smart. So he said, "Just a minute, ma'am," and he took the calf's head into the room back of the shop. Pretty soon the lady heard a lot of clatter. The butcher came out of the room and handed her the wrapped package. He said, "That'll be seventy cents, ma'am." She was very pleased at the saving, paid up and started for the door. But she was curious. So she asked, "Isn't this scab calf's head the same as the union head you tried to sell me for a dollar?" The butcher said, "Yes, ma'am, it is. I just knocked out thirty cents' worth of brains!"

The American folk genre that commands most attention is song. Such items are sometimes found in the yellowed pages of labor's annals as well as in current pocket songsters. At times, unionists ask whether old pieces are sung today. This question can imply mere historical curiosity, or it can signify deep concern with the health of the labor movement itself. Do workers still sing on picket lines? Is trade unionism close enough to its folk roots to express values in traditional form? Can an impersonal institution retain folklore while employing highly sophisticated bargaining processes and modern fiscal techniques?

Perhaps answers to these rhetorical queries can be sought in a handful of songs. Unfortunately, pre-Civil War union songs were not searched for by our first generation of collectors. America's greatest ballad scholar, Francis James Child, knew intimately the quality of work-life, for his father was a Yankee sailmaker, but nothing in Child's adult experience prepared him to gather labor lore, traditional in his lifetime. It was not until 1925 that George Korson, a Pennsylvania newspaperman in the anthracite country, began to collect mining lore, including strike songs. Korson, in his books and on two related Library of Congress record albums, presented a tremendous body of industrial material, carefully identifying those items of specal trade-union content or meaning.

The contrast between general industrial material and labor lore *per se* is seen in two Korson-collected songs. During 1940, David Morrison, eighty-one years of age, recorded "Two Cent Coal," commemorating a disaster on the Monongahela River after the operators cut wages. Following the freeze, the ice broke and tipples at the water's edge were swept down river. The miners saw in the calamity retribution against the bosses:

Oh, the bosses' tricks of '76
They met with some success,
Until the hand of God came down
And made them do with less.

They robbed the honest miner lad
And drunk his flowin' bowl.
Through poverty we were compelled
To dig them two cent coal.

But workers could not always wait for divine intercession. In Homestead, Pennsylvania, members of the Amalgamated Association of Iron and Steel Workers were locked out of their jobs by Andrew Carnegie and Henry Clay Frick in 1892. The dispute led to the use of Pinkerton armed guards against the unionists and many lives were lost in this crucial drama. During 1940, Peter Haser, seventy years of age, recorded "The Homestead Strike":

> We are asking one another as we pass the time of day,
> Why workingmen resort to arms to get their proper pay,
> And why our labor unions they must not be recognized,
> Whilst the actions of a syndicate must not be criticized.

The imperatives of industrial expansion by trusts and monopolies in the late nineteenth century indeed made it difficult to criticize the syndicates, whether by Knights of Labor partisans or by American Federation of Labor skilled mechanics. But in 1905 a number of radical unionists met in Chicago to organize a new front, the Industrial Workers of the World. In time the militants who formed the group's cadre came to be called "Wobblies" or "Wobs" (itself a designation that is more folklore than history). I.W.W. philosophy was as native as Douglas fir or Anaconda copper; it blended Jeffersonian libertarianism and Jamesian pragmatism, but, characteristically, was labeled "direct action" by the men on the job.

Unlike many folk groups, the Wobblies were highly mobile, ethnically heterogeneous, and intensely conscious of their roles in society. Yet they developed a fine body of traditional song lore. Such pieces were initially printed in little red songbooks provocatively labeled, "To Fan the Flames of Discontent." A typical piece employed the gospel melody of "Take It to the Lord in Prayer," but used it with pungent humor:

> Are you poor, forlorn and hungry?
> Are there lots of things you lack?
> Is your life made up of misery?
> Then dump the bosses off your back.

Such a number was a call to action. Others expressed the ultimate goals of the rebels. To the tune of the popular song, "Darling Nellie Grey," the Wobs stated their idealism:

> But we have a glowing dream
> Of how fair the world will seem
> When each man can live his life secure and free;
> When the earth is owned by Labor
> And there's joy and peace for all
> In the Commonwealth of Toil that is to be.

During the Great Depression, these themes gave way to cries of bitter despair. Sarah Ogan Gunning, daughter, sister, and wife of Kentucky coal miners, retained old mountain songs, but also composed new pieces to mark the times. She fused the message of sectarian unionism with the Appalachian ballad style to create some of labor's most poignant songs:

> I hate the company bosses,
> I'll tell you the reason why.
> They caused me so much suffering
> And my dearest friends to die.

Workers at the bottom of the pit who faced both the hopelessness of unemployment and the gunfire of thugs and vigilantes also were burdened by servitude. Sometimes they could ward it off by jest. Poet Carl Sandburg sang away oppression in this ditty, which foreshadowed Merle Travis' hit, "Sixteen Tons":

> You live in the company houses,
> You go to company schools,
> You work for the company,
> According to company rules.

We all drink company water,
We all use company light,
Company preachers teach us
What the company thinks is right.

In the mid-1930's workers who framed answers to suffering and servitude formed the Committee for Industrial Organization— later renamed the Congress of Industrial Organizations. Many C.I.O.-ers seemed particularly conscious of labor lore's utility in union education. They took advantage of radio and tape recordings to popularize folksongs and to create pieces which entered tradition. Tarheel tobacco workers first turned the sacred number "We Shall Overcome" into a C.I.O. piece, thereby preparing it for an eventual role as the civil rights movement's anthem:

We shall overcome, we shall overcome,
We shall overcome some day.
Oh, oh, down in my heart, I do believe
We shall overcome some day.

But labor's task did not end in the New Deal years, nor with the subsequent unification of the A.F.L.–C.I.O. In 1966, Mexican and Filipino agricultural workers in California vineyards pressed their own grapes of wrath in a strike for organization which recalled previous turbulent efforts in these fields. On a pilgrimage to Sacramento, the state's capital, the *huelguistas* (strikers) sang:

Yo no vengo a cantar   I do not come to sing
Porque mi voz sea buena,   Because I have a good voice,
Ni tampoco a llorar   Nor do I come to cry
Mi mal estar.   Of my unhappiness.

A paradox in these times of instant, electronic communication is the difficulty in amplifying the lonely voice of a handful of grape pickers on a dusty road. The *huelguistas* stem from a fully traditional society in Mexico with a rich heritage of folklore. Their present-day union songs are linked by content, style, and function to decades of history. But we cannot yet assess whether their numbers will be heard by fellow unionists who have accepted mass society's image of popular "protest songs."

This brief survey of a few labor terms, anecdotes, and lyric fragments overlooks many genres: legend, slogan, aphorism, ceremony, token, custom. Even my repeating a Neuhaus tale or a Gunning song does not reveal how union men actually distilled beliefs into verbal, graphic, and dramatic form. A full gathering of labor-lore genres and careful exposition of its genesis is not yet available. However, we know where it was conveyed: on the job, in the hiring halls, union temples, caucuses, conventions. The site or time was never so important as the message. Indeed, many individuals first heard labor's word following the tragic death of a fellow worker. From the needle trades' Triangle Fire to the maritime trades' Bloody Thursday, labor buried its dead in solidarity-creating rituals which helped the living to find identity.

Some workers, then, do hear and pass on lore that wells from and documents their experience. But the American labor movement, like other institutions—schools, churches, civic or fraternal organizations—is ambivalent about the use of folklore. Old marching banners can be housed in glass cases after Labor Day parades are given up in favor of packaged leisure. But what does one do with old songs? Literally, some are encased in glossy collections and some are preserved on disk and tape (in archives), but most are forgotten. In traditional society the act of forgetting is matched by the act of creation and re-creation. Today, persons concerned with the quality of American life are uncertain whether folklore can survive in Nashville and Hollywood. Labor unionists more properly should consider whether work-derived traditions will survive in automated factories and computerized offices.

The formal problem of labor lore's vitality concerns neither the A.F.L.–C.I.O.'s top leadership nor most of its many million rank-and-file members. But a few partisans are concerned. A contemporary example of excellent use of union tradition was demonstrated in the publication of *Rebel Voices*, compiled in 1964 by Joyce Kornbluh. This book selects from a half century of I.W.W. reportage and graphic art numerous examples of song, tale, and dialect.

Rebel Voices was intended for those with an affection for our nation's past and concern for its future. It was well received by professional scholars, popular journals, *The New York Times*, and by some big-business house organs (whose sponsors were once terrified by Wobs at the fence). One of the few uncertain reviews to greet the anthology was that of *The Industrial Worker*. Editor Carl Keller did not like his organization to be treated as a monument nor to be remembered by verbal oddments rather than by socio-economic challenges. His reservations about the included folklore led to a Wobbly blast: "Like the boys sifting out the sawdust floor-sweepings in the back yard of an old saloon for long-lost coins, [folklorists] turn up a lot of junk. Unlike the boys, they are not always able to distinguish the real McCoy from the worthless."

Perhaps in Keller's bittersweet response to lore which he helped shape as a youngster we see the pattern of labor's, as well as large society's, need for and discomfort in its past. Who is to assay the lost coin? Is it to be treasured as a memento or to be spent on today's market? What can an antique coin buy: herbs and incantations or wonder drugs and Laser-ray surgery?

Rebel Voices does not tout Davy Crockett, Johnny Appleseed, or Paul Bunyan; rather it memorializes Joe Hill, Frank Little, Wesley Everest. We find it painful to remember the martyrdom of these stevedores, seamen, hard-rock miners, harvest hands, and loggers who gave their lives to achieve social justice and to enlarge the horizons of workingmen. We also are uncertain whether labor martyrs are truly legendary. Are Hill, Little, and Everest forgotten Wobblies or folk heroes? Possibly we are all too grown up to believe in folk heroes and their songs unless they are certified by the media of popular culture. "The Commonwealth of Toil" seems more distant than Cinderella's slipper, yet this song was important to unionists a few decades ago. No matter how far we leave work-associated tradition behind, work continues to shape people's lives, and labor lore still holds the potential for enriching the American dream.

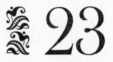

The Hillbilly
Movement

D. K. WILGUS

I find it quite difficult to discuss hillbilly music because no one can determine exactly the limitations of the subject. Hillbilly music may be seen as the style and repertory which developed through the interaction of Anglo-American folk music, Afro-American folk music, and American commercial popular music in the uplands and lowlands of the southeastern United States. Hillbilly music may be seen as a commercial enterprise to purvey standardized musical packages to the rural folk of the United States. Both statements reflect reality, and—as usual—truth encompasses both viewpoints.

One could certainly apply the term "hillbilly" with good reason to specific developments in the folk music of the southeastern United States. But through an accident—lucky or unlucky—the term "hillbilly" has been applied to a historical process and its various results. "Hillbilly" is a pejorative term applied to back-country whites for a longer time than noted in our dialect dictionaries. When a group of Southern folk musicians inadvertently christened themselves "The Hill Billies" at a 1925 recording session in New York, they reflected the attitude of sophisticated America toward their music. But they also fostered a term which was applied not only to hill-country folk music but to all white folk music which was to be commercialized by the many facets of the entertainment industry.

Anglo-American folklorists, particularly in the early years of this century, held an exceedingly romantic view of folk music and folk performers. When they were not speculating that ballads were some sort of survival of poetizing by a primal horde, students of folksong considered only a domestic tradition of singing. The medieval minstrel was generally ruled out of court as a serious contributor to the historical development of the ballad, and folksong was felt to be the production and occupation of the kitchen, the front porch, and the sheepfold. Too many students had only an antiquarian concern with song texts. Students who took account of the music and the performance of folksong were acquainted only with traditions lacking instrumental accompaniment. Thus when the great English folk-music collector, Cecil J. Sharp, made his historic expeditions to the southern Appalachians, he reported that musical instruments were virtually unknown. Yet less than a decade after Sharp's experience, this very area had produced for the radio and recording industries a vigorous tradition of instrumental music and instrumentally accompanied song. This tradition could not have developed and did not develop in such a short time. And the reasons Sharp did not hear this music tell us a good deal about the tradition, as well as about the collector who overlooked it.

A folksong collector usually finds what he is looking for. Cecil Sharp was basically looking for old tunes, imported from the British Isles and surviving in isolated areas of the South. He found them. He was looking for unaccompanied folksong. He found it. The evangelical folk religion of the South was more than suspicious of musical instruments. The best people, the most respectable people, avoided them. A folk musician would not bring out his instruments for a respectable stranger who wasn't interested in them and probably didn't ask about them. Sharp was aided in his search by the settlement schools, which— to their credit—respected and fostered the older folksongs of the population. But the settlement school workers, as well as the local supporters of the settlement schools, were opposed to the new music and especially to its cultural background. For it *was* new, not a quaint survival among the American peasantry. It was not a pure Anglo-Saxon inheritance, but a hybrid influenced by rural Negro music and urban commercial music. It was not only instrumental music, but it flourished in the railroad camps, in the coal camps, in the new mill towns. It was associated with the frolics, at which not only dancing but liquor was in evidence. It was often purveyed and spread by professional or semi-professional musicians: a lone blind ballad singer with a battered fiddle, banjo, or guitar; a small string band performing beside a mine pay shack; a troupe accompanying a touring patent medicine show. This was not respectable music, and what respectable person would want to listen to it, let alone call it folk music?

It is then no surprise that this music was in effect "discovered" by the commercial music industry and ignored when not denounced by folklorists, many of whom had never met folksong outside a book anyhow. This was not a music foisted on the American folk, but a music exploited by a music industry in search of wider markets. And there was certainly a rush of musicians wishing to be exploited. Though they came first from the rural South and Southwest, they came eventually from such unlikely areas as Nova Scotia and the state of Oregon. This was a music that rural America understood. As George D. Hay of radio station WSM once intimated, the listeners wanted not Grand Opera, but Grand Ole Opry.

Certainly the South and the southern Appalachians had a good deal to do with the development of hillbilly music because of their isolation, but not the isolation which supposedly resulted in communities which in 1920 "spoke Elizabethan English and didn't know the Civil War was over." It was an isolation from the precise pattern of industrial development of the northern United States. It was an isolation that permitted the preservation and development of a strong folk culture that was not uninfluenced by general American culture, but made selective adaptations of such cultural elements. Consequently, to a smaller extent than elsewhere, its folk music did not simply erode. It developed a vigorous hybrid, widely recognizable but with distinct regional variations.

The prehistory of hillbilly music—before it began to be well documented in the 1920's by commercial recordings, radio, sheet music, and movies—this prehistory may never be fully known. What elements of this music existed before the Civil War we cannot determine, although we would certainly expect the white folk musician to have adopted the banjo from the Ethiopian minstrels at the very least. But the postwar development of railroads, mining, and logging brought a fruitful interchange of white and Negro folk music and commercial popular music. The folk musician who had alternately sung verses and played the tune on his fiddle now learned to adapt the banjo to his musical style, and even to sing with the fiddle. He developed a new repertory of railroad and river songs, often borrowed and reshaped from the songs of Negro workers. He heard the sentimental parlor songs and often adapted them to his tradition of lyric song. The mills and the mines were disrupting his traditional way of life without altering his basic value system or providing him with the economic and intellectual background necessary to procure and accept many elements of the dominant culture. So he created his own cultural variant.

By the turn of the century, the basic elements of hillbilly music were in existence. There were annual fiddling conventions in many localities. Every fair, court day, or even religious convention would be graced by the presence of itinerant musicians, often performing ballads celebrating recent local or even national events. Another war had enlarged the horizon—incidentally introducing the Hawaiian guitar—and all kinds of instruments were becoming available through mail-order houses. In the West were migrants who had carried their musical culture with them and borrowed from and contributed to the musical repertory of the Western frontier, which itself had already backtrailed to the eastern South. In Louisiana and in Texas, rural white musicians were being influenced by the music of French and Mexican cultures. Out-migration from rural areas had spread the music and—most important—the taste for hillbilly music throughout the nation. A market existed, but it was being supplied only by small numbers of local or itinerant folk musicians, unexploited by the Northern entertainment industry.

In 1920, radio entered the field of mass communication and entertainment, seriously challenging the recording industry, which was forced to look for new materials and markets. The hillbilly musicians themselves were looking for new media. On June 30, 1922, A. C. Robertson and Henry C. Gilliland, folk fiddlers from Texas and Oklahoma, induced the Victor Recording Company to accept two performances. The recording was not issued until April of the following year, with no important result. On September 9, 1922, "Fiddlin' John" Carson, a local folk musician of Atlanta, Georgia, began broadcasting on WSB, followed by other performers of the area, such as Clayton McMichen, Riley Pucket, and the singing family of the Reverend Andrew Jenkins. In the spring of 1923, Virginia folk musician Henry Whitter set out for New York and managed to record two sides for the Okeh label. These were promptly shelved. But on June 14, 1923, Ralph S. Peer, in Atlanta to record local talent for Okeh Records, was induced by a local dealer to wax the efforts of "Fiddlin' John" Carson. Despite Peer's misgivings, the record, which he called "pluperfect awful," was released, first for the Atlanta market only. Its success led to a regular release, the dusting off and release of the Whitter recordings, and the search for similar talent by Okeh and other record companies. Thus began the commercialization of the American folk music called hillbilly after 1925.

This commercialization was not the attempt of music merchants to corrupt the tastes of the American folk. The merchants were merely packaging a commodity already existing. And they were at first hardly aware of what they were doing, except trying to make a profit. They sought out local musicians in the South, recorded and released the results, and hoped for sales. The type of material and performance which sold naturally became the subject of further search, and also imitation.

If commercial hillbilly music began with the confrontation of a folk musician and a recording engineer, it soon became the object of manipulation by shrewd executives and performers. Many of the early recordings had relatively limited appeal, representing strong regional traditions. A popular recording artist of the period was Marion Try Slaughter, a light-opera tenor who performed sentimental and "coon" songs under the pseudonym of Vernon Dalhart. Learning, in a somewhat garbled fashion, "The Wreck of the Old 97" from Henry Whitter's recording, he rendered it in an accent resurrected or imitated from his youth in Texas. While his first recording for Edison was only moderately successful, the 1925 Victor release of the ballad, coupled with "The Prisoner's Song," was a national hit. Thus entered a new factor, the city imitator, but with country roots.

What developed was a new broadside tradition, analogous to the printed sheets distributed by ballad hawkers in Britain from the sixteenth century onward. Ironically, when the broadside tradition had been superseded in the United States by the urban music industry, it lingered in the hinterlands and supported many of the musicians who later became a part of the commercial hillbilly industry. This broadside tradition was to add to the old techniques the new media of mass communication. The recordings first reached beyond the range of even battery-powered radio—but radio was nevertheless an early and integral part of the new broadside tradition. Following the lead of the local program, regional shows took shape. The earliest was launched in 1924 on WLS, the Chicago station owned by the mail-order house which had already aided in the development of hillbilly music. WSM's "Grand Ole Opry" followed in 1925, and radio became a substantial part of the tradition, which still included all the old devices. The emphasis in this broadside tradition was on the performance of the song, but the performer peddled broadsides and song folios. In the early years, the performer used radio time—for which he was seldom paid—to announce his personal appearances and later to sell souvenirs. Even recordings, for which he usually received only a flat fee, were little more than side lines or promotional attractions. Eventually all these techniques were to be integrated into a well-organized show business, a gigantic broadside industry.

A broadside tradition has at least a symbiotic relationship to folk tradition. It is a borrower and a lender. Entering the commercial hillbilly tradition were first the active carriers of the most current folk styles and repertory. Their performances were invariably accompanied, generally self-accompanied. In addition to dance and frolic pieces, the performers had a wide repertory of songs. It included a sprinkling of very old ballads; a small amount of other Old World ballads; a good many native American ballads of tragical, criminal, cowboy, railroad, and miscellaneous themes; and a wide variety of lyrical songs of various ancestry. The last group ranged from an ancient stratum of British country song to Ethiopian minstrel pieces and sentimental parlor songs of the nineteenth century and after. Finally, the performers always included religious songs—a few of the early white spirituals, but most from gospel song tradition and the current Holiness revival.

These songs, particularly local and individual variants, were given increasingly wide distribution. A successful performance on one label or on one barn dance had to be "covered" by parallel outlets, which induced the spread of songs among performers and consequently among the folk audience. The need for new material made collectors of the performers, whether they sought out the material or accepted the contributions of their listeners, who were gracious donors. The performers were often folk composers, and the new opportunities stimulated their production as well as the production of others seeking to capitalize on a new market. Thus Polk C. Brockman, who was responsible for "Fiddlin' John" Carson's successful pioneer hillbilly recording, commissioned the Reverend Andrew Jenkins' composition of "Floyd Collins," now firmly established as an American folk ballad. In fact, the composition of such so-called "tragedies," topical ballads of current disasters and crimes, became a small industry in the late 1920's. Though most of these ballads are now known only to the collector of the old records and song folios, many became established in oral tradition at least firmly enough to be accepted into published collections of folksong.

Before the Great Depression brought the recording industry to a standstill, the knell sounded for the "citybillies" like Vernon Dalhart, whose general appeal had been so lucrative. There emerged folk performers with a wider appeal, particularly a Virginia group called the Carter Family and a tubercular ex-brakeman named Jimmie Rodgers. By the time the recording industry was recovering from the staggering effects of economic collapse, the hillbilly industry had undergone a substantial change. The street minstrels and ragged local bands were being succeeded by thoroughgoing professionals—still somewhat subject to fleecing by music merchants, but musically sophisticated and performing for an audience whose tastes had been sharpened by a variety of performances. The music was not homogenized. But this was the great period of smooth harmony singing, often by sibling teams. The remaining fiddle bands became smoother and more proficient before dropping into the background. While the older repertory still lingered, an increasing number of "heart songs," or sentimental lyrics, arose. The influence of Negro music continued, either directly or through the intermediary of "white blues." And in the Southwest, jazz and country bands began to interchange members, resulting in a new hybrid of honky-tonk music.

On the eve of World War II, commercial hillbilly music still covered a multitude of variants, from the dulcet singing of Western movie stars to lone performers who wandered among rural radio stations or performed in seedy bars in the little Kentuckys and little Tennessees of Northern industrial cities. But gradually the older musicians, the older styles, and the older songs were being crowded out by new material and techniques. The juke box and the radio record show were beginning to threaten the live local performer. The electric guitar was altering the sound of music and bringing it closer to the mainstream of American popular music. Indeed, in the Southwest, string bands had developed into full orchestras which were to spawn the hybrid called "western swing." The music appealed less and less to the old folk values and became more and more a bridge between the rural folk culture and the urban mass culture. The war made the bridge a solid structure.

The war brought Northern servicemen into the South and into closer contact with hillbilly music in the services themselves. The war brought Southerners and hillbilly musicians into Northern war industries. Out of the war years grew a wider and altered market for hillbilly music, now rechristened "country western" music. It became big business indeed. It spawned its own Tin Pan Alley and invaded the mainstream of popular music, to which it was now more and more responsive. The star personality, the hit record, and the hard-sell disk jockey became the pattern of the industry. No one, at least within the established limits of academic discipline, will call this folk music. Yet it has great relevance for at least the study of the disintegration of the rural folk culture of the United States. The rude confrontation of rural and urban living, the further polarization of secular and spiritual values, the breakup of the rigid family pattern, are reflected in various stages—whether in the nostalgic affirmation of dying values or in the celebration of the "Slippin' Around" in a sordid "Back Street Affair."

Though country western music has no longer a vital relationship to the kind of music the folklorist collects and studies, the folk base of the music has not totally vanished. Most of the old performers who could not or would not convert to drumming accompaniment, lush violins, and spangled uniforms remain at best on the fringes of the business. The most prominent survival of the "old timey" music is in "bluegrass" style, a highly sophisticated and artistic development of certain regional and individual elements—a likely candidate to become merely a stylized fossil. But the field of country western music cannot escape its folk roots. The performers—new and old—came from the folk. And songs from their native repertory are still poured into new bottles. The local performers, professional and amateur, still survive on local television, at country auctions, and at local folk gatherings. Their repertory and style still blend the old and the new.

A knowledge and understanding of hillbilly music is an essential part of the equipment of the American folklorist, whether he be collecting songs from the mouths of the folk or studying the collections of the past half century. But certainly more important is the wider recognition of the significance of hillbilly music in the total American culture. Such recognition and study is now promised under the auspices of the John Edwards Memorial Foundation at the University of California at Los Angeles. Here, with the aid of a growing number of dedicated students, may be written the history of the hillbilly movement.

24

Negro Music: Urban Renewal

JOHN F. SZWED

There are not many people left´ who would question the importance of the great musical amalgamation that occurred when the music of Western Europe met the music of West Africa within the process of slavery in North America. There is no longer any room to argue over the lasting value of Afro-American music as a source of inspiration for the world's musical experience. Factors of social and historical concern were certainly important in shaping the conditions which led to rapid world-wide acceptance, but it is inside the music itself—in its very spirit—that one must look to find the explanation for the music that had perhaps the greatest impact of any music since the Renaissance.

Nor is there any question that this music is completely "Afro-American," for no precedent can be found anywhere in the other major culture areas of the world. Unlikely as it seems, it was in that "peculiar institution" of slavery that this artistic flowering took place. Perhaps an eighteenth-century musicologist could have written a doctoral thesis predicting that West African rhythmic complexity and open singing style would be the perfect mate for European melodic formalism and harmony; but no one could have so easily shown the ease with which white Europeans and Negro Africans would be dazzled by each other's music. The slaves' songs were both the least threatening and yet the most powerful human expression that emerged within the incredible social restrictions of slavery. With European instruments and England's language, the Negro of America emerged the aesthetic master, and we have yet to see the end of that conquest.

The American rural South was the source of Afro-American music, not because it was rural, but because that was where the Afro-Americans were. But the bias of folklore has inclined toward the agrarian, and most interest in the musical expression of the Negro has been centered within the old South. Like the increase of interest in British folklore after the rise of the industrial revolution, serious interest in Negro folklore developed only after the end of slavery. With the collapse of agrarian life, this interest, too, waned.

Folklorists aside, American Negro life went on outside of the South. As the South's agricultural importance declined and industrialism in the North increased, a great migration began to the cities. In the decade following 1910, Harlem doubled and Chicago trebled their Negro populations. In the cities of Chicago, New York, Philadelphia, and Detroit, the Negro population quadrupled between 1910 and 1930. This was not a temporary reaction but the beginnings of a long-term process, one that has increased continually throughout the years. As an example, between 1950 and 1960, Mississippi alone lost 323,000 Negroes. But if the folklorists are insisting that the farm is not the factory, and that changes do occur, they are right. Northern city life brought American Negroes improved education, closer contact with the mass media, greater independence through better wages and more jobs, greater mobility, and some degree of greater personal freedom. On the other hand, patterns of segregation assured that Negroes would re-form folk-like communities in the shape of ghettos, and that their visibility as a minority group would assure them separation from a considerable portion of American life. In fact, it is safe to say that racial separation in the cities assured a degree of ethnic identity that might be even greater than that of the South.

Since the music of American Negroes was, like the Negroes themselves, not a part of the central tradition of the country, it does not surprise us that it spread most rapidly after the neutral, depersonalized mechanism of the phonograph record intervened. Unquestionably, the record was the single most important factor in explaining the direction of Negro music in the twentieth century.

Almost by accident, the improved prosperity of Negroes in the 1920's led to the development of "race records," made by white-owned recording companies and aimed exclusively at Negro buyers. Like no other recording activity before or since, race records were designed to fulfill the musical demands of a given social group. At the same time, the flexibility of the record increased the range of taste of its buyers by reducing geographical and social differences between Negroes of various parts of the country. Those Negroes still living in the South heard records of the new city music, while long-settled urban Negroes heard once more the voices of their own traditional past reaching them from the South via the phonograph. (The same process might have occurred for white record buyers who, in the 1920's, could have heard hillbilly recordings, but the ethnic diversity of urban whites made this a more difficult feat.)

What did the record do for the Negro music? First, it allowed a flexibility (almost experimentation) seldom to be duplicated again. Artists of no name and sometimes even with no professional performing background could appear on records to be spread across the United States. It was thus that local traditions (such as the singing style of the Mississippi Delta) were spread far beyond their geographical bounds. Records also gave solidity to groups of singers and musicians who would have otherwise never been brought together. Musicians could appear on records even without there being any demand for live performances. For jazz, this was the single most important factor in its development. Many—perhaps most—jazzmen came to their music not by hearing jazz live, but by listening to the records of obscure, seldom-employed musicians in distant cities. The development of jazz did not depend so much on financially successful trends in music as it did on who was put on records at a particular time.

The technological limitations of phonograph recording were also important to the music heard on them. Since most records pressed at 78 r.p.m.'s had a three-minute time span, the recordings shaped the very form of the music. Live jazz normally depends on a small amount of ensemble playing with a large amount of soloing, but the brevity of records demanded that a framework be created wherein a maximum number of musicians could solo within a limited span. The result was increased concentration on arrangement and composition. Blues singers were also constrained by the demands of recording. The need to limit the verses on a given record forced singers to make choices that finally led to a formalism that can be identified as a new development in traditional blues. Finally, the length of the record helped to determine the length of the dance before the advent of live music.

Although almost all types of Negro folk music were continued after the move to the city, a few forms predominated, and characterize the entire aesthetic direction of Afro-American music: the blues, gospel music, and jazz.

THE BLUES

To speak of the blues, even country blues, as being folksong is misleading. The blues are a highly personalized form, performed solo, and are thus quite unlike the central tradition of American Negro folksong. What's more, the close relationship between the accompanying instrument and the singer suggests art music more than it does folksong. The complete blues performance was attempted by only a few singers. For American Negroes as a whole, the blues were listened to more often than they were sung.

Yet it is still not quite right to talk of the blues as art song: the blues did not "entertain," nor were they art "objects." They were, in their folk setting in the American South, something akin to religious chants (although never a part of orthodox religious belief). Emotionally charged, deeply personalized, the blues were in part a problem-solving technique, closer to the confessional than to the stage. The blues audience responded to the common plights presented to them by the singer as personal experience. As the singer overcame his problems, or was overcome by them, so the listeners shared in the catharsis.

When blues first spread outside of the rural South, it was not the country product that was heard. Mamie Smith's 1920 recording of "Crazy Blues" was the beginning of a long outpouring of what has come to be called the classic blues—formal, neatly structured songs usually accompanied by a piano or jazz-oriented instrumentalists. Absent were the irregular lengths of traditional blues, the rough shouts, grunts, vocal tricks, and most notably absent were the men who had sung the blues in the South at picnics, lumber camps, and bars. Female singers were the first blues performers heard on records, reflecting current tastes in Negro theater and minstrelsy, where they were accompanied by polished urban pianists. But whatever the reason, the theatricality of the female blues singers struck a compromise between the local traditions of the rural Negro South and the commercial productions of white show business. Both Negro and white Northern audiences found the classic blues exciting. By 1922 the blues had become something of a "craze," to use the slang of the day. Today it seems incredible that a concert and dance at the Manhattan Casino in January 1922 could have featured a blues contest—which Trixie Smith won—viewed by Fiorello La Guardia, Mme. Enrico Caruso, Irene Castle, New York Governor Nathan L. Miller, and such leaders of society as the Harrimans, the Whitneys, and the Fairchilds.

The amazing success of the blues created a rush to issue as many recordings of Negro artists as possible. It was thus that the blues came to be the financial backbone of the race record catalogues, although vaudeville and religious tunes still constituted the bulk of the output. The blues did so very well that by the mid-1920's the record companies had begun to run out of blues singers and began to scour the South on what they called "record expeditions." (During the same period and often on the same expeditions, white hillbilly singers were equally sought after.) Paradoxically, then, it was not until the second wave of recordings that the originators of the blues were being heard from. The record companies' quest led them not only to farmhands and sharecroppers but also to street singers, bar entertainers, and medicine show attractions around Birmingham, Memphis, and Dallas. In Texas, Arkansas, and Louisiana they discovered that the piano—like the guitar in other areas of the South—was the accompanying instrument, played in a rural, blues-fed style that was later to form the basis for boogie-woogie in Midwestern urban areas.

But country blues were not so popular among white audiences, and there was little work for the singers outside of recordings. Instrumental jazz and ragtime piano had cut deeply into the popularity of the blues. Worst of all, though, was the depression, which drove many race labels out of production, although a few managed to maintain at least minimal sales with extremely popular singers such as Leroy Carr.

As the American economic crisis eased somewhat in the middle and later 1930's, RCA Victor's subsidiary Bluebird began to record some of the newer male blues singers. Most of them were accompanied by small groups of musicians who played with a jazz-like rhythm that came to be known as the "Bluebird beat." By this time blues recordings were being played in bars and restaurants and thus were in competition with other forms of popular music on one hand and noise on the other. Newer blues singers such as Tampa Ted, Sonny Boy Williamson, and Blind Boy Fuller became great successes with a long series of "party blues"—*double entendre* songs.

World War II was a great leveler, and musical tastes were no exception. The heavy swing of the big dance bands became the norm for popular music, and even the shyest forms of country music responded. For blues, this meant the adoption of the electric guitar, bass, and drums. In Chicago, former rural blues singers such as Muddy Waters converted to electricity, and blues were less listened to than danced to. But a touch of the country remained in the choice of melodies, the essential guitar styles, and in Muddy Waters' use of the harmonica—an instrument widely used in the South—as a part of his blues band.

It was Memphis, Tennessee, however, that seemed to be the new center of blues creation after the war: singers such as Gatemouth Moore and Johnny Ace, and later, Bobby Bland and B. B. King set the style of blues that remains most popular with younger Negroes today. Memphis-style blues are accompanied by big bands and choirs, and, overall, appear much closer to modern gospel singing than to traditional blues.

The blues have taken an interesting but not unpredictable change in direction—from quiet, almost introspective self-accompanied solos before small groups of listeners to loud, quasi-choral arrangements sung before large audiences—and to say that the blues have simply moved out of the realm of folk music into that of mass culture would be to miss the point. Modern blues are still highly personalized experiences, and the lyrics still deal with the basic issues of life in an unromantic manner. Charles Keil, in *Urban Blues*, makes a strong case for the fact that most sophisticated blues performances today still constitute ritualistic experiences, those in which singer and audience are interlocked in an artistic problem-solving venture. "Mass" they may be in terms of over-all framework and appeal, but the traditional core of performance style and meaning remains quite unchanged from its rural roots. A. B. Spellman's book, *Four Lives in the Bebop Business*, quotes Negro jazzman Cecil Taylor's revealing insight into the differences between white Euro-American and Negro American approaches to the same musical contents. Comparing British singer Petula Clark to modern blues singer James Brown, Taylor said: "It got very humorous because she was screaming and she was trying to look composed at the same time. But when James Brown goes into his thing, he goes; it's like a complete catharsis. He goes . . . That's the technique of rhythm and blues singing, man, and no academy but the genuine tradition of a people can give it to you."

There remains one portion of blues history to be commented on: rock-and-roll. In the early 1950's a few white singers—for example, Elvis Presley—established a strong link with blues tradition by emulating the spirit (and sometimes even the letter) of urban blues. As their audience was composed almost exclusively of adolescents, the frank and adult subjects of most blues were not used. Instead, a kind of teen-age blues tradition was established by commercial songwriters who aimed their material at the problems of youth. One Negro blues singer, Chuck Berry, wrote and performed highly complex and rhythmically exciting blues-oriented songs that stressed instrumental virtuosity as well as adolescent themes. It is to his "Roll Over Beethoven" and "Memphis" that one can most clearly trace the influences that shaped the English (and later, American) rock-and-roll explosion in the mid-1960's.

GOSPEL

The extraordinary popularity of the Negro spiritual among both whites and Negroes reflects Alan Lomax's statement that it was the perfect musical form to merge African rhythm and vocal mannerisms with European melody, harmony, and Christian ideology. The source materials were the orthodox Protestant churches and their ministers, while the African tradition of group improvisation and transformation was the means of change. To Negroes, the spirituals' usage of Old Testament characters and situations provided ritualistic release from the oppressive conditions of slavery; whites, on the other hand, found the image of the Negro presented through the spiritual reassuringly humble and submissive.

For whatever causes, the spiritual was almost universally popular in the United States in the later 1800's—a situation that was to turn the spiritual from a functioning folk form into an art form. By the late 1880's this was precisely what happened when the Fisk University Jubilee Singers became leading concert attractions and the best-known exponents of gospel song. The Fisk recordings today strike us as frozen, formal versions of what we have heard since from field recordings of rural Southern churches. Yet in the large urban churches one can still hear versions of the spirituals that reflect attempts to produce respectably white versions of Negro music.

Elsewhere, in the tiny backwoods churches and in the urban storefront sects, the Holiness, Pentecostal, and Sanctified evangelistic movements sought a release from this formality with a return to earlier and less European musical influences. Groups such as the Church of God in Christ, organized in 1895 in Mississippi, were noted for their exuberant, shouting songs (called "gospel," for they were said to be the "truth"), songs always accompanied by instruments alien to the European religious tradition: guitar, piano, trumpet, and drums. These instruments, coming from an existing secular musical background in the Negro community, already had techniques and styles appropriate to other music, and in the church shaped a new approach to songs of worship.

Gospel singer-instrumentalists were often skilled at more than one kind of music. Many guitarists (such as Skip James and Charlie Patton) were equally adept at the blues and gospel songs, and managed to record both. Some, such as Thomas A. Dorsey, dropped one in favor of the other. Tom Dorsey was the piano accompanist of classic blues-singer Ma Rainey, and had himself recorded as a blues singer under the name of Georgia Tom. Abandoning and disowning the blues, he became the most prolific and successful composer of the new religious music. Some have argued that the depression helped create modern gospel song, and certainly the failing market for recordings, combined with the general atmosphere of "bad times," helped to move many singers and musicians to the church as a source of employment as well as inspiration. Many of today's most successful gospel singers had their start in the blues: one thinks of such as Sister Rosetta Tharpe and Blind Gary Davis. Today, the same process works in reverse: gospel singing acts as training for popular singing. Dinah Washington, Sarah Vaughn, Sam Cooke, Aretha Franklin, and Nancy Wilson all began in choirs or gospel quartets.

It is difficult to point to given songs as "gospel," for there are no tightly identifiable forms. Yet there is a style, an approach, to modern Negro religious song that can be generally described. Gospel singing (particularly as compared to spiritual singing) is strongly rhythmic in the manner of jazz; it is filled with patterns of call and response between singer and orchestra and singer and chorus; it is built on a tonality common to the blues, and is heavy with melisma (the singing of a single syllable with more than one note). Most notable, however, is the social framework within which the gospel song is performed. Although gospel singing is sometimes done in concert fashion, it is most often used as a part of a church service and is sung by a regular choir. A lead singer sets the direction of the song and is involved in interplay with the rest of the choir. On the surface, this seems no different from the performance of the spiritual, which involved a minister who led the congregation in song. But the congregation does not sing in the modern gospel. Frederic Ramsey, Jr., says that the congregation's "emotional participation has become externalized; the leader and singers of the young Gospel group act out the old emotions and music, while the real congregation identifies with the performance."

JAZZ

To many people, Negro music in the city can only mean jazz. Jazz, after all, is sophisticated, complex, and one normally hears it only in cities of some size. Historically, it is certainly true that jazz developed only in areas where ethnic musical traditions were exposed to each other and where minds were open to artistic innovation. But most important, it was the cities that could afford to maintain musicians who might be free to experiment consciously with tradition to bring forth the bright and forceful music that Whitney Balliett has called the "sound of surprise."

Cities—New York, St. Louis, Chicago, New Orleans—made

possible the innovation, but jazzmen did not (and still do not, for the most part) come from the cities themselves. North Carolina, Florida, and Missouri are typical source areas for jazzmen; Harlem has still to produce a truly important figure. It was in the border states and in the Deep South that the folk elements of Negro music that contributed to jazz were most active. Samuel Charters and Leonard Kunstadt's detailed study of jazz in New York City (*Jazz: A History of the New York Scene*) clearly shows that the settled Negro residents of the big Northern cities fully accepted a heavily diluted blend of white and Negro music as their own until musical immigrants from New Orleans and elsewhere shook their complacency with newly revitalized Negro instrumental music. The huge military brass bands such as those led by James Europe and Egbert Thompson in New York between the late 1800's and 1920 were a far cry from the tiny, loosely strung New Orleans band of Louis Armstrong or that of Johnny Dunn from Memphis. As a consequence, Northern Negroes and whites alike were startled by the brash music coming out of the South and the Midwest.

Definitions of jazz have been numerous, but pleasantly vague. Vagueness seems necessary, though, since it is the custom of jazz to absorb and use everything in sight. The earliest jazz musicians in the United States played with elements drawn from brass marching bands, Spanish dances, English religious song, piano music of the romantic period, Negro folksongs and spirituals, and West Indian religious cult music. Later, theater songs, gospel tunes, and non-Western music were all drawn upon. This great receptivity to sources is a result of the central emphasis in jazz: improvisation. It has always been at improvisation or the feeling of improvisation that jazz writing has aimed.

If it is difficult to define the content of jazz, there is no problem in pointing to the social group that produces the music. Jazz musicians have always constituted a subculture of music, a cultish but scarcely organized body of self-selected instrumentalists, only a few of whom have ever managed to make a living from their music. The musicians of jazz have, until very recently, been unschooled in their chosen music, except as they have imitated recordings or other musicians directly. Never accepted by academics, only partially accepted by the public, jazzmen formed a closed community, but one in which innovation is valued more than tradition. The jazz community is aesthetically anarchistic, both within itself and in its relations with the larger society. Clearly, that jazz musicians are usually Negroes from the South or the Midwest is related to the fact that they are individuals who were raised outside of the mainstream of American aesthetics and have never accepted the pluralistic blend of music which makes up the core of popular music in America. Jazz musicians are not folk musicians by any standard, but they are important as an artistic development built entirely on a basis of shared folk music experience.

The music of Negroes in the cities functions as a part of mass culture: there are the economics of making a living, of records, night clubs, and concerts. Even a street singer (if he is allowed to work) must have a license and must hustle to continue to exist in music. Yet Negro music—for reasons of cultural continuity as well as of segregation—has not yet become a part of the popular mainstream. One still hears the rhythmic and vocal complexity of nineteenth-century work songs, the "blue" tonality pervades church song, and even the most popular "hit" record of the day is closer to Mamie or Bessie Smith than it is to the British ballad. In fact, underneath all Negro music in America today there is a firm base of similarities, a common traditional core, which makes social function the only means of separating one musical genre from another. The blues and the older church music can sometimes be distinguished only by the words; the same can be said for modern urban blues and current gospel song. Jazz was built directly on a basis of blues and church music, and yet in the 1930's jazz strongly influenced the course of developing gospel style. In the 1960's, younger jazz musicians have again begun to show the influence of gospel music in their playing. Such musical continuity and integrity is seldom seen in the compelling intercultural squeeze the world is experiencing today.

25

Folklore and the Big Money

JOHN GREENWAY

If there is anything anthropologists learn in studying the varied peoples and cultures of the world, it is that, so far as man is concerned, reality has no chance at all of competing with unreality. Images are what count in men's minds, and man has the most phenomenal ability to make what is into what he would like to be. Take Americans, for instance. They have the curious idea that what the rest of the world admires and wants in their culture is immaterial things of an idealistic and nebulous nature, and it distresses them to find that people of other countries approbate those parts of American culture that Americans abominate. Anthropologists who have seriously concerned themselves with human behavior know that man's works—which they call "culture"—are vastly more important in understanding his behavior than man himself. So when the culture of America is seen manifestly and inescapably to be oriented toward materialism, it is only the stubborn and impractical idealist who insists on seeing the primacy of spirituality in the nation's ethos. And when culture pays big money to an activity, it is because culture, wiser than either the individual or the aggregate of its people, values that activity. People of other countries, standing off in a more objective view of America than Americans have, agree with American culture. Folklore—especially folksong—is big money in America, and Americans don't like that reality very much; but the other nations of the world see and approve. Let me give you an example or two.

As a working anthropologist, I recently spent some time in one of the most isolated areas of the inhabited world—the far northwest corner of South Australia. This is a place of frightening solitude and barrenness; it is the center of 300,000 square miles of virtually uninhabited semi-desert, where one can travel in any direction for three hundred miles without striking a town or a village. The only human beings who make this dry wilderness their permanent home are a few hundred aborigines, the most primitive people on earth. Except for the barest superficialities, these natives of the dead heart of Australia live in the Old Stone Age. Their tools are made of wood and stone and those few bits of iron that filter in from the outside. They have no farming or other controlled food resources, no houses or shelter, and only rags of clothing given them by the dozen or so missionaries and government workers who venture into the Australian center. They are almost as far from civilization as we are from the moon.

We went into their country to study their electrolyte metabolism—to see how they cope with an atmosphere whose evaporation rate is ten times its precipitation—a subject that permitted more of their children to be present at our work than anthropologists ordinarily see. At the end of one day of sweat sampling and blood testing, I gathered a half dozen small children around my tape recorder and asked them to sing for me. I expected a childish imitation of the strange, cascading chants of their parents, for these children had never been in a town, had never seen a motion-picture theater, had never put a record on a phonograph, and had never sat goggle-eyed before a television set. In fact, they knew no English at all, yet what they sang into my microphone was "Davy Crockett, King of the Wild Frontier." There is a tragi-comic irony in this vignette: the grandchildren of my friend Tom Blackburn, the composer of "Davy Crockett," don't know the song at all, for it belonged to an age group just beyond theirs!

Stone Age children singing of a partly fictional American congressman is not an isolated or even an unusual instance of the fantastic penetrating power of American folksong, real or artificial (the folk nowhere make the niggling distinctions between "genuine" and "factitious" that folklorists do, so long as the article feels right in their culture). A few years ago my university sent a team of scientists to the island of Puka Puka in the remote South Pacific Ocean to observe an astronomical event. Since the work was mainly a job of waiting for the proper celestial conditions, our men whiled away the waiting by recording the voices of these unspoiled peoples of the unspoiled Pacific singing their unspoiled melodies. One of the Polynesian songs my colleagues brought back on their tape recorder was "You Are My Sunshine," and that, of course, was an example of another American politician getting into the culture of an exotic people. "You Are My Sunshine" was composed by the former governor of the state of Louisiana, Jimmy Davis.

The most intractable of our own Red Indians still accept no musical instruments from the white man, but sing, in meaningless syllables to the accompaniment of a native drum, songs they imagine to be ancient in their tradition. Yet a recording made among the Hopi, one of the most conservative tribes still holding themselves apart from American civilization, finds them singing "Dixie." These, I believe, are southern Hopi.

It is easy to sympathize with people who judge these changes in romantic cultures to be neither interesting nor amusing, but just deplorable. When I returned to Australia after an absence of ten years, I was grieved to hear people talk in the accent of New York announcers instead of the dinkum Aussie I had come —with some difficulty—to understand and love. Television changed Australian speech in less than a decade; it will do the same with other tongues and other tastes. We like best the culture, the ways, the world we were reared in, even when that world was one of deprivation, and therefore all change is in some measure regrettable to our emotions if not to our intellects. But change is one of the hard facts of life; it is as necessary and as inevitable to the cultural organism as it is to the biological organism. We change or we die, for life is a constant process of adaptation to a constantly changing environment, and all we can do is try to see the best in the change.

The mass media of communication are a catalyst, enormously accelerating the changes that would have occurred in any event. What might have taken several generations to accomplish is now done in a few months—and this is what most of us cannot abide, so we tend to flee back into a past that was never really our own. For us folklorists, that Golden Age was rural Scotland of a century ago, and it is quite impossible for many of us to appreciate the dismal fact that the illiteracies of the Scottish hill folk are not in any objective way better than the illiteracies of the Appalachian hill folk. For our own peace of mind, we must adapt, because the movement is inexorable, and it will not adapt to suit us.

It is conceivable that we can adapt. When the first serious exploitation by the mass media of our folklore was perpetrated —the several enormously popular *Treasuries* of American folklore written by B. A. Botkin—folklorists almost unanimously condemned it. But Ben Botkin and his books are now quite respectable and indeed are looked back upon somewhat nostalgically in this age when the younger "degeneration" thinks them square. Time heals all vulgarity.

Consider the first reprehensible exploitation of folk material by the mass media in English, William Caxton's mutilation of Sir Thomas Malory's *Le Morte d'Arthur*. This first important work printed in English always appeared to be a badly edited book, with characters born in terminal chapters dying in beginning ones, but we never knew how badly Caxton chopped, cut, and pasted the original manuscript until a near copy was found in 1934 in the cellar of the Fellows' Library of Winchester College. Caxton, we know now, was as tasteless, insensitive, and vulgar as any Tin Pan Alley composer working a folk ballad into a pop tune. It is doubtful that anyone of literary acumen read the Caxton-Malory book with approval in the fifteenth century; they cultivated polished writers like Lydgate and Hawes and Hoccleve—writers so dead today that surveys of English literature often dispose of the entire century by representing it with the popular folk ballads (whose origins were in fact elsewhere in time.)

But this book for all its faults became the great treasure of English literary inspiration. It matters not at all that its events, its characters, and its ethos, though based on folk originals, were distorted beyond recognizing by its jailbird author and its businessman editor; *Le Morte d'Arthur* is impregnably a work that the world will not willingly let die.

What England and France of *Le Morte d'Arthur* had in the way of real knights and Arthurian heroes could be compressed into the same space of time that America knew real cowboys. Launcelot had less reality than television's Billy the Kid, and Galahad less morality than Marshal Dillon. The point I am trying to make (with some apprehensiveness about how it will be received by my colleagues) is that the world of the cowboy, created out of a few dirty, generally shiftless, and altogether inconsequential saddle tramps who assisted ignorantly in the establishment of the Western American cattle industry—this romanticized, idealized, heartwarming, inspiring, exciting, and superbly entertaining world of the movie-television cowboy could be America's own Arthurian legend if we could put aside the stuffiness of our own time's Roger Aschams, who excoriated the literature of his time's folk for its open manslaughter and bold bawdry, and accept our incipient literary legend the way Caxton's readers, the mass for whom his medium was invented, accepted theirs. It would not displease me personally to think that American literature will be remembered for its *High Noon* sheriffs long after Edward Albee and Tennessee Williams have joined John Lydgate and Thomas Hoccleve in oblivion.

The exploitation of folk materials in the fifteenth century by the mass medium of books was restricted to what could be taken in by the mind; in our time it has evolved to what can be taken in by the ear, for the ear leads not only to the mind but to the senses. Nearly all commercial use of folklore in America has been of its music. When the mass media take notice of the spoken lore, it has usually been to express amazement at its existence and disapproval of its persistence. Newspapers regularly print as factual occurrences items spread wide in folklore's time and space. The scholarly journal *Western Folklore* keeps a regular department to chronicle such self-deceptions by the American press.

Acoustical recording—the most influential medium of mass communication to use the materials of American folklore—is in most of its developments a wholly American invention, so its exploitation of folk music is at least in the national family. Thomas Edison unwittingly began the exploitation as well as the invention—the first articulated sound he recorded was a fragment of a nursery rhyme. He also cut cylinders of folk musicians years before their use became commercial. You have read in a previous chapter the history of commercial recordings of hillbilly music, and hopefully you are at least willing to give that fascinating material a fair hearing. In this chapter I want only to call your attention to the growth of the mass medium, a growth that came of feeding upon the folksong of the Southern mountains, centering upon that area's most important city, Nashville, Tennessee.

On the evening of November 29, 1925, a radio announcer and entrepreneur named George Dewey Hay brought before the microphone of Station WSM in Nashville an old-time fiddler, Uncle Jimmy Thompson, and began the "Nashville Sound." The program grew in size and popularity, and in 1927 it was given its permanent name, the "Grand Ole Opry," to distinguish its home-spun music from an hour of classical and opera music that preceded it. In 1943 the "Grand Ole Opry" broadcast coast to coast, and in the same year it was distributed by the American Armed Forces Radio around the world.

Today, over forty years later, Nashville has become in fact what it calls itself in pride: "Music City, USA"—a $65,000,000-a-year industry. One out of every two phonograph records sold in the United States is made in Nashville. The city has 120 music publishing firms, 870 singers and musicians, and 4,500 composers, all purveying that evolutionary phase of American folk music known as "country western." More than two hundred radio stations in the United States program nothing but this kind of music; another two hundred give most of their programming time to country western song. And how does the rest of the world relate to this saturation of the airwaves by American hill-billies? Well, there is a "Tokyo Grand Ole Opry" now, featuring such typical Oriental musicians as Jimmy Tokita and His Mountain Playboys and such typical Oriental songs as "Sixteen Tons."

The mass media are not exclusively purveyors of white hillbilly music; most of the infinite variety of sounds created by America's multi-cultural folk communities are available from Brazil to Brazzaville. A descendant of American folk expression recently become popular internationally is the so-called "Detroit Sound," described as a "sophisticated, slicked-up, unique Rhythm and Blues sound that is an amalgam of gospel harmonies, a blues beat, symphonic effects, electronic gimmickry, and a 'sweet' kind of rock 'n' roll." Like Detroit itself, the "Detroit Sound" is a combination of not only these musical heritages, but of cultural legacies as well, converged into a vehicle of expression largely by one Negro record company, Motown (for Motor Town). Motown's record buyers only a few years ago were the half million Negro residents of Detroit; today this Negro-owned and Negro-

operated company has licensees and distributors all over the world
to help conduct its $15,000,000-a-year business.

What one can legitimately deplore in the use of folklore by
the mass media depends on what beliefs, tastes, and standards—
and prejudices—one brings to the exploitation. There is much
that I have not been trained to like in what the mass media give
us, but there is little that I find deplorable. Of that little the
worst, in my prejudiced opinion, is the use made of folk materials
by political conspirators whose purpose is to fan the flames of
discontent or to initiate arson wherever they imagine there is
combustible fuel. If one compares the British leftist magazine
Sing with the Australian *Singabout* and the American *Sing Out!*
one notices not only a similar format and similar titles, but similar exploit and exploitation: perhaps 70 per cent genuine or
equivocal folksong and 30 per cent of what our C.I.A. men call
"hitchhiking"—the plausible song of protest riding the back of
the genuine article into the minds of readers too young or too
naïve to know better. I don't like it, but I have to admit that
many more people in the United States subscribe to *Sing Out!*
than subscribe to the *Journal of American Folklore,* and tolera-
tion of *Sing Out!* is one of the payments we must make for the
good things in a democratic system. This is a free country, unfortunately, and we must take the bad with the worse.

And it is a consolation to know that *Sing Out!* makes far less
mischief than its editors and publisher like to believe. Its readers
are chiefly young people whose only knowledge of hard times
and discontent occurs when their parents cut their allowance.
They get over this childishness as soon as they have to put down
their guitars and go into the world to make a living, but for the
time being they have fun singing songs they don't understand.
Sing Out! imagines it is subverting the government and the social
organization of the United States, and everyone is happy in his
illusions except the folklorists, who take this sort of thing seriously.

We can leave the correction of the mischief to Madison Avenue
and Tin Pan Alley. In 1963 these entrepreneurs of the mass
media found out that hundreds of thousands of young potential
customers had an in-group term, "hootenanny," to describe folk
musical free-for-alls. The term was certainly brought to popularity by the organizers of the singing subversives who now write
early American folksongs for *Sing Out!,* but Madison Avenue

deterged the term with such capitalistic efficiency that no self-disrespecting Communist would now be caught dead using it. In that memorable year of 1963 the American Broadcasting Company produced and presented a television series featuring folkniks, folksongers, and a few folksingers, and called the show "Hootenanny." It lasted just long enough to spawn a number of fascinating if not elevating by-products, like the movie "Hootenanny Hoot," unmentionable numbers of record albums with the adjective "Hootenanny" in their titles, and two nationally distributed magazines, *Hootenanny* and *ABC–TV Hootenanny*, which, before their quick demise, printed useful articles like "How to Write a Folk Song."

It is all undeniably deplorable, but I must confess that one of the most exciting experiences I have had in this business—I mean this profession—was to act as a master of ceremonies at the 1960 Newport Folk Festival, a weekend orgy of folksinging attended by some thirteen thousand young people who came by every means of transportation, from shanks' mare to hearses, to that dying resort of our nineteenth-century robber barons. Whatever one thought of the primitive aesthetic sensibility of the pubescent audience, one was caught up in their infectious enthusiasm, at the base of which lay a genuine patriotism, a love for the folk expression of the nation. And the Newport Festivals have had a laudable effect on the course of folk scholarship: as a profitable non-profit organization, the Festival was able to plow very much money into enterprises impossible to finance otherwise. One of its accomplishments was the physical discovery of scores of early folk and hillbilly singers whose talents did not survive the stoppage of commercial recordings by the Great Depression and whom we thought time and age had taken away forever. To see these forgotten performers brought up and honored by their grandchildren's generation was worth all the irritation of the Hootenannies and *Sing Outs!* that indirectly brought the Festivals into being.

The character of a nation is revealed by the use it makes of its folklore. In countries like Ireland, in danger of being swamped out of existence by more powerful neighboring cultures, folk materials are used as a nucleus of what anthropologists call a despair cult, an exaggeration of the worth and importance of the folk soul to rally its more effete descendants to their lost pride. Some other nations extract what they need from the national

Geist for the purpose of absorbing their neighbors as well. Whether Americans like it or not—and they don't—we are a commercial nation, and it is our manifest destiny to make things work for commerce, and thereby, I am convinced, for the good of mankind. There is no competing with it, that is certainly sure. Even Communist China and East Germany are forging models of American guitars and American autoharps—I know this, because I have seen and played on them (badly, because they are pretty bad forgeries), and when they have attained America's production and sales rate of one million and more guitars a year, perhaps things will be better for them. As it will be better for us when we learn to appreciate what we are good at.

For the moment, no polite person outside the United States would mention Elvis Presley in the presence of an American; it would be like forcing vodka on a Muslim or pulling a Greek patriarch by the beard. Even folklorists abominate Elvis. But Elvis Presley was born and reared in Tupelo, Mississippi, and what he made a musical rage around the world can be heard on records made by folklorists among Tupelo and other Negroes, many before Presley's birth. Even the little that Elvis seems to have added in performance style has been traced to the influence of the Negro blues singer Arthur Crudup. As an American and as a folklorist, I am impressed and pleased by the knowledge that Presley's records were prime contraband for smugglers in places where American culture was forbidden entry, and though the sounds he makes may not impinge upon my ears with exquisite pleasure, I am willing to entertain the possibility that what is, is right. Or at least, what most of the world believes is right, is right. As a believer in democracy, I could do no less.

Index